Armed Conflict and Security in South Asia

Armed Conflict and Security in South Asia

Brig. J. N. Mehta (Retd.)

Neha Publishers & Distributors

Published by:
Neha Publishers & Distributors
4832/24, Prahlad Lane, S-207 Ansari Road,
Daryaganj, New Delhi-110002

ISBN: 978-93-80318-81-3

Price: 1295/-

Typesetting: JEE-VEE Graphics

First Edition: 2015

Printed by: Neeta Press

Preface

South Asia, otherwise, normally should encompass a much wider geographical construct. Be that as it may, what is striking about the South Asia region is that it has stood engulfed in conflicts, ever since the British partitioned India into the two successor states of India and Pakistan.

Perhaps the biggest single factor that has shaped the significant global decline in the number of armed conflicts and casualty rates since the end of the superpower confrontation of the cold war has been the dramatic reduction in major powers engaging in proxy conflicts.

The presence of numerous actors, role of civil society, space and rules of bargaining, lack of bargaining tools, independent inputs or the lack of it, level of external support, all these factors play an important role in sustaining the peace processes.

South Asia has numerous, long standing conflicts left over from history. In the last few years several other issues have been added to the portfolio of security issues. Economic development in South Asia is being threatened by burgeoning human security issues. Many security issues such as demography, economic security, environmental security, terrorism, etc., are issues requiring cooperation among countries of the region. Most states in South Asia are vulnerable to non-traditional security threats. South Asia lacks capabilities and mechanisms to deal with these issues.

It is further hoped that the book will prove to be of immense value to teachers, students and researchers.

—Author

Contents

Preface (vii)

1. South Asia Conflict Resolution Impediments 1
2. Trade-Conflict Model in South Asia 11
3. Conflict and Development in South Asia 35
4. Climate Change, Migration, and Conflict in South Asia 57
5. China Debates the Future Security Environment 90
6. South Asia and the Security Dilemma 154
7. Security Challenges in South Asia 197
8. Cooperative Security Work in South Asia 222
9. Peace, Security, Development, and the Environment 242

Bibliography 301

Index 303

1

South Asia Conflict Resolution Impediments

AN ANALYSIS

General Background: South Asia as the successor term to the Indian sub-continent was brought into usage by the United States and Britain presumably to de-emphasise India's natural predominance in the sub-continent and to soothe their protégé Pakistan's sensitivities in not being viewed as part of anything termed Indian. South Asia, otherwise, normally should encompass a much wider geographical construct. Be that as it may, what is striking about the South Asia region is that it has stood engulfed in conflicts, ever since the British partitioned India into the two successor states of India and Pakistan.

South Asia has witnessed five major armed conflicts in the last 50 years or so. Four of these armed conflicts were unleashed by Pakistan i.e. 1947-48; 1965; 1971; and 1999 (Kargil). The fifth was the Chinese attack launched in 1962. India's responses to such a hostile security environment in South Asia has been to build up a sizeable conventional military force as part of its defensive doctrines and lately a nuclear deterrent.

South Asia Conflicts-The Narrow Prism Approach of The West: It has been fashionable for Western leaders, political commentators and strategic analysts to define South Asia's conflicts through the narrow prism of what they term as Indo-Pak rivalries over Kashmir. So much so, that in the last decade or so, a new myth has been created by the United States policymakers that Kashmir has become a nuclear flashpoint and therefore merits external intervention in terms of conflict resolution.

United States and Western policy makers are noted for their high levels of intellectual calibre, rich backgrounds of professional experience and razor-sharp analytical skills. It is therefore intriguing that when it comes to an analysis of South Asia's conflicts, these qualities recede and get overtaken by a single point obsessive reference to Kashmir i.e. convergence with the same single point agenda of Pakistan.

Obviously, when it comes to South Asia and the Indo-Pak conflict which predominates the region, intellectual integrity has to take a backseat when fig-leaves have to be found to screen strategic interests of the United States and the West. Kashmir and specifically the Kashmir Valley (a fraction of the entire Jammu & Kashmir state) is the Western fig-leaf.

South Asia minus Pakistan has been devoid of any inter-state conflicts. Therefore, in terms of viewing South Asia in terms of conflict resolution, the reference point for the impediments have to perforce focus on Pakistan, as that is where inter-state conflicts in South Asia get generated and proxy war and terrorism engineered

Pakistan's Strategic Rationale for Existence as a Nation State: Pakistan's strategic rationale for existence as a nation state has been the "two-nation theory" i.e. a separate nation for the Indian Muslim. Pakistan's claims on Kashmir are neither legal nor historical but framed in the mould of the "two-nation theory". What is irrefutable is that this theory stood negated in 1947 itself, when only eight million Indian Muslims of the then 40 million Indian Muslims in India migrated to Pakistan.

The day the Indo-Pakistan conflict fades away, for whatever reason, Pakistan's strategic rationale for existence as a nation state disappears. This was so stated by Ross Masood, Director of the Pakistan Institute for Strategic Studies in an address in New Delhi in the early 1990s.

Pakistan, therefore has a major vested interest in the perpetuation of conflict in South Asia as General Musharraf, the military ruler of Pakistan put it so succinctly, that even if Kashmir is resolved, there will be many more Kashmirs.

Such attitudinal fixations in the Pakistan hierarchy is a major impediment for conflict resolution in South Asia.

Pakistan's Build up as a "Spoiler State" in South Asia- The External Inputs in Conflict Generation: Pakistan's propensity for resorting to armed conflicts stands greatly enhanced by the bestowal of a "spoiler state" status conferred on it by the United States at frequent intervals and China persistently since 1962.

The United States in the pursuance of its regional balance of power policies against India, found a willing proxy in Pakistan. Weapons and weapons technologies attendant in United States military aid packages were basically offensive-doctrines oriented. With superior technology of the day, the United States thereby imparted to Pakistan, deep strike capabilities against India.

China's role was more sinister in terms of upgradation of Pakistan's military capabilities. They not only provided sizeable conventional arms packages to reduce the gap in India's conventional military, but also built up Pakistan's nuclear weapons and missile arsenal to enable Pakistan to offset India's conventional might.

Pakistan today cannot even stand on its legs without the political, military and economic support from the United States and China. It was ending up as a "failed state" and "rogue state" till the precise moment of the morning of 9/11 when the Islamic Jehadi bombings took place in New York and Washington.

Pakistan has convinced itself and has been led to believe so by the United States and China, that it can continue with its armed conflicts and proxy wars with India and that if Pakistan gets hard pressed by India militarily, they will bail out Pakistan by coercive pressures on India.

Conflict resolution in South Asia, therefore stands greatly impeded by these external inputs of conflict generation from the United States and China.

Conflict Resolution in South Asia-"No Honest Brokers": Even if the above-analyzed impediments to conflict resolution stood diluted somehow and one was to look around for some "honest brokers" to mediate in the conflict, the short answer would be: "NO HONEST BROKERS EXIST".

Of the five members of the UN Security Council, two i.e. United States and China stand disqualified for their role in conflict generation in South Asia. They are unacceptable to Indians for their partisan role. The third, Britain, has vested interests right from the inception of the partition plan. The other two i.e. Russia and France, do not carry much strategic weight today.

The Islamic countries rule themselves out automatically. The major ones like Saudi Arabia have not only financed Pakistan's nuclear and missile arsenal but also Pakistan's proxy war against India. The other liberal democracies in Europe and Asia Pacific have strategic linkages with the United States and are therefore susceptible to American pressure in policies towards South Asia.

The absence of "honest brokers" for negotiating an end to South Asia's Indo-Pak conflict seriously impedes any conflict resolution process. South Asia Conflict- Civilisational and Historical: People outside South Asia and not conversant with Indian History cannot fathom as to how South Asia's conflicts could be characterized as civilisational and historical. Even the Indian pseudo-liberal establishment puckers its noses at this thought, because it distracts them from their Utopian dreams and brings them to face this reality.

The founder of Pakistan, Mohd. Ali Jinnah has gone on record to state that the seeds of India's "two-nation theory" were sowed when the first Muslim stepped on India's soil. Couple this psyche with nearly 700 years of Muslim despotic rule over India and one finds the answer to Pakistan's attitudinal fixation of unwillingness to accept its asymmetric status in contemporary South Asia, today.

Even if one were to find "honest brokers" for conflict resolution in South Asia today, their efforts would get impeded and marginalized by the attitudinal fixations of Pakistan's elite born out of these civilizational and historical roots.

Concluding Observations: South Asia conflict resolution efforts can only succeed and the region emerge as a conflict free zone, if the following developments could emerge:

* United States and China de-link themselves as external inputs in South Asia's conflict generation. This would then end Pakistan's continuance as the "regional spoiler" state challenging the natural balance of power in South Asia by external infusions.
* United States and China conceding India's status as the regional power in South Asia and consequently the prevailing over Pakistan to give up its oversized strategic ambitions in South Asia. In return they could provide some strategic guarantees to soothe Pakistan's strategic fears.
* It dawns on United States and China that regional stability can only be best served by regional powers and not by building up regional "spoiler states." "Spoiler states" are like hand maidens, adept and prone to promiscuous strategic relationships. Pakistan is a prime example with its nuclear weapons proliferation to North Korea even after 9/11 and thereby creating new threats for United States in Asia Pacific At the time when Pakistan's sins were being redeemed by the United States 'beatification' of General Musharraf, he was busy merrily passing on nuclear weapons equipments to North Korea.

Emergence of the above developments would exceed the bounds of optimism, because neither the United States nor China have so far displayed any trends to move in these directions.

What is not being adequately appreciated and recognized by Western policy makers is that their tinkering with the natural balance of power in South Asia and their marked proclivity to be permissive of Pakistan's strategic delinquencies could spark India to build and upgrade her strategic military might. Such a strategic build up would be one that Pakistan could not afford nor Pakistan's external patrons be in a position to offset by their infusions.

POTENTIAL CHINESE USES OF ARMED FORCE AGAINST TAIWAN

The West's concern about China's military capability is focused mainly on potential military action against Taiwan. China has threatened to take military action if Taiwan declares independence from the mainland or indefinitely prolongs the unification process. While the modernization of China's military forces currently under way may facilitate a potential attack on Taiwan, it does not make success a forgone conclusion for the foreseeable future. Reviewing potential uses of armed force by China, this section concludes not only that Chinese capabilities are limited now, but also that given the slow pace of modernization, China's capabilities for attack on Taiwan are likely to remain limited for the next 10-15 years.

Combined Arms Attack and Invasion

In theory, China could launch a combined arms amphibious and airborne assault on Taiwan. China's current forces do not include enough transport assets to accomplish such a task, however; and there is no evidence that China is building up larger numbers of amphibious assault ships or large cargo aircraft. Current military doctrine calls for a 5-to-1 attacker to defender ratio for amphibious assaults. Today China can only transport 1 armoured or 3 infantry brigades with its amphibious ships, which would be completely inadequate for an attack on Taiwan. The use of commercial and fishing vessels (for example, splitting a company of troops among 4 fishing trawlers) could not substitute effectively due to communication problems and the resulting inability to coordinate units. An amphibious assault would only be conducted with control the skies over the Strait, which the Chinese Air Force probably cannot accomplish. The weather and terrain of Taiwan favours the defender, with high waves and wind in the Taiwan Strait, combined with cliffs on the eastern part of Taiwan and expansive mudflats on the western coast. Finally, Taiwan and the United States could see an invasion coming many months before the event, because it would take that long to prepare if China did have the forces to attempt the effort.

Missile Attack

China could attack Taiwan with a few hundred DF-15 and DF-11 conventionally armed missiles; but history suggests that such an attack would probably not force Taipei to capitulate (compare, for example, Britain in 1944-45, or Serbia in 1999). These missiles are not accurate enough to be precision weapons against airfields, radar, transport nodes, etc. They would have to be used more as a terror weapon, against cities and town. if only conventional warheads were used, damage would not be any more significant than that from a large natural disaster, such as the one Taiwan survived in 1999 (a major earthquake near Taipei). Since China only has a limited number of DF-15 and DF-11 missiles, a long-lasting missile siege would be difficult.

Blockade

China's navy could attempt to blockade Taiwan, forcing ships to dock at Chinese ports before proceeding on to the island. If the number of China's large surface ships (frigates and destroyers) continues to increase, such a blockade would be easier. China currently has more ships than Taiwan, and could attempt to enforce a blockade with a combination of naval vessels and mines. And despite the lack of sophistication of China's submarines, Taiwan has limited ASW assets to counter China's large submarine fleet. As with a missile attack, a blockade would bring international condemnation and, as a result, hurt China's economy, even if it were technically legal under international law (with Taiwan recognized as part of China).

INDIA AND PAKISTAN-NUCLEAR STATES IN CONFLICT

When the British withdrew from the Indian subcontinent after the second world war, it was divided, primarily on religious grounds, into the two states of India and Pakistan. At that time Kashmir was included in India, but the issue of which state it should belong to has been contested ever since, largely because Kashmir's population is predominantly Muslim. In 1947 a United Nations resolution called for a referendum in Kashmir to settle the issue on the basis of what the people wanted. It was, however never carried out and it is generally assumed that the reason for this is because the Indian government feared the popular vote would support unification with Pakistan on religious grounds. Many in Kashmir campaign for independence, a position that neither India nor Pakistan supports.

Around 30,000 people have died in Kashmir in the last 11 years. What happens in Kashmir is at the heart of the continuing tension between India and Pakistan. The possibility of the world's first direct war between two nuclear-armed states occurring is very real. The history of the conflict over Kashmir is well documented with three India/Pakistan wars taking place since 1947. But this time it would be with both sides having access to nuclear weapons. Since the attack on the Indian Parliament building in December 2001, the tension and rhetoric have grown considerably. India accused Pakistan of supporting terrorist groups. Pakistan, in turn, pledges its support for Kashmiri freedom fighters. One state's terrorist is another's freedom fighter. Since the attack in December, Pakistan has arrested around 1500 'militants' and banned five groups, two said to be sectarian, one pro-Taliban and two who have been fighting Indian rule in Kashmir. However, Gen Musharraf has pledged continued support for Kashmir.

Many people living along the border close to Kashmir have fled the area due to the large military presence being built up by both sides. From the end of 2001 there were clashes virtually every night in that border region, with sometimes one or two people being shot. There are claims that large numbers of military silos have been destroyed. In an atmosphere of increased tension and sabre-rattling rhetoric on both sides, this led to the situation in May 2002 where upwards of a million troops were gathered near the border. Any mistake or small incident runs the risk of setting off something far, far worse.

The Current Situation

All this, of course, is fuelled by the continuing rhetoric on both sides. Officials in both countries claimed that they would not use nuclear weapons first, but they seem remarkably keen to use them second. Given the proximity of the two states, it is clear that millions of their own people would die along with millions of their nearest neighbours. India has said that it would not use nuclear weapons first, while Pakistan has clearly stated that it would. Whilst a 'no first use' policy is an important step towards disarmament, it is all too often used as an excuse to build a large 'second use' capacity. Eventually, of course, the 'second use' becomes indistinguishable from the 'first use'. As the tension mounts, the temptation grows to get your retaliation in first. But what are the immediate reasons for the current increasing tension and the risk of war? India appears to be escalating events but its argument is that it is following the lead of the US and the west by zero tolerance of terrorist attacks. It has identified what it sees as terrorists being harboured by another state so it threatens military retaliation.

Both sides have had internal problems as well. In Pakistan, Musharraf has been promising a democratic election ever since the army took control, but there has been only a referendum. Though it was boycotted by many political parties, Musharraf claimed it as a mandate for him to continue. Meanwhile in India, the ruling BJP has lost every state election for over a year, so now uses the well-known tactic of uniting the country against an outside 'threat'. Whatever the reasons for the tensions, the crucial aim is to avoid the devastation of nuclear war.

The British Prime Minister, Tony Blair, visited the region in January 2002 to try to persuade both sides that a war was not a good idea. This took place against the background of the bombing in Afghanistan, in which Britain was an enthusiastic participant. His approach raised concerns about Western hypocrisy, as if war is fine for some countries but not others. The sincerity of Blair's mission was also in question after it transpired that his plea for peace preceded two British trade missions to Delhi in February, both designed to sell weapons to India. Defexpo is an arms fair whose promotional material pushes the weaponry on sale, with everything from small arms to missile systems. India and Pakistan have long been valuable markets for British arms manufacturers. So this arms fair, combined with the resumption of arms sales to Pakistan, as a result of its support for the war in Afghanistan, means that Britain will be arming both sides in any future war. This is, of course, not unique. A similar thing happened during the Iraq-Iran war.

So, what's the answer? The situation in south Asia shows the importance of nuclear disarmament. A war even with conventional weapons would be an appalling waste of life. But this would be turned into a complete disaster on an unimaginable scale if nuclear weapons were used. In the short term there must be more diplomatic language and there must be proper international negotiations at the UN to resolve the problem of Kashmir. Our own politicians could do more to help. How can the British Government's attempts to calm the situation be taken seriously when the Defence Minister, Geoff Hoon, appears on television saying that he would use nuclear weapons against any state if necessary? In the long term, the declared nuclear weapon states (NWS)-US, UK, France, Russia and China-must carry out their obligations under the nuclear Non-Proliferation Treaty (NPT) and get rid of their nuclear weapons. The NPT was drawn up in 1968, giving the definition of a NWS as one that tested nuclear weapons before then. Because India was preparing its nuclear programme at that time, it would not sign. Because India would not sign, neither would Pakistan. Therefore, they cannot sign the NPT as NWS and, since the nuclear testing by both sides in 1998, they cannot sign as non-nuclear weapon states. The NWS made statements at the time of the tests saying how appalled they were at this development. But after 11 September, the US lifted sanctions imposed on both sides, in order to boost its coalition in the 'War on Terrorism'.

If the NWS put the words of the NPT into action, they would be in a position to push India and Pakistan to sign the NPT themselves. After all, part of the excuse given by India and Pakistan for the 1998 nuclear tests was that those nuclear weapon states had done nothing about their NPT commitments, so if nuclear weapons were good enough for them...

Both sides need to be persuaded that nuclear weapons make the world a more dangerous, not a safer, place and to take a step back and realise that peaceful resolutions to conflict are the best way forward. This should happen through the UN. But the UN also needs to look at the continuing nuclear policies of the NWS. There are peace activists in both India and Pakistan working hard to get their views across. Their work has been particularly difficult since the nuclear tests carried out by both countries in 1998. They have the entire might of the government and military propaganda machine ranged against them. We should do all we can to support them.

2

Trade-Conflict Model in South Asia

To what extent has economic and trade interdependence heightened or deterred military conflicts in South Asia? In a world with increasingly interdependent economic relations between states, military conflicts on any scale are more influential on the world stage as a whole. However, it is not necessarily evident whether expanded trade relations would help prevent issues from being fought out militarily between nations, or whether they would heighten armed conflict. I hypothesize that trade interdependence in South Asia has led to more stable security in the region, since conflicts would be less likely to be dealt with using military force. Contrarily, some scholars contend that the number of military conflicts have actually increased in the world in recent years. This opposing argument could be supported by the idea that more interactions between two states could result in more chances for tensions to arise. Moreover, it could also be claimed that economic relations are less important to states than political motivators when deciding whether or not to go to war.

The relationship between trade and conflicts between countries in South Asia is important to examine because of the rising prominence of this region of the world. Security issues are of utmost concern when considering the damaging effects that armed conflict has on global economic relations. Therefore, it would be useful to examine whether South Asia has become more stable and less conflict prone as a result of increasing trade relations between countries that have had a history of tense interactions, such as India and Pakistan or India and China. The opposing viewpoints on this economic relations- security relationship seem to align with the liberalism-realism dichotomy in international relations theory. Liberals would argue economic interdependence lowers the prospect of armed conflict because the value of trading would outweigh any benefits that could result from aggression.

On the other hand, realists contend high interdependence would actually increase the likelihood of war. In an anarchic international realm, as realists see the world to be, states continually fear for their security. As a result, interdependence between two states could make them seem vulnerable and it gives states an incentive to go to war, since they need to ensure they have ongoing access to materials and goods they need. Though both sides have their merits and their fair share of scholars who support liberalist and realist doctrine, I believe the argument for liberalism when dealing with international economic relations and security is more applicable. In South Asia, a region which has seen years of constant tensions between the major players of India and Pakistan, India and China, and India and Bangladesh, among others, it appears as though the proclivity for armed conflict has actually decreased in the past decade or so, even as trade relations between the pairs of nations have increased. It would definitely be important to examine the interactions between South Asian countries to see what has led to this shift toward more peaceful relations between the formerly constantly feuding neighbors.

THE TRADE-CONFLICT MODEL: TWO PERSPECTIVES AND IMPLICATIONS FOR SOUTH ASIA

Scholars have long argued over the applicability of certain international relations theories to the trade-conflict relationship. The two dominant perspectives in international relations- realism and liberalism- each claim that they can explain whether increased trade and economic interdependence amplifies or reduces military conflicts in the world (Copeland 1996). While realists argue that increased interactions lead to a heightened security dilemma, uncertainty, and more conflict, liberals assert that surges in interdependence reduces armed conflicts between state actors.

Thus, the existing literature on the trade-conflict model is centered on the dialogue between proponents of the realist emphasis on security dilemmas and anarchy and the advocates of the liberal "democratic peace" theory (Barbieri and Schneider 1999).

However, there exists limited research that has delved into an analysis of the extent to which increased economic interdependence in South Asia, an area of increasing critical interest and importance, has heightened or deterred conflict in the region. My study aims to encompass this focus on South Asia that has not been investigated by other scholars in the discipline and its results will support whether the realist or liberalist perspective of the relationship between trade and military conflict is more applicable to the South Asian region of the world.

Realists argue that their perspective of the trade-conflict model is the most applicable and supported of all the international relations theories, as increased economic interdependence leads to heightened uncertainty in an anarchic world, which then results in more military conflicts. One factor that realists claim explains why states that have increased levels of economic exchange will actually engage in more armed conflicts is that the states fear they will profit unequally from the relationship with their trade partners (Barbieri and Schneider 1999).

One of the most prominent advocates of this realist theory is Kenneth Waltz, who wrote that "close interdependence nears closeness of contact and raises the prospects of occasional conflict" (Waltz 1979, 138). Furthermore, various scholars over the years have found that countries that are more open to interstate trade have a higher probability of war.

This argument is founded on the premise that "multilateral trade openness decreases [both] bilateral dependence to any given country and the cost of a bilateral conflict" (Martin et al. 2008, 865), so for nations in close geographic proximity to each other, trade has had a significant effect on their probability to engage in military conflict. Perhaps the most well-known study that shows that extreme economic interdependence actually has the greatest potential for heightening the probability of conflict is one conducted by Barbieri (1996).

Even though studies of this nature appear to be justified in their conclusions, there are some fundamental flaws that should be addressed. Primarily, even though multilateral trade allows state actors to receive goods from numerous other nations, it does not necessitate a reduction of bilateral dependence to a given country. If two nations engage in bilateral trade of weapons, for example, then even if one of those countries trades other goods with multiple actors, it would not reduce that nation's dependence on its original partner for arms. Moreover, the costs of a bilateral conflict would still be significant enough to influence a state's actions toward another, which would most likely involve trying to avoid military engagements. Finally, while Barbieri (1996) does find evidence that supports her claim that increased trade interdependence heightens militarized interstate disputes, or MIDs, she actually changed the theoretical requirement and measurement of her study. After accounting for this alteration and controlling for temporal dependence, considerably strong support is found for the liberalist belief that economic interdependence has an influence on the reduction of conflicts (Oneal and Russett 1999). Therefore, even though the realist perspective does have its merits, it is the less likely option between realism and liberalism to be applicable to the study of the trade-conflict model in South Asia.

On the other hand, scholars who believe in the liberalist approach to the trade-conflict relationship often cite the works of Kant and Montesquieu, focused on the liberalizing effects of trade and cost-benefit analysis (Barbieri and Schneider 1999), to argue their point that economic interdependence lowers the prospect of armed conflict. Liberalists argue this correlation exists because the value of trading would outweigh any benefits that could result from aggression. According to liberal theorists, "commerce promotes peace because violence has substantial costs" (Hegre, et al. 2010, 763) that nations do not want to pay. Trade provides benefits and profits for both sides that would be lost if the states went to war.

Liberalists may then ask this fundamental question: if trade is beneficial to both sides, why would state actors ever go to war? They would be harming themselves if they did since "states are deterred from initiating conflict against a trading partner for fear of losing the welfare gains associated with the trading relationship" (Polachek 1980).While this reasoning is logical, it does not explain why some studies have found that increased trade actually results in more MIDs. This apparent discrepancy between what the liberalist perspective on the trade-conflict model predicts will happen and what data from the world actually shows appears to be a flaw in the liberalism argument. However, other scholars have shown that the "interdependent states would rather trade than invade" (Copeland 1996) concept may still be substantiated with further research into this topic.

Some proponents of the liberalist perspective argue that they have been able to account for the instances when both economic interdependence and military conflicts increased. Most of these scholars provide explanations for this apparent discrepancy between liberalist theory and reality in the trade-conflict model by introducing various other conditions that affect whether trade leads to conflict or by explaining alternative variable construction that can influence the outcome of scholarly research already conducted. Several studies found that two factors that have an effect on the extent to which trade influences conflict are nations' sizes and the distance separating them. Some other conditions that may influence the trade and conflict relationship include the presence of asymmetric information (Barbieri 1996), the "contrasting effects of bilateral and multilateral trade openness" (Martin et al., 865), and the aversion that democratic leaders have toward conflict versus that of autocratic leaders (Gelpi and Grieco 2008). Meanwhile, sometimes the definition of variables such as "trade" or "conflict" can have an effect on the results of studies, since some authors may use trade dependence to measure trade, while others may focus on trade share or trade openness (Gartzke and Li 2003), and still others consider trade efficiency (Hegre 2004). Thus, liberal theorists have been able to explain most of the flaws in the findings that show that trade interdependence actually heightens military conflict rather than deters it.

After reviewing the most pertinent literature on the trade-conflict model, it is evident that the bulk of these studies "support the hypothesis that interdependence, measured in terms of trade, inhibits violent conflict" (McMillan 1997, 33). Even though this hypothesis, a central tenant of liberalism, appears to be the more pertinent theory in the analysis of the effect of trade interdependence on military conflicts in South Asia, it does have a few shortcomings that must be resolved. Primarily, scholars who espouse the liberalist perspective often make assumptions about trade interdependence and conflict that are more theoretical in basis and less data-driven. While for some studies the theory portion may be adequate evidence of a correlation, in an examination of the extent to which economic interdependence either heightens or deters military conflicts in South Asia, it is important to compare trade and MID statistics for each pair of nations in the region to reach a sufficient conclusion. This comparison using data sets from the Correlates of War database is something I will be doing to address the question at hand. Rather than solely depending on international relations theoretical perspectives, I will use statistical data to determine whether there is a positive, negative, or no correlation between trade interdependence and MIDs in South Asia. The results can then be associated with either of the two major schools of thought, or neither one.

My study will contribute to the gap that currently exists in scholarly literature with regards to the increased economic interdependence in South Asia and what the influence of this change in trade levels has had on military conflicts in the region. Since South Asia has historically been an area of considerable conflict and tensions between state actors but has recently undergone fast-paced economic development, any changes in the frequency and likelihood of MIDs in the region can conceivably be linked to the increased levels of bilateral trade. Among the limited scholarship that exists on this topic in South Asia, one scholar has determined that economic cooperation between India and Pakistan, two dominant rivals in the region, has the potential to create positive security spillovers (Sridharan 2005). These positive spillovers will most likely come in the form of reduced MIDs, which I can confirm after the completion of this study. Since South Asia is becoming an area of considerable strategic interest in contemporary times, it would be extremely beneficial to determine if, and to what extent, trade interdependence in the region can help stabilize it and deter the occurrence of military conflicts. Security issues are of utmost concern when considering the damaging effects that armed conflict has on global economic relations, especially when prominent economic markets, such as the one found in India, are involved.

Some people may question whether there are confounding variables that result in the correlation found between trade and conflict, but Oneal and Russett (1997, 1999) did control for possible sources of a spurious correlation in their research. Since Oneal and Russett found that the correlation between trade and conflict does exist and there are no conceivable confounding variables on the relationship, I feel secure enough to bypass the use of controls for my study. Instead, I will focus wholly on the two variables of interest, degree of economic interdependence between two South Asian nations and militarized interstate disputes between the two countries during the same time period, and determine if there is a correlation between the two. I will also be including China in the study because even though it does not fall under the category of a South Asian nation, its interactions with countries in the region, such as India and Pakistan, have considerable influence on the security of the region as a whole. My results can then be used to support or refute the predictions of the trade-conflict relationship by the two major schools of international relations thought- realism and liberalism.

AN INVESTIGATION INTO THE RELATIONSHIP BETWEEN THE LEVEL OF TRADE AND MILITARIZED INTERSTATE DISPUTES (MIDS) IN SOUTH ASIA

In this study, I used statistical software to determine whether a correlation exists between the trade level of a dyad in South Asia and the occurrence of MIDs between the two states. After I found whether or not a statistically significant positive or negative correlation exists between trade interdependence and MIDs using a bivariate regression, I then extracted case studies of dyadic country pairs that had at least five occurrences of MIDs. The reason I chose my cutoff to be a minimum of five MIDs is because for states that had less than five MIDs in a nearly 50-year time span, it was difficult to find a correlation between the two variables of interest that could be used to draw overall conclusions. For these case studies, I used a time-lag linear regression to investigate whether a change in the direction of the relationship results in a better approximation of the correlation between trade interdependence and MID occurrence. I used the time-lag regression by switching the independent variable from trade independence to MID occurrence from the previous year. Then, I reviewed my results in order to see which of the two linear regressions- the first one with trade interdependence as the independent variable and the second one with MID occurrence from the previous year as the independent variable- best approximated the relationship between the two variables of interest. If I found any major deviations from the trend I had established using quantitative methods, I investigated a bit using scholarly research done on the subject, which comes under qualitative methods.

I used pairs of countries in South Asia- some of the important ones being India-Pakistan, India-Bangladesh, and India-Sri Lanka- to conduct my study of whether or not trade interdependence decreases the level of military conflicts between countries. Since there are several varying classifications of which countries are included under the heading of "South Asia" by different organizations, I decided to use the World Bank as my reference. I believe the categorization provided by the World Bank is most relevant to this particular study because it examines trade data, most of which originates from the World Bank. Therefore, I used trade and MID datasets for the following South Asian nations for my research: Afghanistan, Bangladesh, Bhutan, India, Maldives, Nepal, Pakistan, and Sri Lanka. However, I also included dyadic relationships involving China and South Asian nations, such as India-China or Pakistan-China, because even though China is not considered a South Asian country, it does play enough of an influential role in the region with respect to trade levels and military conflict incidence to be included. It would be negligent not to incorporate data on whether or not increased trade interdependence between South Asian countries and China has altered the level of military tensions that has historically existed in the region involving China.

Since I believe that increased trade interdependence between nations leads to fewer occurrences of MIDs between the two countries, the key variables I need to define are "trade interdependence" and "conflict." For the purposes of this particular study, it is the most rational to examine dyadic trade interdependence using trade dependence statistics between the two sovereign states in question, as the scholars Oneal and Russett did.

For the bivariate linear regression, I plotted the dyadic trade interdependence data for two countries against the number of MIDs between the two nations for corresponding years. After plotting dyadic trade interdependence as the independent variable and MID occurrence as the dependent variable, I looked for the dyads that had at least five instances of MIDs. For these dyads, I looked at the datasets of trade interdependence and MID occurrence and decided to investigate the relationship between the two variables further. Therefore, I used STATA to run a time-lag linear regression, which means that the independent variable- which I switched to be MID occurrence- would be matched up with the dependent variable- trade interdependence- from the following year. I then compared my results from both linear regressions to see which best-fit line approximated the dyadic relationships better. While it is not possible to account for every variable that may have an effect on the occurrence of dyadic MIDs, the fact that the numerous country pairs being analyzed do not share many characteristics in common does help reduce the chance of having an omitted variable bias.

The data sources for bilateral trade and dyadic MID statistics are both datasets that can be found on the Correlates of War (COW) Project website. By using the COW Project for my datasets for both trade and MIDs, I ensured that the country codes for both are comparable, which then enables the two datasets to be combined in SPSS. The reason the bilateral trade data on the COW website is reliable is because it is derived from the World Bank's database and it is compiled in such a way that is conducive to using it in conjunction with the MIDs dataset from the COW Project. With the bilateral trade data provided by the COW Project, I used the Penn World Table to obtain GDP data on countries from the 1950s onwards. I used the GDP data from the Penn World Table, created by Heston, Summers, and Aten (2011), so I could input the figures into the formulas given above to calculate trade interdependence. Additionally, since the dyadic MID dataset on the COW website is only compiled from 1993 to 2001, I used the EUGene data management program to expand the years covered. The EUGene program, created by Bennett and Stam (2000) allows me to create the dyadic MIDs dataset from 1950 to 2001 that I need to use for my research.

As my research design demonstrates, my study is mainly quantitative in nature, but I did include aspects of qualitative research when I could not explain the trends I observed using quantitative methods. The reason I focused on quantitative methods is I believe that a study of the overall relationship between trade interdependence and dyadic MIDs is best completed using statistical data because theoretically, the issue can be argued either way. Depending on whether one decides to use a realist or liberalist- or perhaps even Marxist- approach to International Relations theory, the predictions of whether increased dyadic trade will heighten or reduce dyadic MIDs will vary. If a quantitative approach is used, it is more difficult to argue the issue based solely on theoretical frameworks. Once a positive or negative correlation was established statistically, I isolated particular case studies that had at least 5 MID occurrences between the dyadic pair and use further quantitative methods to investigate whether the causal relationship I expected between the two variables of trade interdependence and number of MIDs is, in fact, better explained by switching the independent and dependent variables. Finally, if necessary, I went back and did some qualitative research to look for reasons why certain time spans in a particular dataset did not follow the overall trend established by the regression models.

The primary tools I used for this study are the EUGene data management program and SPSS and STATA statistical software. I used these programs to establish whether or not a causal relationship exists between trade interdependence and the prevalence of military conflicts in South Asia- and if it does- what the direction of the causal sequence is.

FINDINGS OF THE RELATIONSHIP BETWEEN LEVEL OF TRADE AND MID COUNT IN SOUTH ASIA

After importing the trade and MID datasets into SPSS, I ran an analysis on the two variables of interest- trade interdependence and number of MIDs- for each South Asian country pair per year. The result of the correlation test for the two variables of interest was a slightly positive correlation that is not statistically significant at the 0.05 level. This finding is contrary to what I had expected, which is a negative correlation that is statistically significant.

However, the results are still inconclusive for the most part, since the correlation I found was not statistically significant and the linear regression for the best fit line only had an R^2 value of 0.003, which is a measure of how well the regression line approximates the real data points. Therefore, the regression line that is derived for the overall dataset only approximates 0.3 percent of the cases well. Since no statistically significant correlation was found and the R^2 value for the regression line is negligible, these results neither confirm nor refute my hypothesis that increased dyadic trade interdependence leads to decreased numbers of dyadic MID occurrence between two nations in South Asia.

Since my analysis of the overall dataset delivered inconclusive results, I decided to remove country pairs that did not exhibit any signs of conflict in the years recorded. The reason for this omission is because a relationship between the two variables of interest cannot be established if no instances of MIDs were reported throughout the history of two countries' trade relations. Then, I ran a bivariate linear regression again for the dataset with omissions and the results showed a slightly negative correlation that was not statistically significant at the 0.05 level. Next, I decided to focus on the dyads that had at least five MID occurrences in the time range specified, since any fewer MIDs would not help me find conclusive evidence of a relationship between trade interdependence and occurrence of MIDs that could be generalized for the South Asian region as a whole. Thus, I broke down my data into separate datasets for each dyad that showed at least five occurrences of MIDs in the years of interest and then I re-analyzed the datasets for possible correlations between the two primary variables- trade interdependence and number of MIDs. After excluding the other country pairs, the dyads I focused on are the following: Afghanistan and Pakistan, China and India, India and Bangladesh, India and Pakistan, and India and Sri Lanka.

Of the pairs listed, only one resulted in a correlation that was statistically significant at the 0.05 level- China and India- and it was a moderately negative correlation, which is consistent with my expectation of a negative relationship between the two variables of interest. Moreover, the regression for the China-India data subset has an R^2 value of 0.089, which means the line can approximate 8.9 percent of cases well. Accordingly, compared to the overall dataset, the China-India subset displays a significantly stronger correlation between the variables of trade interdependence and MID occurrence. Meanwhile, of the remaining pairs, the only dyadic pair that had a correlation that was significant at less than the 0.07 level also had a negative correlation. That pair was India and Sri Lanka, which had a moderately negative correlation that was statistically significant at the 0.065 level. The linear regression test for India-Sri Lanka resulted in a best fit line that approximates well for 6.6 percent of cases.

The rest of the dyads had correlations that were not statistically significant at less than the 0.65 level and the regression best-fit lines approximated well for 0.5 percent of the cases or fewer. Thus, the R^2 values for the remaining dyads of Afghanistan-Pakistan, India-Bangladesh, and India-Pakistan are not high enough for the linear regressions to approximate occurrences of MIDs in the remaining dyads. As a result, I decided to look at each of the five dyads as miniature case studies and use further quantitative research in order to understand whether the direction of the relationship I had predicted may have been reversed and which perspectives of International Relations theory, liberalism and/or realism, are evident in the trade-conflict model in South Asia.

Afghanistan-Pakistan

Upon closer inspection of the trade interdependence and MID dataset for Afghanistan and Pakistan, I noticed that drastic drops in trade interdependence most often occurred following an MID the previous year. This observation prompted me to re-analyze this specific data subset using trade interdependence as the dependent variable, rather than the independent one, and MID occurrence from the previous year as the independent variable. In order to accomplish this reversal in variables, I used STATA time-lag regression, which allowed me to use the MID count from the previous year to correspond with the trade interdependence number for the following year. Demonstrate that for this particular dyad, the causal relationship between MID occurrence and trade interdependence is statistically significant at the 0.06 level and it is in the opposite direction from what I had expected. Essentially, according to the time-lapse linear regression from STATA, MID occurrence in the previous year leads to a drop in trade interdependence the following year. However, the first time-lag linear regression, which covered all the years from 1956 to 2001, only had an R^2 value of 0.056, which means it only approximates 5.6 percent of the data points well.

China-India

The initial bivariate linear regression I ran with trade interdependence as the independent variable and MID count as the dependent variable resulted in a statistically significant, moderately negative correlation at the 0.05 level between the two variables of interest. When I ran the time-lag linear regression with MID count from the previous year as the independent variable for the years from 1950-2001, however, the results also came out with a statistically significant, slightly negative correlation between the two variables of interest. While these results may seem contradictory, since the independent and dependent variables are switched, it is not necessarily the case. First of all, the first bivariate linear regression has an R^2 value of 0.89, which means it only approximates well for 8.9 percent of real data points and the time-lag linear regression has an R^2 value of 0.0581, which means it approximates well for another 5.81 percent of real data points. Therefore, realistically, it is possible for one of the linear regressions to predict well for certain years of the China-India dataset, and the other one to predict well for another time range in the same dataset. Furthermore, the relationship between trade interdependence and MID occurrence could be a self-fulfilling cycle in which a drop in trade interdependence leads to more MIDs, which then leads to a drop in trade levels, and so on.

Meanwhile, the trend seen between the years of 1988 and 1989 is quite opposite in relation to the one exhibited between 1954 and 1956: even though there was no report of an MID occurrence in 1988, the trade interdependence between India and China still dropped considerably in 1989. When I investigated this slight blip, I found that Rajiv Gandhi, the prime minister of India at the time, had visited China in December of 1988 in an effort to alleviate growing tensions between the two nations. However, most scholars agree that the trip resulted in meager outcomes that did not accomplish much. Moreover, Gandhi was severely criticized by the Indian media for conceding that Tibet was an internal Chinese affair, which implies that many people within India were not content with the way China was dealing with Tibet (Ganguly 1989). This internal discontent with China might have contributed to the decrease in trade between India and China that is seen in the dataset.

India-Bangladesh

The India-Bangladesh dataset is the one with which I could not find a statistically significant relationship between trade interdependence and MID count. When I ran the dataset in SPSS as a simple bivariate linear regression and later in STATA as a time-lag linear regression, I found a slightly negative correlation between the two variables of interest that was not statistically significant at the 0.05 level or even at the 0.1 level. Therefore, of all the datasets, it appears as though India-Bangladesh is the only one that does not depict a strong correlation between the two variables- trade interdependence and MID occurrence. However, when I went back and looked at the dataset by hand, I noticed one particular time period of interest during which I could focus my research.

Between the years of 1973 and 1988, the trade interdependence and MID counts for the dyad pair both followed and diverged from the general expectation that either increased trade interdependence would lower conflicts or more conflicts would reduce trade interdependence in the following year. Some years, even if India and Bangladesh engaged in no armed conflicts, trade interdependence between the two nations would decrease; while other years, even if the two nations engaged in conflict, the trade interdependence would continue to rise. In order to investigate this interesting trend, I looked to scholarly journals that focused on the topic of India and Bangladesh's relationship in the 1970s and leading into the 1980s. Through my research, I found information about Bangladesh after its independence in 1971 that could help explain the trend- or in this case, lack thereof- I noticed between the nation and India with relation to trade interdependence and MID count. In the 1970s, Bangladesh was grappling with its newfound independence and efforts by India to make it a dependent state. Due to India's economic, military, and political superiority over Bangladesh, it was difficult for the latter country to maintain its sovereignty (Maniruzzaman 1977). This struggle to avoid Indian dependence could explain why the relationship between Bangladesh and India was volatile and unpredictable during the early years of Bangladeshi independence.

Overall, I think that the India-Bangladesh relationship could be explored further in order to determine if any other variables could help explain the level of trade and conflicts these two nations have engaged in over the past 30 years. However, this study will delve no deeper into this subject- this is a topic that can and should be addressed by future research.

India-Pakistan

The case study of India and Pakistan is an interesting one because the numerous linear regression tests I ran produced varying results. The original bivariate linear regression run in SPSS resulted in a slightly positive correlation between the variables of trade interdependence and MID occurrence, but it was not statistically significant at the 0.05 level. Moreover, the R^2 value was 0.002, which means the best fit line approximates well for only 0.2 percent of the data points. Next, when I turned to STATA to run the time-lag linear regression with MID count from the previous year as the independent variable, the results showed a slightly positive, statistically insignificant correlation between the two variables of interest for the years 1950 to 2001. Furthermore, the R^2 value was 0.0001, which means the best fit line for this particular time-lag linear regression could only approximate well for 0.01 percent of the data points. Since I was unable to derive a conclusive relationship between the two variables of interest, I decided to then turn to breaking down the dataset into subsets for certain time ranges.

India-Sri Lanka

The last dyad pair I investigated for my case studies is India and Sri Lanka. When the bivariate linear regression I ran for this country pair using trade interdependence as the independent variable and MID count as the dependent variable resulted in a moderately negative, statistically insignificant correlation, I decided to run the time-lag regression next. When I ran the time-lag regression in STATA for the entire time range of 1950 to 2001, the results showed a slightly negative relationship between the two variables of interest that had a p-value of nearly zero. The fact that the p-value was rounded to zero is important because the closer the p-value is to zero, the more statistically significant the results are. Therefore, the relationship I found between the variables MID count from the previous year and trade interdependence from the following year is one that definitely exists. However, the R^2 value for the time range of 1950 to 2001 was only 0.0661, which means only 6.61 percent of the data points can be approximated well by the regression best-fit line.

MAIN TRENDS OF RUSSIA'S FOREIGN POLICY IN TRANSFORMING EAST AND SOUTHEAST ASIA

In order to understand Russia's foreign policy toward East Asia we should take into consideration the current state of affairs and main trends in Russia and the region. Then it is possible to project what Russia should do to provide its interests in East Asia. So what is going on in Russia? Vladimir Putin inherited the country from Boris Yeltsin with a ruined economy, smoldering armed conflicts, and a poor populace. According to official statistics, under Yeltsin Russia's GDP declined by roughly 60% - which is unprecedented in peace time - with all the ensuing consequences. Russia became weak and concentrated upon domestic problems, and by 1998 it had lost its erstwhile role and almost all influence in East Asia. Under Vladimir Putin, Russia managed to match its own GDP of 1990 only in 2006! Putin proved effective at stopping political and economic chaos, soothing armed conflicts inside Russia, and restoring a level of social and economic development. As a result, Russia has returned to the world stage as a strong state. It is expected that new president Dmitry Medvedev will continue that political course and that the energy dimension will become more considerable in Russia's foreign policy as President Medvedev previously served as Chairman of the Board of Directors of Gazprom.

CHANGING CALCULATIONS IN EAST ASIA

During Russia's decline, the situation in East Asia, including Southeast Asia, changed a lot. First of all, the region as a whole has undergone rapid economic development and is transforming in a China-centric way. There are several important reasons for the increase of Chinese influence over the last 10 years. Most generally, China has shown impressive economic growth, and the regional balance of power has essentially shifted in China's favor. The financial crisis of 1997-1998 created conditions especially favorable for Chinese economic and political expansion. Some Southeast Asian political leaders accused the U.S. of organizing this crisis, and Beijing recognized the opportunity. China began to undertake a very active policy in the region: it refused to revalue its currency and even provided direct support to the most affected countries.

After the crisis, when the ASEAN countries had lost considerable amounts of foreign direct investment, China proposed the creation of a free trade area, excluding Japan and South Korea, and received support at the 2001 ASEAN summit in Brunei. Japan is the most economically developed East Asian country, but it has foreign military bases on its territory and Japan's foreign policy in the East Asian region is considered to be dependent on decisions taken by the U.S. War crimes committed by the Japanese army during World War II are still remembered by the local populations in China, both Koreas, and Southeast Asian countries. The unfortunate historical background and associations make modern Japanese dominance difficult; in a mid-term perspective Japan has no chance of being accepted as a regional political leader to promote East Asian interests.

China's "ASEAN Plus One" plan (in Russia, it is usually called "China Plus ASEAN") was motivated more by politics than economics; in the economic aspect China-ASEAN cooperation is much more favorable to the ASEAN countries than to China. All these factors contributed to the rising of local pan-Asian ideas. In the context of current financial instability in the U.S. and the falling dollar, for example, the concept of an Asian currency unit (ACU) should be noticed.

It was proposed in 2006 as a weighted index of currencies for ASEAN Plus Three (China, Japan, and South Korea) to stabilize the region's financial markets. The improved financial interaction between related central banks could prevent such events as Asian financial crisis of 1997-1998.

China's increasingly centrality in regional affairs will underline this pan-Asianism, and it poses both challenges and opportunities for regional community building. Southeast Asia considers China as a new regional leader that could provide more favorable opportunities to ASEAN countries in their economic development, and in fact can provide an economic umbrella.

The creation of China-centered free trade area in East Asia in general is not difficult to imagine, and China's economic growth and centrality will inevitably be converted into political influence and will provoke significant security changes first in Southeast Asia and later in East Asia as a whole.

In context of practical absence of regional security system, the rise of China will obviously provoke a significant change in East Asian order. Such a China-centered transformation of the region would be contrary to U.S. interests.

The Vietnam question

In these circumstances, Vietnam is viewed as an especially significant country in Southeast Asia because of its geopolitical disposition on the continent, close to China. Vietnam remains a flashpoint of rivalry between major powers, not only because of its strategic location along vital Asian trade routes, but also because of the vast prospected oil reserves under the South China Sea. It is clear that intelligent use of the Vietnam factor could either hamper or accelerate China's southward strategic expansion. Various dispositions are considered not only in Washington, but also in Beijing, Hanoi, and Moscow; the players involved in these geopolitical calculations are mutually suspicious, and the future alignment of forces is not clear yet.

But the "battle for Vietnam" will have far-reaching consequences for regional development, and so far China has acted more successfully than the others. Beijing is helped both by its own economic success and growing power, and recent international events.

Despite its increasing positive influence in Hanoi, China is very sensitive to recent contacts between Vietnam and the U.S. As reported in the Russian mass media in 2005, "... the U.S. Deputy Secretary of State Robert B. Zoellick's visit to Vietnam provoked real turmoil in Beijing.

The Central Committee held an extraordinary session and the whole evening was devoted to discussion of the 'Vietnam question.' The phantom of 'color' revolution appeared in the region which is considered as a main direction of economic and political Chinese expansion... In late May, Hu Jintao gave a special paper at a closed Party conference...'To win opposition without fire: how to prevent U.S. and European attempts to organize 'color' revolutions in China's neighboring countries and how to destroy U.S. plans to organize 'color' revolution in China.'"

According to American experts, Vietnam should seek an alliance in order to offset the unfavorable balance of power that is evident in its rivalry with China over small islands in the South China Sea.

In this connection Vietnam is viewed by the U.S. as a natural alliance partner. But in the context of previous wars, recent American ideological pressing on "human rights" and "religious freedom" is considered by Vietnamese authorities as the threat to the stability of their regime. Vietnam is regarded by the U.S. as one of the most effective tools that could stop Chinese expansion in a southward direction, but some recognize that "Vietnam will never want to be seen as part of a containment policy against China." Hanoi is certainly worried by a possible regional stand-off between China and the U.S. and does not want to be played in the same way Afghanistan was as part of efforts to contain the Soviet southward expansion 30 years ago.

Existence between hammer and anvil is not new to Vietnam and the general rule is the same - the more powers involved in the geopolitical game, the more space Hanoi has to maneuver. So the question of which orientation (toward Beijing or Washington) is more favorable to Vietnam in the current geopolitical situation remains open. It is well-known that Vietnam is very skillful in balancing between major powers, and through its history has traditionally followed a very flexible policy.

In this context Russia is the only involved country which never invaded Vietnam and has always maintained a balanced policy vis-à-vis Hanoi. Conversely, Vietnam is viewed in Moscow as a traditional and reliable friend in Southeast Asia. East Asian powers, including Russia, could influence the development of a China-centric Asia by their foreign policies vis-à-vis Vietnam, but of course the situation will also depend on the position that Vietnam develops independently.

DEVELOPMENTS IN RUSSIA'S FOREIGN POLICY

The issues of "unilateral and illegitimate actions" as well as "disdain for international law" and "uncontained hyper use of force" were brought up by Vladimir Putin at the Munich Conference on Security Policy in February 2007, and his views are supported by many countries. Asian governments fear that the U.S. will use the "war on terror" as a pretext to interfere in their internal affairs. Such an attitude toward U.S. policy in the "non-western world," especially in the context of events related to the former Yugoslavia, Afghanistan and Iraq, has provoked the regional arms race in East and Southeast Asia. As a result, there is the strong wish to foster regional integration and to find a reliable security umbrella provided by local, East Asian power.

During the "reforms" of the 1990s, Russia lost influence in East Asia. Later, as Russia went forward and began to develop its economy, its activities in East Asia became more and more numerous and reasonable.

Indeed, the East Asian region will play a steadily increasing role in Russia's foreign policy. Russia's strategy in the region is aimed at maintaining the status quo and the balance of forces between the major powers.

The smaller states of the region conduct a policy of maneuvering between the United States and China, but as noted above, in the last 10 years they have become oriented more and more toward Beijing. The Southeast Asian countries view China-centered regional cooperation as a model that could protect them from the influence of "hostile forces." They regard China's economic growth and prospective political umbrella as an opportunity for developing their own economies.

Now Russia has come back ready to take a more active part in world affairs. Russia is consistently developing multivector cooperation with various nations not only on a bilateral level but also in the framework of key international and regional organizations.

The current state of affairs in East Asia should be viewed as one of unstable equilibrium. There are several high intensity points around China (the Korean peninsula, the Taiwan Strait, the South China Sea, Vietnam, Tibet, the Xinjiang Uyghur Autonomous Region, and Central Asia). Each of these flashpoints has huge destructive potential and could be regarded as a part of U.S. power projection system.

A reanimated Russia and a rising China are members of UN Security Council and Shanghai Cooperation Organization (SCO). For example, in August 2007, the Russian and Chinese Ministers of Foreign Affairs proposed ASEAN countries to advance security cooperation in the frameworks of the SCO. Russian President Vladimir Putin took part in various summits: Asia-Pacific Economic Cooperation, Organization of the Islamic Conference, and the East Asia Summit. All these activities enhanced Russia's cooperation with East Asian countries and reinforced its role in regional affairs.

Energy security is one of the most discussed topics of Russia's foreign policy. The East Asian region is a net oil importer, as is well-known, and the problem of energy security is extremely important. As East Asia is the fastest developing region, its dependence on crude oil imports will rise in the foreseeable future.

This has prompted Northeast and Southeast Asian countries to display a growing interest in energy cooperation with Russia, recognizing that Russia is the world's second largest oil exporter after Saudi Arabia, and has the biggest gas reserves. Russia plans to make its contribution to regional energy security by building pipelines from its oilfields to Nakhodka (Kozmino) with a branch line to Daqing in order to support the growing demand for oil in East Asia.

Realization of this project could considerably increase energy security in East Asia and will enable Russia to play a more significant role in regional integration; in these ways Russia could support stability and economic growth in East Asia.

The most important strategic goal of Russia's foreign policy in East Asia is to become involved in regional integration, primarily with neighbor countries and traditional allies, in order to have more opportunities to develop East Siberia and the Russian Far East.

So the main directions of Russian foreign policy in the region support that goal. Russia hopes to advance cooperation with China, Japan, North and South Korea, and the ASEAN countries. Russia will try to maintain the balance of power and develop large scale economic cooperation with East and South East Asian countries. At the same time, Russia should promote its interests strictly and avoid any possible confrontation or destabilization, especially along its borders, as well as in the Korean peninsula and the Taiwan Strait.

Russia is vitally interested in the maintenance of peace, normalization, and predictability on the Korean peninsula, because it still plans to develop one prospective project – a railway through Russia connecting both North and South Koreas to the EU. Realization of such a plan will help transform the current stand-off to a situation of mutually beneficial economic cooperation. The

Korean part of this project is exceptionally important. That is why Russia is deeply involved in the Six-Party Talks and supports denuclearization of the Korean peninsula, but North Korea's concern over "unilateral and illegitimate actions" also should be taken into consideration.

The problem of North Korea's security is really difficult, because "firm guarantees" and general declarations are not believed any more. This problem was highlighted by Vladimir Putin in Munich when he mentioned "guarantees that were made and that are not being observed today" regarding current NATO expansion toward Russia's boarders. This lesson was soon learned by the international community, first of all in East Asia, and it resulted directly and immediately in a lack of trust and an unprecedented arms race.

The Taiwan Strait is relatively far from Russian borders, but the situation there could affect China, Russia's strategic partner in the framework of the SCO.

In 1992 Russia tried to advance economic cooperation with Taipei, but this idea was soon rejected. Later Russia's position was definitely clarified, on July 18, 2000.

According to the Beijing Declaration, Russia recognizes that "the government of the People's Republic of China is the only legitimate government representing China, and that Taiwan is an inalienable part of the Chinese territory ... The Taiwan issue is exclusively the internal affair of China and involvement of outside forces is inadmissible." Russia is very sensitive to security developments along its borders. Any conflict with China or North and South Korea would affect Russia, because it would mean a considerable destabilization of the entire East Asian region with unpredictable consequences.

During the last eight years Russia has acted as a responsible member of international community, and according to its foreign policy priorities, all conflicts should be resolved on the basis of international law. In this regard Russia's position is very clear and predictable. One of Moscow's main tasks is to build a constructive relationship with the United States, an extremely important component in preserving the equilibrium and balance of power and enhancing stability and security in East and Southeast Asia. The diversification of Russia's exports, which so far are limited mainly to raw materials, military-technical cooperation, and energy security issues, remains one of the most essentials tasks. But in comparison with the 1990s, current results could be considered as significant progress.

It is supposed in Asia that Russia does not pose a threat to any country in the region and could strengthen regional security and stability by its role in international affairs. The Russian Federation does not need any kind of conflicts and does not have plans to overthrow local political regimes through "peaceful transformation" or "color revolutions." Russia therefore is considered in East and Southeast Asia as a reliable and responsible partner which is open to honest cooperation with all countries on the basis of mutually profitable economic relations without confrontation and ideological stereotypes.

3

Conflict and Development in South Asia

South Asia is the second most violent place on earth after Iraq. While conflicts in Afghanistan and Pakistan have attracted global attention, parts of India, Sri Lanka, and Nepal have also experienced long-running conflict. The result is human misery, destruction of infrastructure and social cohesion, and death. The knock-on effects are huge. What is conflict? Where is it concentrated? Is conflict a problem *for* development, or a failure *of* development? What should policymakers do?

Conflict is a clash between two opposing groups, external or internal to the country. An example of external clash is state-to-state conflict, which is on the decline. Internal conflicts have resulted in three times as many deaths as wars between states since World War II (Fearon and Laitin 2003).

There are two types of internal conflict. The first is conflict against the state or civil war. Examples of this are terrorism, which is an extreme manifestation of conflict and reflects a certain degree of organisation of conflict. It is carried out by a relatively organised group of non-state actors, and directed against the state. The second category includes people-to-people conflict, or ethnic conflict. Examples of this include localised land conflicts, religious and ethnic riots, homicides or other crimes (Stewart 2008, Varshney 2002).

These two types of conflict have evolved differently in South Asia. People-to-people conflict has declined. In India, communal and ethnic riots between Hindus and Muslims are on a downward trend but terrorism has increased.

Is conflict a problem *for* development, or a failure *of* development?

Figure 1 plots conflict rates (number of people killed in terrorist incidents normalised by population) and real per capita income for a large group of countries. The downward sloping line suggests that countries that have low per capita income have higher conflict rates. This is consistent with other findings that report higher conflict rates in low income countries (Collier et al. 2003).

The relationships between conflict, income, and poverty are much more complex than is commonly supposed. High income does not guarantee peace and stability. Figure 1 shows that the relationship between conflict and per capita income is not very tight – there are many countries which are outliers. What is even more striking is that these outliers are concentrated in South Asia. Most South Asian countries (except for Bangladesh) have much higher conflict rates for their stage of development.

It is not possible to infer *causality* from Figure 1. If it is conflict which holds back development, then policymakers should focus on controlling conflict, i.e., increase military and police interventions to reduce conflict. But if it is low income and high poverty which cause conflict, then the focus should be on direct policy interventions to reduce poverty and human misery. In India, there is evidence that states that had higher incomes and fewer police had less violence than ones that had more police and less income (Justino 2009). There is also some evidence that horizontal inequalities (inequality between identity groups) can be a factor in causing conflict (Stewart 2008). This suggests that it is not enough just to have "development" but it must be shared fairly across groups.

Given the inverse association between conflict and per capita income, we would expect that conflict rates should be much higher in lagging regions within countries – i.e. those regions that have lower per capita income compared to national average? Indeed, this is exactly what we find – conflict is concentrated in lagging regions within countries.

Figure 2 shows that in India, Bangladesh, Nepal, Pakistan, and Sri Lanka, conflict is concentrated in the lagging regions. Conflict rates are higher in the lagging regions of Pakistan (Baluchistan, Federally Administered Tribal Areas, and North-West Frontier Province), India (Maoist insurgency in Bihar, Chhattisgarh, Jharkhand, and Orissa), Sri Lanka (North), and Nepal. Lagging regions have experienced more than three times the number of terrorist incidents per capita, compared with leading regions, and almost twice as many deaths per head of population in such incidents.

What triggers conflict?

Conflicts can be triggered by low economic growth which leads to a lower economic opportunity cost of rebellion against state in poor areas. Low economic growth in certain areas can be the result of unequal distribution in gains from development or political marginalisation. A second trigger for conflicts is a natural disaster. The lagging regions of South Asia suffer from both types of problems – low economic growth and higher vulnerability to natural disasters. The lagging regions have experienced much slower economic growth compared to leading regions. They are also more vulnerable to droughts and floods. The consequences of conflict on development are more severe in lagging regions because they have weak institutions, poor geography, and are poorly integrated with global markets. These are also the characteristics that limit economic growth in lagging regions.

Leading regions also suffer from conflict and poverty in South Asia but they have managed them better because of rapid economic growth, job creation, and better safety net programmes.

What should policymakers do to reduce conflict?

A speech given by the Prime Minister of India, Dr Manmohan Singh, to a Conference of Chief Ministers on Internal Security and Law and Order in 2005, sums up the story of conflict and development well:

"...Whatever be the cause, it is difficult to deny that extremism has huge societal costs. Investments are unlikely to fructify, employment is not likely to grow and educational facilities may be impaired. In all, the society at large and people at large suffer. Delivery systems are often the first casualty. Schools do not run, dispensaries do not open… the threat of Naxalism is geographically spread out to the more backward regions and districts of our country…"

Reducing conflict is a prerequisite to political stability, which, in turn, is the prerequisite for implementing pro-growth policies. Even in a best-case scenario, the presence of low-level conflict constrains the policies governments can implement to promote growth.

Policymakers in South Asia have tried various policies to reduce conflict. The most common approach to deal with insurgencies, terrorism, or internal violence is to use the police forces to establish law and order in the affected areas. The police forces in South Asian countries, however, tend to be understaffed and underequipped. In cases where police forces are insufficient, the armed forces are called in to deal with the insurgency. In most cases, this has not been a successful strategy. Even when these measures are successful in defeating the insurgents, as in Sri Lanka, the human cost associated with military operations is very high.

A different approach to dealing with insurgencies is to conduct negotiations and sign peace agreements with the insurgents. To be effective, this approach needs two conditions:

- the government must negotiate in a coordinated way and fulfil at least some of the insurgents' demands; and
- the insurgent group must be genuinely interested in joining the political mainstream. This approach has been tried in some areas of South Asia. For instance, the Indian government has signed peace deals with several separatist groups in the northeastern states, granting them a higher degree of local autonomy in some cases. Similarly, negotiations with some Tamil groups such as the EPRLF have resulted in their integration into mainstream politics.

At the same time as the security-based solution, there are economic solutions. These involve the government expanding welfare programmes to reduce poverty in the conflict-affected areas as a means to undercutting the support for the insurgency.

This approach is consistent with economic backwardness as a cause of conflict and has been tried in some conflicts in South Asia, but it has failed because of poor choices of economic policies and poor implementation in conflict regions.

CHOOSING THE RIGHT POLICY

Policy choices and their implementation are critical in preventing an escalation of conflict and in post-conflict reconstruction. Economic policies should be geared not just to maximise growth, but also to address the distributional or political factors that led to the conflict. Policy choices must be structured to reduce real or perceived inequality. Aid agencies should work through the existing government institutions, be pragmatic in order to create jobs quickly, and in most cases, work on short-term economic goals first and address medium-term and longer-term efficiency considerations later. This approach calls for humanitarian treatment of conflict-affected people, closure of refugee camps, and reintegration of refugees within society.

Cross-border cooperation between countries should be an integral part of any strategy to reduce conflict. Many of the internal conflicts in South Asia have cross-border dimensions. The Taliban in Afghanistan obtain significant support from Pakistan's border areas. The Maoists in Nepal formed close links with the Maoist movements in India. Many separatist groups in India's northeastern states have training camps and cells in neighbouring countries like Bangladesh and Bhutan. The Liberation Tigers of Tamil Eelam and other Tamil separatist groups in Sri Lanka have traditionally enjoyed support from the Tamil Diaspora in India and other countries. In such a context, regional cross-border cooperation is an essential part of any counterinsurgency strategy. Considerable potential exists for regional cooperation in reducing conflict, but this strategy has been underused in combating terrorism in South Asia.

Going forward, regional cooperation initiatives, which have so far been underused, are likely to be important in countering terrorism. South Asian governments have taken a variety of different approaches to fight terrorism. Reviewing these approaches in the South Asian and global context, it appears that the armed forces or local militias have not been especially effective in combating terrorism. Strengthening police forces or conducting negotiations to induce insurgents to join the political mainstream appear to be more effective approaches. Social welfare programmes rather than just economic incentives hoping to revive growth can be useful complements to this political accommodation approach. The challenge is to balance these different approaches toward countering conflict, as well as the optimal economic policies to be adopted in post-conflict environments.

ENERGY SECURITY IN SOUTH ASIA: CONFLICT OR COOPERATION

High population growth rate, high economic growth rate, and rapid urbanization have made South Asia a region where energy demands are growing at over 6% – a pace that is far in excess of the region's capacity to meet, unless the countries act in concert innovatively, and bring urgent reform in their internal policies. The fact that a sizeable section of the population does not have access to electricity makes energy security a daunting challenge in the countries of this region namely, Afghanistan, Bangladesh, Bhutan, India, Maldives, Nepal, Pakistan and Sri Lanka.

India, Pakistan, Bangladesh, Nepal and Bhutan import anything between 75%-100% of their petroleum needs. But the region is rich in other sources of energy which are not evenly distributed and are to a large extent untapped. India, Pakistan and Bangladesh have large reserves of gas and coal. The South Asian region has among the world's highest potential for hydel power, with Nepal and Bhutan in the lead. There exists a high potential for renewable energy, with India showing the way in solar and wind energy. Afghanistan, which is strategically placed between the oil rich Persian Gulf and South Asia, can benefit from this proximity and from the transit fee that it can levy from other countries in the region. Sri Lanka is looking to leverage hydel and biomass resources for its energy needs.

Inter and intra-regional energy production, distribution and exchange are beset by several seemingly insurmountable problems. Bickering between two of the largest players in the region, India and Pakistan, virtually eclipses any attempts at regional cooperation. Internally, in the name of expanding access to the poor, all these countries have subsidized their energy pricing -be it kerosene, LPG, or diesel to an extent where they are not just economically unviable but also that they do not reach their target group, the poor. Subsidies are straining the national budgets; for instance, the outgo on petroleum imports and subsidies as a proportion of GDP is the highest in India. Issues of price controls, lack of transparency and faulty planning are factors that militate against sound energy policies being followed among the countries in the region; this in turn impedes private investments in the power sector in this region.

Road and rail infrastructure for transporting coal or conveying gas are woefully inadequate in these countries. India has therefore turned to import of coal, while in recent years Pakistan has taken Chinese help in building roads, ports and airfields to gain access to its untapped coal reserves in the Thar region bordering Gujarat. In India, Pakistan and Bangladesh, the problem of access to land for building roads and pipelines is exacerbated by the fact that many of these areas are insurgency prone. Within these countries lack of consistency in policies is reflected in the disputes over royalty sharing between the Federal government and the states as can be seen in the case of Baluchistan and Islamabad. In India lack of governance manifests itself in intransigence in tackling the high transmission and distribution losses and loss making state electricity boards. It is proven that energy shortages are feeding unrest in the region and Pakistan is said to be a prime example.

The benefits of sound country wise and regional policies in the energy sector are manifold. Bringing electricity to the millions of poor in the region will alleviate people from much misery. It will give people access to better education, health, water and sanitation services, technologies that will open up communication, information sharing, storage of food grains and several other societal benefits that will bring peace and cohesion to these societies. The 1020 MW Tala Hydel Project in Bhutan contributed as much as 10% to the nation's GDP growth. In the interests of the people of the region, the states of South Asia need to come together with a plan that can look into the energy needs of the region for the next 50-75 years. India is best placed to take the lead in this movement, being blessed with size, location, stability and a large talent pool possessed of the technological know-how.

But India has to overcome its poor legacy in formulating policies in this regard. The Iran-Pakistan-India, the Turkmenistan-Afghanisthan-Pakistan-India and the Oman under sea gas pipelines are all mired in regional and international politics. India has frittered away its traditional affinity with the countries of the region through lack of strategic foresight and vision. Mishandling of issues such as bringing gas from Bangladesh to India by creating pipelines via West Bengal, or exploring the oil blocks in Myanmar where India had an initial advantage, have provided an entry point to China in this region.

According to Dr. Charles Ebinger, Senior Fellow and Director, Energy Security Initiative, Brookings Institution, USA, to loosen the investment environment and address the needs of the energy sector, the business communities in these countries need to come together. New Delhi must be the prime mover and has to strengthen ties with countries in this region. Citing Germany's claims of phasing out nuclear power over the next decade and stepping up production of solar power, Dr.Ebinger said that the country has already heavily subsidized its wind farming and the situation is untenable. Soon, Germany may be importing n-power from France and Czechoslovakia. Clearly, in the near term, solar power production cannot be stepped enough to provide for the growing energy needs of South Asia. He called for elimination of subsidies to different segments in the power sector, a radical step. Speaking at an interactive session organized in Mumbai by the CII, Dr. Ebinger called for intensified research in the area of clean energy from coal using carbon capture and sequestration technologies. With countries struggling to meet rising import costs of fuel, it may well be an exercise in self preservation for them to leverage regional cooperation to move towards greater energy security.

PEACE AND SECURITY POLICY COOPERATION IN SOUTH ASIA

South Asia is one of the most conflict prone regions of the world as it is marred by numerous local, national, bilateral and regional conflicts of varying intensity and dimensions. Relations in the region are dominated by the bitter rivalry between India and Pakistan for strategic influence, the power struggle between India and China for political, economic and military dominance in South Asia and the violent conflict in Afghanistan with a dangerous political vacuum looming after the withdrawal of the NATO-led ISAF forces in 2014. Unresolved border issues keep fuelling simmering tensions between the neighbours, most prominently in Kashmir and the Durand-Line, but also in repeated standoffs in the border region between China and India. Adding to that, South Asia is the only region in the world where three nuclear powers share borders: China, India and Pakistan.

Violent conflicts in South Asia are at the same time the symptom as well as the cause of a lacking regional security architecture. Looking at the various and overlapping conflicts, cooperating institutionally in the field of peace and security policy is deemed necessary but because of persisting tensions, seems rather unlikely.

There are currently no regional organizations that have the scope or mandate to actively contribute to regional cooperation in security policy and conflict management. The South As*ian Association for Regional Cooperation* (SAARC), focussing mainly on economic, social and technical co-operation, mostly excludes working on security issues and by principles keeps aside bilateral issues and involvement in internal issues of member states like insurgencies. SAARC does provide the framework to act on multilaterally agreed topics like cross-border terrorism and fighting international organized crime and drug trade. But even these initiatives never took off as the unresolved Kashmir conflict between India and Pakistan have generally prevented South Asia from deeper integration and especially from cooperating in security and defence issues. Another reason for the lack of regional integration is the enormous trust deficit between most neighbours.

So where does India stand in the region? India is perceived as the political and economic power house in South Asia. Therefore, future developments in the region also depend largely on Indian foreign, economic, and environmental and defence policies. From its status as the future's most populous country and largest democracy in the world as well through its role as a rising economic power, the political leadership for example deflects India's claim as a regional and global power and to a permanent seat at the UN Security Council. So far India has, however, failed to show that it contributes effectively to stability and peace in the region.

India and China are constantly competing for strategic partners in Asia. A major concern for India is China's increasing economic and military footprint in South Asia. Smaller countries like Bhutan, Myanmar, Nepal and Sri Lanka have increasingly used China as a counter-weight against Indian influence. China has also been a close strategic partner for Pakistan, much to India's discomfort. However, economic interests seem to dominate China's agenda. Economic cooperation between China and South Asian countries (including India) has increased in recent years. China seems less interested to involve itself in internal conflicts of South Asian countries than before and more interested in arrangements securing resources and energy. Military and security cooperation with China by South Asian countries seems not to be focused against India anymore due to shifting threat perceptions and changing economic prospects. China's influence, some argue, should therefore not be seen as an obstacle for security cooperation in South Asia.

India and Pakistan on the other hand have already endured four wars and numerous bilateral crises and ongoing bilateral tensions keep dominating regional developments. After the Mumbai attacks of 2008, all bilateral ties had been disrupted. While relations seemed to have improved in the last few years and visa and trade negotiations were resumed, armed borders skirmishes at the Line of Control (LOC) in the disputed Kashmir-region in 2013 have been described as the worst fighting in a decade which has destroyed years of diplomatic efforts, damaging the peace process.

The relations between India and Pakistan are also relevant for the future of Afghanistan after the troop withdrawal of NATO-led ISAF forces. The conflict is often perceived as a proxy war between India and Pakistan, each one eyeing the strategic moves of the other country with suspicion. The planned post-2014 scenario presents an opportunity for Afghanistan's neighbours to strengthen their roles in securing the future of Afghanistan. A peaceful stabilization of the conûict in Afghanistan is key to securing the fragile region from current and future threats. Cooperation between India and Pakistan for the stabilisation of Afghanistan is crucial. As such, the process has to be based on constructive regional cooperation between India and Pakistan and of Afghanistan with all its neighbours. For this, serious trust-building is necessary. While economic cooperation between India and its neighbours has improved, mutual distrust remains a challenge. Supporting intra-regional cooperation and particularly peaceful dialogues with India's neighbouring countries are a much-needed contribution. Track II trust-building dialogues are a promising forum to discuss political, security and economic issues which should be discussed at the government level, but due to political sensitivities cannot be discussed.

As regional institutionalized cooperation in the field of security policy seems unlikely, the countries of the region could increase their (military and defence) cooperation by building on existing bilateral confidence building measures (CBMs) like the DGMO meetings between India and Pakistan as well as fortifying mechanisms between India and China to better deal with border incidents.

There are also other encouraging signs of cooperation, e.g. by the establishment of the South Asian University, fostering regional cooperation and trust building through people-to-people contacts, knowledge exchange, academic debates. There are also a growing number of initiatives ranging from regional academic networks to support track I with informed and sound advice on regional cooperation in UN Peacekeeping missions to the establishment of policy groups in Afghanistan, Central Asia, India and Pakistan by high-ranking experts closely linked to track I to lobby for joint policy suggestions intended to feed governments with starting points for regional cooperation.

These initiatives have come up with implementable ideas like joint military and strategic trainings for UN peacekeeping operations or joint maritime exercises in the Bay of Bengal and anti-piracy efforts in the Indian Ocean. These non-sensitive CMBs might provide the basis for further cooperation by improving the flow of information between the military and security establishment on either side, so that lasting communication channels are established, that do not break down even in the case of an armed conflict.

These are encouraging developments that provide the governments in the region the right support and information to deepen cooperation in the region as long as there is political will. The alignment of threat perceptions e.g. of China with South Asia countries regarding the spread of terrorism are slowly changing the regional setting, opening channels for communication and joint action for example in Afghanistan. India and Pakistan also seem to realize that peace in the region can only be achieved by their constructive cooperation in Afghanistan.

Through is various trust building dialogues, FES India supports these track 1,5 peace processes from Afghanistan's neighborhood in the west to Myanmar in the east of India (Bay of Bengal Initiative).

MILITARY DEVELOPMENT

Chinese analysts often point to Russian military power as one of the key factors contributing to its continued existence as a major nation in the world and believe that in international affairs it will rely on its military strength while it copes with its domestic economic and political problems. However, the Russian military, while strong, still can not compare to that of the Soviet Union. One author writes about Russia's current force: "Its military power has declined and its defence capability has seriously weakened.... Russia inherited most of the former Soviet army's weapons and equipment, but less than 20 percent of those meet the requirements of modernization; its military power has seriously weakened."

A CICIR study stated, "Following the collapse of the Soviet Union and the fall in Russia's Comprehensive National Power, Russia's armed forces sank into a severe decline." It went on to sum up several problems Russia will have to deal with in its efforts to modernize and develop its military:

- "The largest difficulty currently facing the Russian military is that funds are seriously insufficient."

- "The serious shortage of funds greatly influences the Russian military's work in troop training, logistics supplies, equipment renewal, professionalizing troops, and other projects."
- "Troop replenishment difficulties have brought the Russian military one disaster after another. Because of unrest in the Russian political situation and the low level of the troops' social position and living wages, young people's enthusiasm for participating in the military is universally low, and evading military service is extremely common."
- "Various objective factors are causing a sharp rise in the crime rate in the Russian armed forces."
- "In the war in Chechnya, the Russian military revealed that its command coordination was not at its best, its coordinated fighting was in chaos, its information reconnaissance was sluggish, its logistics safeguards were lacking, it had low officer-soldier morale, and there were many other weak points."

However, according to the study, Russia's military reforms may speed up because of its problems in Chechnya, which "critically influenced Russia's military reform process," even though Russia still "lacks a clear military reform strategy." Failures during the war in Chechnya resulted in much attention from Russia's highest decisionmaking levels, so that the entire plan for military reforms is also being "tensely deliberated and drafted."

One area of Russia's military force that Chinese analysts assess as balancing these inadequacies is its arsenal of nuclear weapons. "On the one hand, Russia is still a major nuclear power and the second largest military power in the world; on the other hand, the shortage of military funds, the slow renewal of equipment and the irregular training have greatly lowered the Russian army's effectiveness." Chinese authors point out that, "given the fact that Russian national power has dramatically declined and its conventional forces have been reduced on a large scale," Russia has no choice but to "stress the deterrent role played by the nuclear force in safeguarding its national security." A *People's Daily* article stated,

Russia, not reconciled to having been reduced to a "second-class country," tries hard to restore its status as a big country with its "nuclear shield." ... After beginning to expand eastward, NATO has steadily closed in on Russia, and Russia has been reduced to an inferior position with regard to the balance between Russia and Western countries in conventional military forces. Thus, Russia should all the more attach importance to the nuclear weapons in its hands. The chapter predicts that Russia will invest heavily in the development of nuclear technology so that it will retain its military power: To balance its nuclear weapons with those of the United States, Russia has still allocated a huge sum of money, despite its financial straits, in order to accelerate development of the "White Poplar M" intercontinental guided missiles. This year, Russia will deploy this new kind of guided missile to replace gradually the SS-25 powered intercontinental ballistic guided missiles. Russia is also developing a new series of fourth-generation nuclear submarines called "God of the North Wind," and the first modern nuclear submarine, named "Dorglooge," had also been put into use.

A particularly negative assessment of Russia's military capabilities was put forward by Shen Jiru, Director of the International Strategic Research Section of the Institute of World Economics and Politics at CASS. He also believes that Russia's only option is to rely on its nuclear forces. He writes:

Few Russian army divisions are completely equipped nowadays. As its navy cannot even afford fuel, its aircraft carriers have had to be sold as scrap metal. Under these circumstances, Russia can only barely manage to keep up its nuclear forces, but nothing else. Russian military personages have said that, in the future, Russia will have to be more and more reliant on nuclear forces. Therefore, in conducting any future military activities, Russia has lost the possibility of making choices. As far as Russia is concerned, it either fights or does not fight. But if the latter is chosen, it is very probable that it will have to use nuclear weapons, because any other weapons link for Russia is now incomplete. Russia would be unable to operate militarily in a normal way due to financial problems as well as a shortage of military staff. Frankly, it just lacks the material base to adopt any strategy and tactics which would escalate step by step.

Despite Russia's weakened military force, Chinese analysts emphasize that it still is quite powerful when compared to that of other countries. According to Chinese assessments, Russia currently has the second most powerful military in the world after the United States, and in the short term no other country will be able to surpass it. For example, Yan Xuetong of CICIR writes, "Russia's superiority over China, Japan, and Germany in the areas of nuclear and conventional weaponry... can be preserved until early next century." A comparison of the military power of six countries, done by Colonel Huang Shuofeng of AMS in 1996 as part of a study on CNP, found that Russia's military power was 67 percent of the U.S. score, a major decline from the assessment of the Soviet Union's military power by Huang in 1990, when it was 99.6 percent of the U.S. score. However, Huang points out, "Although Russia currently has numerous economic difficulties, the progress of its armed forces reforms is uneven, its national defence expenditures have actually decreased by around 45 percent, and it has suffered a disastrous decline from its position as a military superpower to a very large extent; it can be said that Russia is a military power that is second only to the United States, and it is second only to the United States in terms of the highest military expenditures." China accordingly, still falls behind Russia in military power. Based on Huang's calculations, in 1996, China's military power score was 77.7 percent of the Russian score. In strategic weaponry, China's score was only 0.4 percent of Russia's; in national defence expenditures, China scored 8.7 percent; and in average national defence expenditures per person and annual per capita defence expenditures, China's scores were 4.7 percent and 1.0 percent, respectively.

"Secret" RMA Efforts

As Russia assumes its place as one of the five poles in the multipolar structure, Chinese military analysts believe Russia will also be exploiting the RMA, probably ahead of the declining United States. Two officers at AMS, authors of *America, Russia, and the Revolution in Military Affairs,* describe Russia's fall from its "superpower pinnacle" as the reason Moscow "temporarily will be unable to compete with the United States in this new RMA." They add: "In the new RMA tide that is currently rising in the world, the United States without a doubt is in the central position that is the focus of attention." However, they contend that several factors favour a surprise, and Russia may do better at the RMA than the United States: "Because military power has today become practically the only pillar supporting Russia's position as a major nation, its strategists will place top priority on using the new RMA to maintain its military superiority in a position of top priority in its national strategy. Currently it is secretly taking aim at America's commanding position in the new RMA and actively planning, preparing, and carrying out the new RMA." The orthodox had viewed that Russia will achieve sustained growth after 2005, and recovery suggests to PLA authors that Moscow will be able to exploit the RMA rapidly, which would enhance Russian military power.

Russian military specialists invited to AMS find their works quoted favorably in Chinese journals. Even though "up to now [Moscow] still has not completely implemented a new RMA plan... this does not indicate that the figures in Russia's military and political leadership and military doctrinal circles lack a full understanding and urgent desire regarding the RMA; also, it does not mean that Russia is willingly allowing its former opponent to get far ahead in the spring tide of this new RMA... they are trying to prepare for the future when Russia will enter the period when it completely carries out the new RMA." Despite its current economic weakness, Chinese analysts such as Gao Chunxiang of AMS see that, "Russia's high-level military and political leadership continually make speeches on issues related to the RMA... [and] draw lessons from the new technology the United States needs to develop the RMA." The place in Russia where this is done is "the General Staff Military Academy and other military learning organizations." The Chinese are aware that Russian doctrine "points out that national defence research and development must first focus on developing new deep-strike weapons, information weapons, and electronic warfare equipment." Moreover, they know the Russian military is "putting forward concepts about 21st century

Russian military structure and has already made public 'The Russian Military's Ten-Year Weaponry Development Long-Term Plan' and 'Twenty-First Century Soldier Equipment Plan.' " Li Qinggong, a Research Fellow at CIISS, writes,

With the introduction of the program of "three-phased military reform," Russia has begun to speed up the process of the new military revolution, with an even clearer objective, i.e., carrying out the professionalization of the armed forces, enhancing military scientific research, updating equipment on large scale, and restoring its position of a major military power. To achieve this goal, Russia on the one hand is adjusting its military structure and reorganizing its military industries, and on the other hand is increasing its input in the development of military high technology, updating its nuclear force and promoting its conventional force. In order to deal with future information warfare, Russia specially held a roundtable meeting, which introduced the "doctrine of information security" and decided to step up its development of information weapons so as to achieve a "new balance of power."

Implications of the Soviet Collapse

As noted in the Preface, Chinese "debates" about the security environment are quite different in style and content from the debates of Western scholars and public commentators. Debates about Russia have been particularly sensitive and secretive in the two decades since the death of Chairman Mao. According to interviews in China, these past debates remain relevant and not all issues in them have been fully resolved. A secretive debate on the character of the USSR was carried out in the mid-1970s through allegorical references to Chinese ancient history by authors using pseudonyms for the individuals or groups involved. The authors pretended to hold "harmless" historical debates. Only after the deaths of Mao Zedong and Zhou Enlai and the subsequent arrest of the Gang of Four did China reveal that the allegorical debates had directly involved Politburo members. Apparently they instigated the scholars' attack on the policies of their political opponents using ancient historical figures in allegory.

From 1978 to 1982, a second debate on the USSR was also largely concealed. The result of the second debate was a sharp reduction in China's assessment of a Soviet military threat. The collapse of the Communist Party in the Soviet Union jolted China. China's leaders had difficulty maintaining their claim that socialism was a superior system that would eventually replace capitalism. Consequently, in the early nineties, a debate ensued over the causes of the collapse and the implications for China. In the first phase of the debate, from 1991-92, the United States was assessed to be completely responsible for the collapse of the Soviet Union through a process of containment and ideological subversion called "peaceful evolution." However, this view was overturned in the second stage of "scholarly" debate in 1992-93.

American Subversion?

Close examination of Chinese commentary from 1990 to 1992 indicates a veiled debate took place among various institutes and individuals about the causes of the Soviet disintegration and its consequences for Chinese communism. The debates were initially restricted to internally circulated journals. Using an old Mao quotation, an initial explanation was attributed to an American strategy, dating back to John Foster Dulles, known by the characters for "peaceful evolution." An early assertion of this cause of the Soviet collapse appeared in Hong Kong in December 1991 in a newspaper affiliated with the People's Republic of China (PRC): The strategy of peaceful evolution created an opportunity for foreign forces, lead by United States, to meddle in, interfere with, and eventually dominate the political and economic affairs of the Soviet Union, and opened the door for them to impose their own political, economic and social values. Its author provides an explicit warning for China when he adds, "It is fair to say that without overt or covert support from the United States, the disintegration of the Soviet Union could not have been realized, nor could it have been achieved so successfully and so precipitously."

According to the "peaceful evolution" strategy, the levers the United States used against the former Soviet Union (and which would apply to China) were trade, economic cooperation, technology transfer, diplomacy, cultural and educational exchanges, religious freedom, and so on. Another scholar estimates that the West enjoyed a superiority in these "weapons." By the mid-1980s, the estimated advantage that the Western countries enjoyed over the socialist countries in material terms was calculated by the Chinese to be 3:1. However, in terms of mass media, the advantage was calculated to exceed 20:1. The analyst argued that Western countries have employed electronic media as a weapon to infiltrate socialist countries and disintegrate them. One internal speech by a Chinese leader warns, In the wake of traumatic changes in Eastern Europe and the August 19 coup in the Soviet Union, the task of countering peaceful evolution has become ever tougher. The developed countries headed by the United States attempt to conquer the whole world in terms of ideology, imposing such Western values as democracy, freedom and human rights... they have already caused revolts in the Soviet Union and Eastern Europe. Now they naturally would target China.

According to interviews conducted by the author, a book entitled *Western Politicians on Peaceful Evolution* contains articles warning about the American subversive strategy for dealing with China after the June 1989 Tiananmen breakdown.

Moscow's Own Fault

The second thesis about the collapse of the Soviet Union was argued by Liu Keming, the former chief of the Liaison Department of China's Central Committee. Liu, a leading Soviet expert, criticized Mikhail Gorbachev's "new thinking" and his personality. In Liu's view, when Gorbachev introduced a multiparty system and separation of powers, he completely negated 70 years of Soviet political structure and brought an end to the Communist Party in power. Gorbachev was a negative example for China; thus Liu asserts that China should avoid:

- The adoption of a multiparty system, which abandoned the leading role of the Communist Party
- A pluralist ideology, in which Marxist-Leninism no longer formed the only ideological foundation
- Talk of democratic socialism rather than communism as the final goal of the party
- Rejection of democratic central control of the Communist Party and its transformation into a loose political organization tolerating overt factions.

Liu's thesis holds that the neglect of politics and ideology by the Soviet leadership, together with Gorbachev's political errors and widespread corruption (including the bribery case of Leonid Brezhnev's son-in-law), all caused the downfall.

By mid-1992, however, a new analysis emerged. Scholars presenting this analysis challenged the idea of Western imperialists pushing peaceful evolution in the Soviet Union. If they had been at it since the 1940s, why did it not succeed until the late 1980s? They asked how hostile international forces could peacefully subvert a 20-million-member Soviet Communist Party without encountering any resistance.

Professor Luo Zhaohong, of the Institute of World Economics and Politics at CASS, directly criticizes the effort to blame Gorbachev alone for the Soviet disintegration. He also attacks the notion of peaceful evolution, arguing that foreign involvement could never play a significant role in the Soviet collapse. Professor Luo puts forward the view that it was an excess of Stalinism and poor budgetary management and errors in economic policy that caused the Soviet collapse.

According to Chinese analysts, the logic of the "peaceful evolution" thesis began to be attacked by many analysts in the second phase of the 1990-1992 debate. For one thing, not a single American soldier had entered the Soviet Union. Chinese analysts instead suggest that problems such as agriculture were ignored; the ethnic issue was mishandled; and the Soviets were overcommitted, especially with the invasion of Afghanistan and generous aid to Cuba. In general, they said, economic factors were key to the collapse.

In an interesting twist, the new argument held that stagnation and isolation had caused the Soviet system to fall behind, along with its highly centralized planning and an excessive military budget.

The implication of this diagnosis was that if China could avoid highly centralized planning, excess defence spending, and isolation, then China could also avoid the fate of the Soviet Union. Professor Luo Zhaohong also criticizes the economic theory of the Soviet Union because it left out of its theoretical foundation notions of value, profit, and competition and it overemphasized state-owned enterprises, which had no autonomy and had their production geared to an arbitrary state plan rather than market commands. This, he concludes, destroyed the vitality of enterprises and hampered the quantity and quality of production. There were no incentives to innovate. Technological progress and competition with the West were impossible.

Professor Luo estimates the Soviet defence budget to have been at 20 to 25 percent of the GNP at the time of the USSR collapse, and almost all the research efforts of the Soviet industrial base served the military.

He quotes former Soviet Prime Minister Nikolai Ryzhkov in saying that 75 percent of the government research and development budget had been appropriated for alternate use, and that the military share of electronics was as much as 50 percent.

Thus Luo concludes that because the Soviet GNP was one-third that of the U.S. GNP, maintaining strategic parity with strategic weapons and surpassing the United States in conventional forces put an unbearable burden on the Soviet economy. The Chinese quote Gorbachev's admission in a speech in February 1981: "This is the most militarized economy in the world."

Gorbachev's personality and policies may have accelerated the economic collapse, but in the Chinese view, decades of overly centralized planning and excessive military expenditures were the root causes of the collapse. The gap between American and Soviet living standards was 10 to 1, according to Chinese calculations, with the per capita GNP in the Soviet Union as low as about $2,000.

The conclusions for China of this new thesis were not that "peaceful evolution" should be cut off by seclusion and isolation from Western cultural influences; rather, the issues would be successful management of the economy to maintain ever higher living standards, further devolution of planning toward a market economy, and efforts to continue technological progress.

After nearly 2 years of debate, in what seems to be a tradition in this policy process, a major conference was held in Beijing in May 1992. The record was published in the journal *World Economics and Politics*. An important element in this policy process was a statement made by Deng Xiaoping during his tour of Southern China in early 1992. In remarks conveyed through intermediaries, Deng supposedly said, "A planned economy does not equal socialism." Whether something is socialist or capitalist, Deng pointed out, depends on whether it will benefit the living standards of the people. He criticized anyone who opposed foreign capital investment in China or joint ventures with foreigners as "ignorant" and "lacking common sense."

4

Climate Change, Migration, and Conflict in South Asia

RISING TENSIONS AND POLICY OPTIONS ACROSS THE SUBCONTINENT

In areas of existing conflict in South Asia, added stressors of climate change and changing migration patterns could be a security concern.

South Asia will be among the regions hardest hit by climate change. Higher temperatures, more extreme weather, rising sea levels, increasing cyclonic activity in the Bay of Bengal and the Arabian Sea, as well as floods in the region's complex river systems will complicate existing development and poverty reduction initiatives. Coupled with high population density levels, these climate shifts have the potential to create complex environmental, humanitarian, and security challenges. India and Bangladesh, in particular, will feel the impacts of climate change acutely.

The consequences of climate change will change conditions and undermine livelihoods in many areas. And extreme events and deteriorating conditions are likely to force many to leave their homes temporarily or even permanently for another village, city, region or country.

Uncertainty surrounding the specific implications of climate change and migration on security and stability is no longer an excuse for inaction. A 2009 Report of the U.N. Secretary General outlined "second-order effects of unsuccessful adaptation in the form of uncoordinated coping or survival strategies of local populations ... [including] involuntary migration, competition with other communities or groups over scarce resources and an overburdening of local or national governance capacities."

The Asian Disaster Preparedness Center recently reported that Bangladesh "is already under pressure from increasing demands for food and the parallel problems of depletion of agricultural land and water resources from overuse and contamination. Climate variability and projected global climate change makes the issue particularly urgent."

Additionally, Thomas Fingar, chairman of the National Intelligence Council, testified to the U.S. Congress that climate change will exacerbate poverty and increase social tensions, leading to internal instability and conflict, and giving parts of the global population additional reasons to migrate.The Pew Charitable Trust's Climate Security Project came to the same conclusion: U.S. national and international security is inextricably linked to global climate change. The project's experts warn that climate change will increase resource conflicts within and among countries, increase migration pressures on hundreds of millions of people, increase the number of humanitarian disasters, disrupt economies all over the world, and threaten military preparedness.

Recent disasters in South Asia demonstrate what could be a more frequent reality for the region. Floods in September 2012 displaced 1.5 million people in the northeastern state of Assam, while Cyclone Aila in 2009 displaced 2.3 million people in India and almost 850,000 in Bangladesh.

The Asian Development Bank 2012 report "Climate Change and Migration in Asia and the Pacific" concludes that while uncertainties exist on where, how, and how many will be displaced by climate change impacts, it is imperative to begin aggressively examining emerging climate challenges to avoid future complex crisis scenarios. The extreme vulnerability of South Asia raises concern of potential changes and increases in both internal and international migration across the subcontinent. In areas of existing conflict in South Asia, added stressors of climate change and changing migration patterns could be a security concern.

The United States has the opportunity to build a vital partnership with countries in the region to mutually cope with climate change. Hurricane Sandy, a record breaking year of drought, heat waves, and extreme weather proved that potential impacts of climate change are not problems of distant shores; they are a globally shared burden. The United States has much to learn and offer in the way of best practices as climate change worsens in the decades to come. Large cities in the United States, such as New York and Miami, will be hit hard with extreme weather in very similar ways as South Asian megacities such as Dhaka and Mumbai. Partnering with India and Bangladesh in complex climate scenarios is smart policy and smart diplomacy for the United States. But in order to do this, the United States needs to understand the factors playing out on the ground.

In this paper we examine the role of climate change, migration, and security broadly at the national level in India and Bangladesh-and then zero in more closely on northeast India and Bangladesh to demonstrate the interlocking problems faced by the people there and writ larger across all of South Asia. As discussed in our framing report, "Climate Change, Migration, and Conflict," we do not assert direct causal relationships between climate change, migration, and conflict. Instead, we understand climate change, migration, and security as three distinct layers of tension and assess scenarios in which the three layers will overlap. The Indian border state of Assam is a case study on where the three factors converge.

Zeroing in on Assam

Assam is located in the northeast region of India, connected to India by a land bridge called the Siliguri corridor, which measures less than 25 miles across. The states in the northeast region are collectively called the Seven Sisters and their cultures and traditions are influenced by greater India as well as bordering Southeast Asia. The consequences of climate change on both sides of the border, existing political issues with migration, and conflict that has plagued the region make Assam a unique case study into the intersection of climate change, migration, and security.

Deteriorating environmental conditions could increasingly influence decisions to move, in addition to social, political, economic, and demographic drivers. Suddenonset and slow-onset climate change events could spark migration in both India and Bangladesh. Sudden-onset events-such as flooding, cyclones, and storm surges-could displace millions of inhabitants within short periods of time, as recent events in India and Bangladesh demonstrate. Slow-onset events-such as changes in precipitation, sea level rise, and land erosion-could have detrimental impacts on key economic sectors-such as agriculture, fishing, and tourism-influencing someone's decision over time to move for greater economic opportunity.

The internal and temporary displacement of people in this region will probably account for the bulk of migration that takes place in the face of environmental changes and degradation. People may move within country for a couple days, weeks, or months, or even years to a new location before trying to resettle in their home towns and cities. Rural-to-urban migration has taken place throughout India and Bangladesh and could be more sought after if climate change threatens rural livelihoods, particularly in the agriculture sector.

International migration may also be an option, particularly to areas in which historical, familial, and cultural ties exist across borders, either through a legal or unauthorized process aided by porous and unguarded international borders. As the Asian Development Bank reports, substantial and established flows of migration takes place between India and Bangladesh, particularly to the Indian states of West Bengal and Assam. The bank's report goes on to say, "It has been suggested that this is the largest single international migration flow, with more people involved than estimated for top-ranked Mexico-United States migration flows."

No reliable numbers exist on Bangladeshi emigration. But any change in existing migration patterns from Bangladesh into India could have security consequences, particularly in Assam. Back in the 1980s a group called the All Assam Student's Union began a movement calling for the deportation of all supposed unauthorized Bangladeshi immigrants, asserting that the immigrants were influencing their economy, security, and political system, as well as their local demographic structure. It became known as the Assam movement and lasted until 1985, causing up to 7,000 deaths.

More recently, members of the Bodo tribe and the Muslim community clashed in Assam over the building of a mosque. It resulted in close to 100 deaths and the displacement of over 400,000, who fled to relief camps in the area.As the conflict escalated, members of the Bodo tribe and a section of politicians began to blame the incident on the increasing number of unauthorized Bangladeshis in the region.In the following days, rumors spread via text messages and emails that Muslim groups were planning attacks on Assamese residents living in other parts of India, particularly in the southern cities of Bangalore and Chennai. Thousands of people native to the Northeast Indian region boarded overflowing buses and returned to the region. As of October 2012, 133,000 were still in relief camps.In the days following the conflict, many in Assam resorted to public demonstration and protests against unauthorized immigrants from Bangladesh demanding their identification and deportation, similar to the fervor during the 1980s Assam movement.

The conflict in Assam caused upheaval across the country, highlighting the issue of unauthorized immigrants, which routinely becomes an issue during elections in Assam. In assessing the security challenges of climate change, Assam provides an example of several factors coming together in a complex way. Climate change will stress existing migration patterns both locally and internationally in Bangladesh. Even more importantly, the *perception* that there has been an increase in immigrants has the potential to stoke tensions over immigration in Assam.

What this means for the United States and the world

Given the likelihood that large-scale climatic events will strike the region in decades ahead, it is important to grasp how the complex historical and cultural issues associated with migration in the region could play out. As the United States shifts its strategic focus to the Asia Pacific, a clear understanding of climate change and human mobility will be central to development and security goals in the region. The United States and international policymakers will need to understand and prepare for the added stresses and risks imposed by climate change and migration globally.

For the international community the extended region located around India, Bangladesh, and the Bay of Bengal represents both an economic opportunity and a massive development challenge. The unique concentration of population will likely play a pivotal role in coming decades-India and Bangladesh must chart a path of sustainable development by which the region can achieve economic growth while maintaining long-term stability.

The United States could be a vital partner in this effort. We propose three policy collaborations that the United States can take up with South Asian partners as complex crisis scenarios unfold in the wake of climate change:

- High-level climate-vulnerable cities workshop
- A dialogue on migration
- Ecological infrastructure development

These three collaborations are detailed further in the conclusion of the report, but let's briefly examine each of them in turn here.

High-level climate-vulnerable cities workshop

The United States, India, and Bangladesh should lead a high-level workshop on climate vulnerable cities. Cities will be a priority as urbanization continues in India and Bangladesh and as extreme weather challenges the resilience of U.S. urban centers. Cities such as New York, Mumbai, and Dhaka can learn from each other.

The goal should be to zoom in and have detailed discussions about resilient infrastructure, disaster relief logistics, and preparedness best practices across countries and government levels. The workshop would be ideally coordinated at a federal level through the U.S. Agency for International Development and the U.S. Department of State with governor and mayor level participants. New York City Mayor Michael Bloomberg and New York Gov. Andrew Cuomo could be in workshop discussions with Mumbai Mayor Sunil Waman Prabhu and Maharashtra's chief minister Prithviraj Chavan as leaders of two cities vulnerable to sea level rise and extreme weather.

A dialogue on migration

The United States and India share numerous concerns about undocumented residents and immigration including social inclusion, path to citizenship, language, cultural differences, deportation issues, border management, and legal status. Comprehensive immigration reform is likely to be tackled in the next four years of the Obama administration. An open exchange between India and the U.S. on immigration would be beneficial to both sides.

Ecological infrastructure development

Ecological infrastructure involves using natural landscapes and ecosystems for the benefit of society. In the case of climate change, natural landscapes that mitigate the consequences of flooding, water salinization, and erosion may be both cost effective and more resilient than traditional infrastructure, such as levies and pumps.

Residents of India and Bangladesh have been innovating ecological infrastructure due to lack of formal structures in many areas. As in the cases of city adaptation and immigration, a U.S. partnership with India and Bangladesh on ecological infrastructure would create a rich depository on adaptation strategies while informing U.S. diplomacy and development programs on the ground.

THE IMPORTANCE OF ASSAM IN CLIMATE CHANGE, MIGRATION, AND CONFLICT IN SOUTH ASIA

Analyzing South Asia through the prism of climate, migration, and security in Assam and the surrounding region provides useful insights into the underlying trends shaping the entire region and the risks posed by current long-term trajectories. While the precise influence of climate change on migration is still the subject of scientific inquiry and debate, the range of issues facing the region calls for a comprehensive assessment of climate change, migration, and their impact on both traditional and human security. We hope the assessment will be a jumping-off point for more empirical research establishing the realities of climate driven migration in South Asia.

To assess these overlapping dynamics, we begin our report with an examination of the climate change, migration, and security issues facing India and Bangladesh before turning in greater detail to the northeastern region of the subcontinent, and specifically the Indian state of Assam.

CLIMATE CHANGE IN SOUTH ASIA

A Framework of Sustainable Development and Human Security

Climate change has attracted unprecedented attention in recent years. It has been referred to as the defining human development issue of our generation. While climate change originated as an environmental problem, it now impinges on every aspect of human life including international peace and security. South Asia provides an interesting case study to discuss climate change as the challenges facing these countries are wide and varied yet they share similar cultural and socio-economic backgrounds. Issues relevant to India which is fast industrializing will be different from the Maldives, which is threatened by submergence due to rising sea levels giving rise to "climate refugees." Problems facing Sri Lanka, an island nation, will be different from Nepal and Bhutan which are landlocked states. At the same time, these countries are plagued by conflict, poverty and malnutrition. The effects of global warming on the Indian subcontinent vary from the submergence of low-lying islands and coastal lands to the melting of glaciers in the Indian Himalayas, threatening the volumetric flow rate of many of the most important rivers of India and South Asia. *(Penny Christopher: 2007).*

The South Asian region is one of the most densely populated and at the same time most exposed regions in terms of the threats of climate change. A considerable section of the South Asian population is dependent on agriculture for their livelihood and they have to bear the brunt of the vagaries of the changing climate. It is estimated that by 2050, the population of South Asia will increase to reach 2.2 billion from the current figure of 1.5 billion. With an estimated 600 million South Asians subsisting on less than $ 1.25 a day, even relatively small climate shocks can cause irreversible damage and push a large number of people into destitution. Over the years the South Asian region has experienced significantly longer summers and in some cases severe heat waves. In many parts of South Asia, the frequency of more intense rainfall has increased-leading to severe floods, landslides and debris flow. At the same time, the total amount of precipitation has declined.

HUMAN SECURITY: A PARADIGM SHIFT

Environmental issues have been seen in the broader context of human security since the end of the Cold War. This marked the end of both the political bipolarity and the narrow, mainly military notion of security concepts and perceptions which dominated the security discourse at that time. A number of United Nations' Conventions directly and specifically address environmental issues that have great bearing on societies worldwide and contribute indirectly to improving several of the dimensions of human security. The *UNDP Human Development Report,* (1994) defined human security as *'safety from chronic threats such as hunger, disease, and repression as well as protection from sudden and harmful disruptions in the patterns of daily life – whether in homes, in jobs or in communities',* and as the totality of economic security, food security, health security, environmental security, personal security, community security and political security. Human security has become *'both a new measure of global security and a new agenda for global action'.* Culture, economies, trade, production-lines, values, politics are no longer framed within national boundaries, peoples of the world are connected through their actions and inactions, and as such threats to security and livelihoods transcend state apparatus.

Human security as a concept first surfaced in the early 1990s when it became increasingly clear that the end of the Cold War would not be accompanied by an end to armed conflict but that instead the nature of violent conflict was changing, away from traditional interstate war towards intrastate conflicts fuelled by ethnic, religious, or ideological divisions. The discourse about security became enriched with the new insight that states are not the only entities whose security ought to concern us. Regions, communities, families, and individuals can only feel secure if they have reason to believe that their continued functioning is not going to be threatened at every turn. Furthermore, the security of the state largely depends on the security of regions, communities, families, and individuals.

And occasionally states fail to fulfil their obligations as security guarantors, even to the point of threatening the security of their own citizens. It was realised that a primary requirement for human security was not merely the absence of war but the absence of structural and personal violence. These realisations informed a shift in perspective from the state as the subject and object of security policy to the human individual as the centre of security considerations – from state security to human security. And since human beings, unlike states, are capable of sensations and emotions, human security was recognised as partly contingent on those particular states of mind that we tend to associate with human well-being.

Human Security focuses primarily on protecting people while promoting peace and assuring sustainable continuous development. It emphasizes aiding individuals by using a people-centred approach for resolving inequalities that affect security. One of the major failings of Human Security, according to its critics, is that it is too all encompassing and that it fails to achieve its ambitious goals for improving the human condition. Still, the relevance of this concept for addressing the world's most pressing issues seems clear. Security has gone global. It is no longer simply related to the security of nation states. The security of the individual now directly impacts the security of the state and vice versa. By the beginning of the 21st century, climate change and harrowing effects of natural hazards like extended drought or extreme hurricanes, crushing economic inequality, disease, lack of resources and resulting migration have all shaped a new reality for the human security paradigm. The paradigm inseparably links humans, their social systems, and their environments and strives to achieve freedom and fear, freedom from hazard impact, and freedom from want. The paradigm has been shaped in part by recognition of the need to achieve greater societal resilience and improved environmental conditions among the world's most vulnerable people.

Human-driven changes in the terrestrial surface of the earth hold wide-ranging significance for the structure and function of ecosystems to the earth system, with equally far-reaching consequences for human well-being. Deforestation and irrigation were the largest sources of human-released greenhouse gasses to the atmosphere until the advent of industrial era fossil-fuel burning, and as much as 35% of the human-induced CO_2 equivalents in the atmosphere today can be traced to the totality of land-use/cover changes. Today, as much as 50% of the earth's ice-free land surface has been transformed, and virtually all land has been affected in some way by such processes as adapted landscapes, climate change, and tropospheric pollution.

The main factor in anthropogenic climate change is the increase in the concentration of carbon in the atmosphere over time. This increased concentration has been caused by the emission of GHGs as a result of economic activities, including energy, industry, transport, and land use, many of which rely upon fossil fuels. The most important GHG, carbon dioxide, CO2, currently constitutes 77 per cent of the global warming potential. Other contributors are methane (from agricultural sources), and land use change such as deforestation. Concentration level has increased because emissions during the last two centuries were in excess of what could be absorbed, and the excess GHGs began to accumulate in the atmosphere. The concentration of CO2 alone has increased by some 100 ppm over this period (Stern 2006). Current global emissions contribute another 2-3 ppm of carbon dioxide equivalent (CO2) GHGs per year.

Climate change has become one of the fundamental concerns of the 21st century. Ultimately, climate change is all about humans acting in socio-ecological settings in which biophysical, socio-cultural, economic, institutional, political, and legal mechanisms operate. It is in this complex system that disasters emerge and that society has to cope with. Human security within the context of climate change remains relatively under explored, whereas the biophysical dimensions of climate change, both on a worldwide and regional scale, are more rapidly addressed by natural scientists. Thus, there is an urgent need to deal with climate change through both adaptation and mitigation.

Climate Change is increasingly recognized as a major human security issue that poses serious global threats. Although climate change affects everyone regardless of race, caste, ethnicity, sex and level of income, its impacts are more heavily felt by poor nations, communities and people, and climate change magnifies existing inequalities. For the world's poor the impact will be most severe, disproportionately affecting their livelihoods and security. Climate change is a grim reality. Scientists tell us that the world is getting warmer by the day. Extreme weather phenomena such as floods, droughts, heat waves and cyclones, experienced in different parts of our globe, are among the far reaching consequences of climate change, giving us a bitter foretaste of what worse may come in the near future.

The link between climate change and human security is now as clear as ever. Dramatic environmental change undeniably places the infrastructure of all countries to the test. But it also poses an even greater threat to developing countries that lack the means, the know-how and the capacity to effectively deal with this phenomena. Add to this the soaring food and oil prices, and the future for millions of people across the globe, particularly those living on the edge struck by poverty or ravaged by war, is ominous.

CLIMATE CHANGE AND HUMAN SECURITY

The literature on environment and security has evolved over the years: from an early focus on incorporating environmental and related concerns into the definition of "security" to a new focus on how environmental change can be a cause or amplifier of violent conflict. An emerging trend within this evolution has been a move toward greater emphasis on the concept of human security.

Human security is not in opposition to the earlier trends of redefining security or of mapping the environmental roots of violent conflict. In fact, it is an outgrowth of these trends. Indeed, many early attempts to broaden the definition of "security" used language very similar to that found in today's discussions on "human security." For example, consider the following definition from Norman Myers' Ultimate Security:... security applies most at the level of the individual citizen. It amounts to human well-being: not only protection from harm and injury but access to water, food, shelter, health, employment, and other basic requisites that are the due of every person on Earth. It is the collectivity of this citizen's needs— overall safety and quality of life—that should figure prominently in the nation's view of security. Those analysts who have focused on explicating the environmental causes of violent conflict have also brought the debate closer to the notion of human security—most noticeably by focusing on intrastate (often conflicts that can...become a feature of state insecurity....If peoples and communities are insecure (economically, socially, politically, environmentally), state security can be fragile or uncertain.

Today, environmental change including climate change presents a new threat to human security and a new situation for migration. By 2050 when human population is projected to peak, some 9 billion people will live on Earth. The majority of them will live in urban areas with crushing environmental footprints. Many megacities are located in areas prone to sea level rise. Climate change will visit urban and rural areas alike with increasingly frequent and violent hazard events. Flooding, intense storms, or droughts, or more gradual but similarly intense changes in regional climates place great stress on livelihood systems.

Research on the effects of specific stressors like environmental degradation on society grew during this time period. Environmental issues have been seen in the broader context of human security since the end of the Cold War, which marked the end of political bipolarity and the narrow, mainly military notion of security that predominated the discourse at that time. The Brundtland report (1987) introduced the concept of sustainable development, followed by broad public discussion and a series of United Nations summits on environment and sustainable development (World Conferences in Rio 1992 and Johannesburg 2002). In this respect, the United Nations Conference on Environment and Development (UNCED), informally known as the Earth Summit, held in Rio de Janeiro in 1992 was a critical point in mainstreaming environmental issues at the international level. The event heralded the development of various UN Conventions dealing with environmental issues, for example, the UN Framework Convention on Climate Change (UNFCCC), the

Convention on Biological Diversity and the United Nations Convention to Combat Desertification (UNCCD). These conventions and conferences directly and specifically address environmental issues that affect human security.

SUSTAINABLE DEVELOPMENT IN SOUTH ASIA

South Asian countries while sharing similar geographical and cultural features, are also very diverse: the region has the country with the second largest population in the world (India), a small island state (Maldives), an island nation (Sri Lanka), land-locked countries (Nepal and Bhutan), two nuclear power states (India and Pakistan), and a country located on a river delta (Bangladesh). They are very rich in biological diversity as the region is home to many tropical rainforests and world heritage sites. South Asia is home to well over one fifth of the world's population and is one of the most densely populated areas of the world. Most countries in the region are prone to conflict and political instability and are also plagued by poverty and corruption. Sri Lanka enjoys the highest GDP per capita and the highest literacy rate in the region while India alone accounts for 5.6 million child deaths per year. According to the World Hunger Index, the region also has the highest child malnutrition rate in the world.

The south Asian region accounts for five per cent of the world's land but houses 20 per cent of the global population. The population density is the highest with 260 people per sq. km. in contrast to the global average of 44 people per sq. km. Also poverty is widely prevalent with one third of the population living under one dollar a day. To add to this, the effects of climate change have been on the rise in this part of the globe. The erratic weather patterns, retreating Himalayan glaciers causing frequent floods and droughts coupled with the diverse ethnic beliefs and internal conflicts further complicate adaptation measures and pose significant threat to national and human security. South Asia is a zone of instability with unstable governments and inter and intra state conflicts. It is also home to some of the poorest countries in the world. In addition to the existing conflicts, climate change throws up new challenges in the form of water scarcity and resultant water disputes and also other national security issues along the unsettled boundaries. On the other hand, India is fast industrializing, and has made tremendous strides in the field of science and technology – it even made its mark on the moon recently. Bangladesh and Nepal are among the poorest countries in the world while the Maldives, consisting of atolls barely above the sea level, is a tourist haven. While Sri Lanka was the first country in the region to liberalize its economy its development efforts have been undermined by the 25 year old civil war that ravaged the country. Tensions have always been high between the two nuclear powers – India and Pakistan. India, by far the largest and the most populous country in the region, has naturally been its dominant political power.

In South Asia there are at least forty-seven million people living in highly vulnerable Low Elevation Coastal Zonesin Bangladesh, India and Pakistan. These zones include one of the most populous delta regions of the world—and megacities such as Mumbai, Kolkata, Dhaka and Chennai—where some areas are only 2–10 metres above the current sea level. As flooding and drought increase in frequency, this will have devastating impacts on livelihoods, and slow economic growth within the countries of South Asia, thereby increasing the number of people living in poverty and the number of triggers for displacement and forced migration. Small farmers living in the coastal zone are particularly vulnerable to storm surges, salt water ingress, and flooding which damages crops and creates conditions for seasonal attacks by insects and rats. Rural wage labourers are even more vulnerable to climate changes as their opportunities for employment will be reduced and as they will have fewer assets to sustain their households during times of disasters. In urban areas, poor households are particularly vulnerable as their members are forced to live in 'high risk areas' due to a lack of affordable housing and to a lack resources needed for adaptation to changing climatic conditions. Effective responses to climate-related displacement need to be informed by a robust research base, with a strong and dynamic social science approach bringing together local, regional and international knowledge and experience.

Data shows that there is a sharp increase in the number of natural calamities with extreme weather events like cyclones or droughts. With a broad coastline and millions calling it home the loss of life will be monumental. Over the past forty years, there have been as many as 1333 disasters in South Asia that claimed 980,000 lives, affecting another 2.4 billion people and causing an economic loss of $105 billion. This number is only set to go higher with further increase in flooding due to the melting glaciers followed by droughts as the Himalayan rivers, once perennial, become seasonal. So, collective action is the way forward with substantial financial and technological help from the developed countries. The South Asian Association for Regional Cooperation (SAARC) the regional grouping of 8 countries has recognized climate change as a key issue to be dealt with at a regional level during their third meeting in Nepal in 1987 and has constituted various committees to look into the affects and suggest mitigation measures. But as a result of various factors like lack of political will, consensus and other priority issues not much substantial has happened since. The broad outcome of all the factors in this region is large scale migration and displacement. Eighty per cent of Bangladesh is prone to submergence due to floods and any sea level rise will result in submergence of a large part of its coastline. This will result in distress migration and scramble for scarce resources. For instance, in 1998, Bangladesh was flooded and submerged from few days to several months resulting in more than a 1000 deaths, half a million homes damaged and about 30 million people displaced. The loss only went up north in November 2007 as cyclone Sidr, the worst cyclone since 1991, battered Bangladesh again killing 3000 people and affecting over seven million people. Similarly Pakistan too is highly flood prone as was witnessed in July 2010. In addition, the sectorial strife, ethnic unrest and political instability can break down the entire federal machinery which might be filled by fundamental elements, a geopolitical nightmare. Other countries in the region Bhutan, Nepal and Sri Lanka too are no different. The disaster management in the region is inadequately prepared to tackle these challenges and there is no gender based approach to address the plight of women, children and other backward societies. A study of the recent flood in Dhaka, Bangladesh reinforces this point where more women lost their lives as they couldn't swim and did not have proper facilities in relief camps such as closed bathing spaces and shelters.

India has been traditionally vulnerable to natural disasters on account of its unique geo-climatic conditions. Floods, droughts, cyclones, earthquakes and landslides have been a recurrent phenomenon. About 60% of the landmass is prone to earthquakes of various intensities; over 40 million hectares is prone to floods; about 8% of the total area is prone to cyclones and 68% of the area is susceptible to drought. A natural hazardous has been happened in Kedarnath valley due to torrential rainfall during 16 and 17 June 2013. From 14 to 17 June 2013, the Indian state of Uttarakhand and adjoining areas received heavy rainfall, which was about 375 per cent more than the benchmark rainfall during a normal monsoon. This caused the melting of Chorabari Glacier at the height of 3800 metres, and eruption of the Mandakini River which led to heavy floods near Gobindghat, Kedar Dome, Rudraprayag district, Uttarakhand, Himachal Pradesh and Western Nepal, and acute rainfall in other nearby regions of Delhi, Haryana, Uttar Pradesh and some parts of Tibet. The range of climate change impacts in South Asia includes: water shortages, increased salinity, inundation of low lying cities, less water for agriculture, soil erosion, increased incidence of disease, extreme weather events and loss of endemic species. These coupled with poverty and conflict, reliance on an agricultural economy and lack of infrastructure and other social safety nets, make the situation rather bleak. *TERI* in its report summarizes the situation:

CHALLENGES IN SOUTH ASIA

Across South Asia there are various 'hot spots' where it is predicted that climatic changes will have a very large impact. These 'hot spots' are: the Eastern Ganges Basin; the major river deltas (i.e. the Ganges-Brahmaputra, the Indus and the Kaveri); the arid zones in Afghanistan, Pakistan and Western India; the Deccan Plateau; the middle hills of the Himalaya and the High Himalayan regions; and coastal areas affected by salinity, extreme storms and sea-level rise. Across the Ganges basin, the specific vulnerabilities to which climate change contributes are droughts, floods, super cyclones and other storms, and sea-level rise. The entire basin is heavily dependent on the monsoonal system. In the upper reaches, the Himalayan glaciers, which provide the winter flows, are experiencing changes in melting rates and density.

Bangladesh will be one of the most severely affected countries because nearly eighty per cent of its total land area is prone to flooding. Every year approximately twenty to twenty-five per cent of the country is inundated by floods from rivers, heavy monsoonal rainfall and storm surges, worsened by poor drainage and haphazard development in urban areas. But with increasing frequency, floods are inundating much larger areas. For example, in 1998, about 80 per cent of Bangladesh was flooded for between a few days and several months. This caused more than a 1,000 deaths, damaged more than half a million homes and affected an estimated 30 million people. In India, monsoonal floods frequently inundate states such as Bihar. This was the case in 2008 when the Kosi River changed its course, affecting 4.7 million people. Cyclones coming up the Bay of Bengal have affected many coastal regions, including the megacities of Dhaka and Calcutta. In July 2005, floods brought Mumbai to a standstill for 48 hours, following a day of record rainfall.

It is a major reason for the increasing impoverishment and marginalisation of rural households and communities. This riverbank erosion is exacerbated by the intensity of floods created by melt water from glaciers, which are expected to increase as the global temperature rises. During the dry season these same populations face water and food insecurity.At particular risk from sea-level rise are the people living on the islands of the Sunder bans in the Bay of Bengal. The decrease in flow of the Ganges River due to the construction of the Farakka Barrage in West Bengal (India) now means that seawater pushes up the delta, creating heavy inland flooding during tidal surges. This has destroyed rice fields and thus forced people to find alternate jobs in Bangladesh. While some employment has been created by the cultivation of shrimp, they are too expensive for local consumption and this has meant that rice must now be imported. This further marginalises the poor, and, with the decrease in employment, forces many men to migrate, leaving behind women, children and the elderly.

DISPLACEMENT AND MIGRATION

A crucial issue that will have to be addressed by the South Asian region is how it will deal with displacement and possible migration due to sea level rise and other severe weather events. This is particularly crucial for low lying cities such as Dhaka, Mumbai and Karachi and small island states such as the Maldives. The entire costal belt of Sri Lanka is vulnerable to sea level rise and already much land has been lost due to sea erosion. The issue of displacement and migration would be a good issue to be addressed within the framework of SAARC. The Stern Report warns that many people in developing countries will be displaced as a result of climate-related incidents: "Severe deterioration in the local climate could lead, in some parts of the developing world, tomass migration and conflict, especially as another 2-3 billion people are added to the developing world's population in the next few decades." It points out that rising sea levels, desertification, and other climate-related events could drive millions to migrate. More than one fifth of Bangladesh could be under water by the end of the century. With a predicated one meter rise in sea levels, the Maldives could be completely submerged as well. A similar fate awaits people living in low lying cities and Small Island states. It has been estimated that 634 million people live in low-lying coastal areas vulnerable to sea level rise associated with climate change and cities from Tokyo to New York would be affected. Migration away from the zone at risk will be necessary. It is generally accepted that sea level rise in the long term will cause displacement of many millions of people currently living in coastal areas: "For the small island nations of the world, especially the many cultural groups living on coral atolls, entire nations face complete submersion."

ASSESSING HUMAN SECURITY THROUGH SUSTAINABILITY IN SOUTH-ASIA

Political scientist Robyn Eckersley has noted that developments after the Cold War placed as potlight on "neglected areas of vulnerability and marginalization," on interdependence between the global natural environment and the global economy, and on the necessity for cooperation at the international level. The interactive relationships between peace, environment, development, and economy as matters of security were successively recognized by the Brandt Commission (1980), Brundtland Commission (1987), the Rio Declaration (Principle 25) (1992), the United Nations Development Programme (UNDP) (1994) (as a component of human security), The Commission on Global Governance (1995), and even, in April 2007, by the UN Security Council.

Eckersley has identified four main themes of a broader approach to security with regard to the environment sincethe end of the Cold War: the emergence of new understandings of "ecological risks" as sources of insecurity; a recognition of new security referents such as the biosphere and "ecological communities"; creative responses to ecological threats based on cooperation and dialogue linked to various levels and kinds of governance; and identification of the prerequisites for "long-term security" and sustainable development, such as ecological and communicative justice based oncritical, Habermasian, and constructivist theories.

Both the equity and connectivity dimensions of climate change underscore the importance of sustainable adaptation.

The broader goals of most sustainability efforts are to foster economic and social practices that contribute to the maintenance of environmental quality, diversity of species and preservation of ecological functions for the benefit of both humans and other living things. Sustainability emphasizes the idea of using natural resources in a manner that meets the needs of the present generation without compromising the ability of future generations to meet their needs. Adaptation to climate change can be described as adjustments in practices, processes, or structures to take into account changing climate conditions, to moderate potential damages, or to benefit from opportunities associated with climate change. Combining aspects of both sustainability and adaptation, the notion of sustainable adaptation entails measures that reduce vulnerability and promote long-term resilience in a changing climate.

Two broad principles define the general concept of sustainable development:

1. "The right to development must be fulfilled so as to equitably meet developmental and environmental needs of present and future generation."
2. "In order to achieve sustainable development, environmental protection shall constitute an integral part of the development process and cannot be considered in isolation from it".

These two principles broadly relate to the notions of inter- and intra- generational equity, respectively. The real challenge, however, is to translate the principles into concrete policies for national development. As an example, none of the countries in South Asia has been able to develop an apex national council or mechanism focused on sustainable development. The misperceptions that economic and industrial development should take precedence and that incorporating environmental concerns would have an adverse impact on development are quite prevalent throughout the region. At the moment the South Asian nations are caught in a vicious cycle of poverty, environmental resource depletion and lack of development.

The existing development paradigm should receive careful consideration and perhaps requires some rethinking, given the prevailing conditions in the region. The primary target of such efforts must be the reduction of poverty in the region, particularly when the number of people living below the poverty line currently stands in excess of half a billion. A number of factors contribute to this situation, including weak incentives for improved service delivery to the poor, rampant corruption, imperfect monitoring and administrative obstacles. The rampant poverty and low quality of life have other indirect consequences, such as increased vulnerability to natural disasters. Poverty can also be linked to a number of "environmental" health problems, including a lack of sufficient and clean water, food, appropriate shelter and fuel, and access to healthy air. The most poignant example of this is arsenic poisoning through drinking water in South Asia, which affects huge numbers of people- over 35 million in Bangladesh, 2 million in India and 100,000 in Nepal. Of the many drivers of environmental degradation, urbanization is perhaps the most significant because of the major trend of increasing urbanization (3.4 per cent annual growth in South Asia's urban population), a lack of proper planning, and the exploitation of natural resources under the urban footprint and the generation of vast quantities of waste. Some of the largest and fastest growing cities in the world are located in South Asia. Industrial growth also poses a challenge, primarily through the production of waste but also through exploitation of the limited natural resource base. For example, an environmental impact assessment (EIA) is still not fully established as a requirement for the establishment and operation of industries.

A major proportion of the land surface in the South Asia region is becoming degrades, leading to a decrease in land productivity and even more importantly, threatening the food security of the countries in the region. The causes of this degradation are many and varied, including declining forest cover, inappropriate agricultural practices, destruction of natural vegetative cover for development, inadequate maintenance and management of the vast canal-based irrigation system, and industrial and mining waste. Climate change and global warming are the most serious environmental threat to the region in many ways. They many reduce availability of water resources and a likely increase in climate-related extreme events. Prolonged drought in south and central Asia over the past few years is a concrete example of such impacts. Conversely, extreme flooding events in Bangladesh and southern India have also become more frequent. Another indirect threat from global warming is sea-level rise, particularly for countries such as Maldives (which could be completely submerged) and Bangladesh (which could lose up to one-third of its surface area) as a result of even a 0.5 metre rise in sea level.

IMPACT OF CLIMATE CHANGE IN SOUTH ASIA

South Asia is one of the most climate impacted regions in the world. Many studies are now available to support that fact. For instance, the World Bank has identified three unique factors that make South Asia vulnerable to the impacts of climate change:

- Poverty and population increase;
- Threats to water supply and agriculture; and
- Vulnerability to natural disasters.

First, South Asia has the highest density of poverty in the world. With an estimated 600 million South Asians subsisting on less than $1.25 a day, even small climate shocks can cause irreversible losses and tip a large number of people into destitution.

Second, South Asia is endowed with great rivers, which are the lifelines of the regional economy. The ice mass covering the Himalayan-Hindu Kush mountain range is the source of the nine largest rivers of Asia, including the Ganges, Brahmaputra, and Indus. Glacial melt coupled with more variable precipitation could severely compromise livelihoods and the future prospects of agriculture.

Third, South Asia suffers an exceptionally high number of natural disasters. Between 1990 and 2008, more than 750 million people - 50% of the region's population - were affected by a natural disaster, leaving almost 60,000 dead and resulting in about $45 billion in damages. As climate-related risks intensify, there will be a need to respond proactively to build resilience through prevention and preparedness rather than through relief and response.

South Asian leaders issued a Statement on Climate Change at their meeting in April 2010, at Thimpu. They recognise that the Member States of SAARC as developing countries face the dual challenge of addressing the negative impacts of climate change and pursuing socio-economic development. The Statement emphasises the overriding importance of socio-economic development and poverty eradication in our region, and that reducing dependence on carbon in economic growth and promoting climate resilience will promote both development and poverty eradication in a sustainable manner.

These points to the imminence of development strategy that is both sustainable and inclusive. South Asian governments have to work together to share knowledge, technology, and finance. Work on this is already underway within the rubric of SAARC as well as various bilateral agreements. This will have to be followed-up with speed and sincerity.

South Asianprivate sector will have to be engaged, because it is they who seek new opportunities to work on. Sustainability is reservoir of opportunities which needs to be dwelled upon by the private sector. It is important for business to realize that they are held back by the same factors that keep individuals and communities in poverty, which is environmental deterioration, and the absence of adequate infrastructure.

CLIMATE CHANGE, SUSTAINABLE DEVELOPMENT AND SECURITY ARE COMING TOGETHER

There is an ongoing debate within the United Nations whether a sustainable development and a security lens will be needed for dealing with climate change, the most important challenge of our times. The new High level Political Forum on Sustainable Development recently established in the United Nations (A/67/ L.72 dated 27 June 2013) to replace the Commission on Sustainable Development will review progress of all major conferences and result in a "negotiated ministerial declaration", blurring the distinction with arrangements like the climate treaty. A recent article in 'Nature' (21 March) argues for sustainable development goals that consider both people and planet. Will the goals now being negotiated in the United Nations General Assembly for the post- 2015 global agenda also deal with climate change along with development?

Responding to emerging challenges, scientific consensus and geopolitical shifts, the G8, in their communiqué of 18 June, have recognised climate change and sustainable development as "mutually reinforcing", while also describing climate change as a security threat. Asia has yet to formulate a comprehensive response to the new global agenda developing in the three parallel negotiations - in the Climate Convention, General Assembly and the Security Council - that will take place between now and 2015. A strategic view is important because the perspectives of the different countries have political rather than scientific or legal dimensions.

Current strategic thinking focuses on the size of the military and the strength of the economy as determinants of the influence countries exert in world affairs, ignoring the role of global rules in maintaining that influence. The design of new global goals provides an opportunity for countries with a bold vision to build a coalition and ensure that the new order serves their interests. The world is at such a defining moment, much like at the end of World War II when the United States established the multilateral system, putting economic concerns under the Bretton Woods Institutions with 'one dollar one vote' and keeping political concerns in the Security Council where the victors had a veto, while humanitarian concerns went to the United Nations with its 'one country one vote'. The leverage that went with that arrangement is now unravelling - China's aid to Africa exceeds the amount provided by the World Bank. It has also become clear that in a multi-polar world the new global challenges can no longer be dealt with in a fragmented system.

THE EMERGING AGENDA

The climate treaty, negotiated in Rio 1992, is an experiment in bringing together environment and development to reconcile a continually growing global economy within a finite global ecosystem. However, international environmental law has not been able to resolve how to accommodate the rising living standards of all those who have so far been excluded from the benefits of globalization through burden sharing. Post Rio 2012, development and environment are coming together around global sustainable development goals to shape patterns, trends and drivers of global change. The new rules for the post-2020 climate regime are also focusing on aggregate emissions pathways rather than percentage reductions in emissions of greenhouse gases. The distinction between climate change, development and sustainable development is blurring.

The political problem is that the billion richest accounts for over 70 percent of world consumption with the poorest billion accounting for only 1 percent of natural resource use, and how the ecological limits are approached depends on lifestyles and associated consumption. These in turn depend on what is used, and how and what is regarded as essential for human wellbeing, and the G8 is reluctant to even put these trends on the global agenda.

The G8 see the collective response in terms of new rules for intervention to meet environmental risks rather than for societal and technological transformations. A redefinition of national security is being pushed by raising the question whether traditional roles of national states and international agreements will prove adequate for dealing with the adverse effects of climate change as a "threat multiplier". The deliberations in the Security Council mirror those in the other forum and have ignored the complex interactions between human activities, ecological limits and international cooperation.

New global goals

The policy issue for China and India is whether to continue with the comfortable but fraying principle of environmental law, 'common but differentiated responsibilities and respective capabilities' agreed in 1992, even as the deliberation shifts to other forums, or acknowledge the significance of the different concerns coming together around human wellbeing and take a more forward looking approach, for example, based on new research like the World Economic Forum's '*Global Risk Report, 2013*, stating that severe income disparity is a greater disruptive risk by likelihood and impact than climate change.

By shifting the global agenda from environmental risk as the overriding concern to seeking human wellbeing within ecological limits, these countries can shape the new global goals to focus on the gaps in the Millennium Development Goals, because eradicating poverty has been central to the agenda of the United Nations since it was established in 1948.

This new global vision will have five key elements.

First, the reduction in poverty in recent decades has been overwhelmingly dependent on the rapid growth in China, which alone accounts for three-fourths of the global reduction and did not adopt a MDG focused policy. A review of past trends suggests that two-thirds of poverty reduction depends on growth and one-third on equality; poverty will be eradicated only when all have assured access to affordable services, like energy, food, housing, transport, education, health and employment. A consensus is needed to define global goals around standards of living that ensure exercise of universal rights and economic opportunities, otherwise we will fool ourselves into thinking, once again, and that poverty is history.

Second, the key global concern should be modifying longer term trends in production and consumption patterns to determine how standards of living can be raised within ecological limits. As developing countries shift to urbanization and manufacturing to provide employment and services limiting the use of natural resources while still achieving high standards of living will require a review of existing global rules (for example, intellectual property rights) and new rules (for example, energy efficiency and sharing biotechnology).

Third, the guiding principle for the new partnership should be "sharing responsibility for the Planet and prosperity of the People". The MDGs, for example, did not include adequate and affordable energy, which has an environmental impact. They also framed development cooperation narrowly as essentially an aid-driven relationship and ignored other policy instruments like trade, investment and technology transfer. New goals will need new rules and a new partnership.

Fourth, all the analyses suggest that the most rapid growth of the middle class will occur in Asia, particularly in populous China and India, and these countries will have to think about global ecological limits in new ways. The volume of urban construction there for housing, office space, and transport services could roughly equal the entire volume of such construction to date in world history. The future health of the global economy, society and environment will, therefore, be increasingly linked to how these countries do —more so than the traditional West – and they must take the lead in shaping the new goals.

NEW CLIMATE FRAMEWORK

The design of a fair climate agreement is already drawing on the wider scientific and policy debate around new global goals, because keeping global emissions within agreed limits has very different implications for fast growing economies and where growth has stabilized. For example, three-fourths of the electricity produced in developing countries is used in manufacturing and any limitations on emissions will impact on economic growth, while two-third of the electricity generated in developed countries is used in buildings, and restrictions will affect lifestyles. Emissions, standards of living and global ecological limits are inter-linked, and cannot be considered in isolation.

Up to now less than one billion people have accounted for three-quarters of global consumption; during the next four decades, new and expanded middle classes in the developing world could create as many as four billion additional consumers. The volume of this urban construction for housing, office space, and transport services could roughly equal the entire volume of such construction to date in world history. Currently, per capita generation of electricity in India is one-fifteenth and in China one fifth that of the United States and the use of cheap and widely available coal will continue because of the imperatives of growth, which also provides opportunities for re-shaping the pattern of demand, or lifestyles.

First, in the face of continuing reluctance of the rich countries to modify longer term trends in consumption and production patterns, which they had committed to under the Convention, and geopolitical shifts in the power of developing countries, a rigid environmental perspective giving sole consideration to risk management is giving place to a more flexible sustainable development perspective of economic growth within ecological limits. Temporarily over-shooting of the global temperature limits using carbon budget or paths over time rather than an end-point is gaining prominence amongst scientists, and is likely to be reflected in any new agreement.

Second, fairness is no longer sought to be defined as differentiated commitments for burden sharing but rather in terms of methodologies for reviewing national actions. There is, however, no agreement on whether this would be based on common accounting rules and a consultative process to enhance commitments or patterns and trends of natural resource use, for example, between 1970 and 2060, should shape the multilateral reporting and assessment of national actions; environment first came on the global agenda in 1972 at the Stockholm Conference and global growth is expected to continue till at least 2060. The fear is that international approval should not be accorded to a lack of ambition on the part of developed countries to the detriment of the others as energy use reaches the planet's ecological limits before comparable levels in standards of living are achieved.

China and India are still building their infrastructure and, according to BP's forecasts in its latest *Energy Outlook 2030*, energy use per capita is predicted to increase at a similar rate to that in industrialized countries in the period 1970-2011, and despite energy intensity of GDP in 2030 being less than half of the level in 1970, incomes and population are expected to drive a 40% increase in global primary energy use. This implies that the international review of national actions should consider national circumstances, or stages of development.

Third, the specificity of the global goals and the monitoring arrangements will depend on the extent to which redistribution, which has so far been kept out of the United Nations, becomes a part of the global agenda. Given the complexity and uncertainty surrounding the environmental, social and economic processes upon which pathways to sustainable development depend, the guiding principle for the new partnership will update the principle of 'common but differentiated responsibilities and respective capabilities' to focus on "sharing responsibility and prosperity". International cooperation will then be seen in terms of sharing technological development and exchanging experiences on societal transformations that will lead to emissions reduction, and not the other way round.

Environmental security

Academic debate on the issue of environmental security is divided, with some concluding – on the basis either of case studies or quantitative analyses of historical and present-day climate-conflict relations – that anthropogenic warming is likely to exacerbate conflict dynamics, with others finding only circumstantial evidence of linkages between the two, and still others refuting the climate conflict thesis altogether.

A redefinition of national security has been gaining political momentum worldwide away from state-cantered and military-focused definitions raising the question whether traditional roles of national states and international agreements will prove adequate for human security. There is as yet no universally agreed definition of environmental security as it involves complex interactions between human activities, ecological limits and international cooperation making it difficult to determine causal relationships other than environmental degradation as a "threat multiplier", with human security defined in terms of a range of elements such as freedom from threats, disruption of daily lives and resource scarcity.

In the context of growing disagreement on sharing responsibility for climate change the emerging powers are blamed for these threats in the thinking of analysts in the old powers, by extending what originated as a the strategic concern of impact on military operations to international relations. Analysts in Asia, despite considering climate change as a sustainable development concern, have not developed a coherent response by extending this perspective to see these threats in terms of equitably sharing global ecological resources so that development, in all its dimensions, is not constrained.

The essential question in considering climate change as a 'threat multiplier' is the nature of the threat - environmental or developmental - and whether the risks are addressed better by promoting cooperation or by preventing conflict? The related questions are whether mediating disputes between States can best be done in the Security Council because it has delegated responsibilities for "maintenance of peace and security "giving the permanent five members immense power to react urgently and set the agenda or whether this composition reflecting the victors of World War II will not build a global consensus? And, whether other regimes, including the UN General Assembly, can set appropriate norms and standards for enforcement short of sanctions and use of force? A global consensus has yet to emerge on these issues.

In the face of scientific uncertainty developing countries have yet to formulate a coherent response. For example, with respect to water scarcity in South Asia the contribution of Himalayan snow melt varies greatly for the rivers flowing on the Northern and Southern aspects. For example, the Yellow, Mekong and Salween rivers get less than 10 per cent of their flows from the glaciers, while the Indus and the Ganges get up to 70 per cent prior to and during the monsoon. Clearly, for South Asia the monsoon, including the resulting snow fall in the upper reaches, is the determining factor in water flows. A recent assessment of the scientific research by the US National Research Council (*'Himalayan Glaciers: Climate Change, Water Resources and Water Scarcity', National Research Council, 2012, United States*) shows that "glaciers in the eastern and central regions of the Himalayas appear to be retreating at rates comparable to glaciers in other parts of the world, while in the western Himalayas glaciers are more stable and may even be increasing in size", and concludes that the consequences for the region's water supply are unclear. Their assessment is that shifts in the location, intensity, and variability of rain and snow due to climate change will impact regional water supplies, concluding that "social changes such as changing patterns of water use and water management decisions, are likely to have at least as much of an impact on water demand as environmental factors do on water supply". These perspectives are not being shared by developing country scientists in intergovernmental processes, such as the IPCC.

The academic and policy discourse within the United Nations on climate change, sustainable development, conflict and security has so far been highly climate-centric and fails to contextualise climate impacts in relation to other broader processes of economic and social change. It is also framed too narrowly around the intersection with poverty and state fragility in Sub-Saharan Africa and the long-term problems in certain small island states, leaving out other areas such as the Arctic and without understanding the complexity of interlinked processes like glacial melt and the monsoon. The strategic community has also ignored current scientific consensus on how to meet the challenge of global change, which focuses on societal dynamics as both the root of environmental problems and the potential solution to them.

The legitimate concern of the non-permanent members of the Security Council is that sovereignty no longer exclusively protects

States from foreign interference, and environmental security should not adopt the principle of 'sovereignty as responsibility' where collective action for crimes against humanity is extended to protect populations from loss of habitat, starvation and mass migration. The emerging trend in the negotiations around the post-2015 global agenda is now stressing the principle of 'sustainable development' with respect to the global impacts of natural resource use. Environmental, technological and societal transformations are interlinked and cannot be considered in isolation, and it would be within the mandate of the Security Council to support peace and security by looking at the longer term future of the planet for sharing responsibility as well as prosperity for human wellbeing.

In the case of climate change the choice for the collective response is between rules for societal and technological transformation and intervention in the face of environmental risks and access to resources. The international community should define 'responsibility to protect' in terms of equal rights of all populations to sustainable development with new platforms for cooperative responses to deal with longer term global change, of which climate change is only a part.

WAY FORWARD: GLOBAL GOVERNANCE

At the global level the issue that must be debated is how a continually growing economic system will fit within a finite ecological system, and identify longer term trends in production and consumption patterns that need to be modified to raise standards of living. Given the complexity and uncertainty surrounding the environmental and economic processes upon which pathways to future wellbeing depend, the guiding principle for the new partnership should be "sharing responsibility and prosperity". The focus will then be on global sustainable development goals and a political agreement in the UN General Assembly rather than legal commitments in an environmental treaty or enforcement through the Security Council.

Developing countries, particularly in Asia, will have to think about global ecological limits in new ways. In an interdependent and multi polar world global goals are more likely to be based on negotiated political agreements in the High Level Policy Forum that has replaced the Commission on Sustainable Development, rather than legally binding commitments in the Climate treaty. As China re-shapes its urban future, with its planned urbanization involving 250 million farmers, its willingness to lead by example in reforming the United Nations, rather than the United States defending the current arrangements, will determine the outcome and the new global rules. It may well be a complete break with the past, equitable and democratic.

5

China Debates the Future Security Environment

OBSTACLES

Some words of caution are advisable to any reader not fluent in Chinese or familiar with Chinese Government-sponsored documents. It is easy to set out the English language words with which Chinese analysts in government research institutes have described the future security environment. It is more difficult to attain a true understanding of the context and what these specific words actually signify to the Chinese. There are at least four obstacles to understanding Chinese views to keep in mind.

Precise Translation

Readers unfamiliar with the Chinese language may not appreciate how wide a range of choice an interpreter has in translating Chinese terms from ideographic symbols, the semantic content of which has developed in a 5000-year-old cultural framework. For example, the Chinese word *sixiang* may be translated as "ideology," "thinking," "thoughts," and "doctrine," among other choices. Chinese verbs have no tense, so tense must be indicated by context, and Chinese nouns do not indicate singular or plural, again relying on context.

Some translation issues create only minor misunderstandings; others can be more significant. An example may help. Chinese writings on the future of warfare and the revolution in military affairs (RMA) frequently use three Chinese ideograms to signify something that can be used in a war that will surprise and overwhelm the enemy, vital parts of exploiting the RMA. The three ideograms (*sha shou jian*) literally mean "kill," "hand," and an ancient word for club, or "mace." U.S. Government translations have rendered this term as "trump card," "magic weapon," or "killer mace." None of these translations is wrong, but none captures the full meaning. The importance of the term can be seen in its continued usage over time, both originally in traditional Chinese novels and ancient statecraft texts, as well as today in the daily military newspaper. Behind these three ideograms may lie a concept of victory in warfare through possession of secret weapons that strike the enemy's most vulnerable point (called an acupuncture point), at precisely the decisive moment. This entire concept of how RMA technology can win a war cannot be fully conveyed by its simple English translation of "trump card."

The Changing Rules of the Chinese Communist Party about Debate

All authors quoted in this study are Party members with access to a system of confidential Party documents, many of which deal with assessment of the future security environment. Debate must remain within the limits of Party guidance. Books by Party members clearly will contrast with the freewheeling debates in American books about the future. In the United States, there is certainly no "party line" from the White House about the nature of world politics in 2020. Yet, as "scientific socialists," the leaders of the Communist Party of China are expected to have an official view of the future security environment and to disseminate this in confidential Party documents to members. The line may be unclear between narrow doctrines that Party scholars are expected to accept uncritically and broad areas that may be debated. Foreign readers, even if they know the Chinese language, can become lost in the woods if unfamiliar with Party context—which points are ideologically mandated and which are open to debate. One clue appears when there is extensive repetition by Chinese authors of "boiler plate" (*tifa*) phrases describing the future. Such repetition probably signals quotations from Central Party documents, but to foreign readers such terms may appear to be an uncanny coincidence of the same phrases used by dozens of Chinese authors.

The Party seems ambivalent about open debates. For 20 years, Party leaders have even debated whether or not to have open debates. The 20th anniversary on May 11, 1998, of the publication of the article, "Practice is the Sole Criterion of Testing Truth," led to numerous pieces in the Chinese press commemorating the debate over economic reform and opening up, that was ignited by the article. Not only do they now praise the past debate, but they also advocate that in order to further carry out China's reforms, the country needs to "inherit the pioneering spirit of the debate... adhere to the ideological line of emancipating the mind and seeking truth from facts, and initiate a new stage for China's development." One book written as part of the commemoration of the "criterion of truth" debate and the reforms that it brought about may itself even be ushering in a new open form of academic debate in China. *Jiaofeng* (Crossing swords), by Ma Licheng and Ling Zhizhun, describes three periods of the "emancipation of the mind" since the end of the Cultural Revolution, in 1978, 1992, and 1997. According to a review in *Ching Pao,* the book broke all of the norms of Chinese veiled debates. "It criticizes people by name in total disregard of their 'face' or feelings. All parties involved in the sword crossing in the book are referred to directly by name and by the title of their works rather than by quoting and commenting on people's opinions as was usually the case in the past. It has been calculated that over 100 articles were cited. Even *Renmin ribao* and *Qiushi* [Party Central Committee publications] were cited. It is really clear where its spearhead is directed against."

Premises about Statecraft Held by Chinese Analysts

The Prologue addresses several important examples of how ancient Chinese statecraft is used as a lesson or metaphor to assess the future. Chinese references to the "Warring States era" of 2,500 years ago remind Chinese readers never to forget the eternal verities of geopolitics and worst case scenarios. The Warring States era as a guide to the future is a rich subject, but it is never spelled out for foreign readers. Though significant, the true meaning of "the words" is never made explicit in a way Westerners need to know in order to understand what is really meant.

The Taboo on Open Discussion of Future Chinese Security

This obstacle can truly confuse foreign readers. China's future role in international politics (which Western scholars often assume will be significant) is seldom mentioned. One explanation is that this sensitive subject can be dealt with only in secret Party documents, not in the open source books and journals upon which this study completely relies. Glimpses of these internal documents sometimes come as "leaks" to the press. In 1994, a Hong Kong magazine, *Cheng Ming,* disclosed that a confidential report about the period 2000 to 2010, "War to be Won," had been circulated to Party members by the Policy Research Office of the Chinese State Council, the Policy Research Office of the Central Military Commission, and the Policy Research Office of the Communist Party Central Committee. The main points are that China's Comprehensive National Power (CNP) will be among the top three in the world and that the two sides of the Taiwan Strait will be unified. China's gross national product (GNP), excluding Taiwan, is estimated to become about U.S. $2.5 trillion by 2010. China will have two to four aircraft carriers and a PLA of 1.5 million, reduced from today's 3 million. By 2010, manned Chinese spacecraft will be launched and will have established a space station. In May 1997, *Cheng Ming* leaked another report on Sino-U.S. relations, done by the Central Policy Research Center, the State Council's Policy Research Center, the Foreign Ministry and Defense Ministry. This second report predicted that war between China and the United States was possible in the future. According to *Cheng Ming,* the report asserted:

With the return of Hong Kong and Macao to Chinese rule, the Taiwan issue will inevitably become China's major event around 2010. If the United States uses force to meddle in China's sovereignty and internal affairs, China will certainly fight a war against aggression, thus leading to a limited Sino-U.S. war. China must be prepared for this. With the change in the international situation, the United States will make use of islands, maritime space, and resources, encourage and support of Japanese militarists in provoking a war against China.... China is the U.S. number one political adversary at the turn of this century. China must make systematic preparations against the invasive war and military attacks unleashed by the United States under any pretext.

If authentic, these documents represent rare samples of the kind of confidential forecasts Party members may be reading about China's future role that cannot be discussed in open books and journals.

These obstacles need not prevent all understanding, but together they limit the probability of fully comprehending China's assessment. Modesty is an appropriate attitude to adopt in any attempt to understand Chinese assessments. The need for further research and more extensive translations should be kept in mind.

PREVIEW OF FINDINGS

The central finding of this study is that China has developed a remarkably detailed picture of the future security environment. The concluding chapter provides details about the range of Chinese debates on the features of the future. The extent of the debate is very restricted when compared to the freewheeling give and take that exists in the West. The mutually exclusive "scenarios" employed by Americans to explore alternative possibilities for the future do not exist in Chinese writings. China's clear picture of the future is an amalgam of Marxism and ancient Chinese statecraft from the Warring States era. All institute authors and PLA officers are members of the Chinese Communist Party, obligated to accept Party doctrine about the shape of the future. According to Deng Xiaoping, in order to preserve this clear picture of the future, Chinese should not "debate" because it can make things "complicated." Nevertheless, reformers continue to challenge orthodox ideological authors on sensitive issues. These debates are an important key to improving U.S. understanding of China. Western understanding of Chinese debates has improved since 1949 because of the remarkable efforts of only a few scholars, mostly Chinese who have emigrated to the United States or Americans. This study highlights veiled debates between reformers and orthodox authors on:

- The future world structure in 2010-2030
- The rate of America's decline

- The future hierarchy of the major world powers in 2010
- Locations and causes of future wars
- Consequences of the RMA
- Prospects for Russia, India, and Japan.

Measuring Geopolitical Hierarchy

Consistent with the texts of ancient statecraft, China's analysts believe in geopolitics. They try to calculate mathematically the hierarchy of the world's future major powers. At least two teams have done so at the orthodox Academy of Military Science and the reform-minded Chinese Academy of Social Science. According to the *military* forecast, China's CNP by 2020 will grow equal to that of the United States in a multipolar structure. Russia, Europe, and Japan will be "poles" three, four, and five, each with half the power level attained by the United States or China. According to the "reform" *civilian* forecast, the United States will lose its hegemony not to China but to Japan. Tokyo's national power will grow equal to that of the United States by 2010, followed closely by Germany. The *civilians* rate China only as number eight by 2010, not even one of the top five "poles." China and Russia score only half as high as the United States and Japan. Given these calculated power scores, Chinese analysts of the future focus intensively on assessing the intentions of Japan and the United States toward China, especially the strength of the "slanderous" and dangerous "China Threat Theory" in Tokyo and Washington.

China foresees a turbulent multipolar world. In contrast to wide-ranging Western debates about scenarios from the "long boom" to a more "dangerous world," since 1986, China's Communist Party has had an almost unchanging assessment of an "inevitable" multipolar future. This Chinese assessment draws heavily on both Maoist, pre-Gorbachev Marxist-Leninism, and ancient Chinese statecraft. It sees a relative decline in U.S. power so that the world will be "multipolar," much like the Warring States era. American security alliances will weaken, the United States will decline to become a regional power, and the post-World War II rules and norms set mainly by the United States and the Allies will give way to China's proposed rules, known as the Five Principles of Peaceful

Coexistence. China's authors warn of future wars. There will be intense competition among major powers to build CNP and to develop the RMA. There will be a danger of frequent "local wars," from future small wars in Africa to wars on the scale of the Korean conflict and the Gulf War. The main cause of wars involving major powers will be competitive struggles over natural resources (oil and gas). The "Yalta System" of stable "spheres of influence" must be replaced by the Five Principles, which have already been adopted by "most countries," including Russia, but not the United States or Japan. Without a new "system," turmoil like that during the Warring States era will continue indefinitely. "Systems" tend to last at least 40 years, according to some Chinese authors.

China calculates power ratios and predicts American decline. Ancient Chinese statecraft from the Warring States era emphasizes the need to calculate future power ratios mathematically. Chinese national security research analysts have quantitatively analyzed the relative power of the nations of this inevitable new "world structure" in which the United States will decline economically, socially, militarily, and internationally to become one of five "poles" in a "multipolar world." Nothing can save the United States from this fate, which will include serious conflict with its former NATO and Japanese allies, a failure to exploit the coming RMA, and a fading away of all U.S. security alliances. Orthodox Chinese analysts predict that 15 to 20 years will be sufficient; reformers argue that it may take longer. U.S. influence is already said to be declining because the multipolar power of other nations constrains U.S. ambition. A domestic Chinese radio broadcast explained, "Even though the United States is currently the most developed country in the world, this does not mean that it can dominate everything as it pleases; and this is specifically the inevitable outcome of the world's accelerated pace toward creating a multipolarized pattern after the Cold War."

Dangers and Opportunities

This new multipolar world will present China with both dangers and major opportunities that parallel those of a rising power during the Warring States era. Some rising states were brutally "extinguished" by the hegemon of the Warring States, a role the United States could play. Ancient strategists deceived or diverted the hegemon and even formed a coalition to balance it. As today's hegemon, the United States may already be maneuvering to prevent ("contain") China from entering this new multipolar world in which China's CNP continues to rise and grow closer to that of the United States. Orthodox authors argue that it is "too late" for the United States to "contain" China. They say U.S. military forces can be defeated through ancient strategic techniques known collectively as "the inferior defeats the superior" (*yiruo shengqiang*). Conversely, other authors assert that the inevitable process of America's decline has not gone far yet. One senior analyst created a probability chart of alternative policies China could pursue in order to delay for 10 years any U.S. military actions that would use force against a rising China to preserve American hegemony. Another author warns that this dangerous threat to China from the United States will not arrive until the decade 2020 to 2030, when the United States finally realizes the implications of becoming inferior to Chinese national power. Both orthodox and reform authors recommend tactical accommodation (including partnership) with the United States. However, both fear that if the China Threat Theory gains more influence in America, the United States will become so alarmed by China's rise that Washington will decide to contain, use strategic deception, or even attack China in order to preserve U.S. hegemony.

China's ancient statecraft urges the development and use of surprise "magic weapons" to win wars, a theory that today appears to influence China's view of the RMA. Five books about the RMA published in 1996-97 are striking evidence of the importance of this subject to the Chinese military. Analysts assert that the *different rates* at which major nations exploit the radical changes in warfare will change the world balance of power, as occurred during the ancient Warring States era. These authors' books boldly predict the United States will lose its initial lead within a decade and then fall behind other nations in this RMA competition. Such a forecast about U.S. failure to take advantage of the opportunities of a potential RMA is consistent with the calculations of other Chinese authors about the future relative decline of the United States. Russia and Japan will surpass the United States in exploiting the RMA, they say. Thus, the effect of the RMA will reinforce the current "inevitable" trend toward multipolarity and the end of America's superpower status.

Future Warfare

There is some evidence that there are three distinct schools of debate about which type of future warfare China will most probably face. There is not a direct debate, so this study labels the different schools of thought the "RMA" advocates, the "Local War" advocates, and the more traditional "People's War," or "Active Defense," advocates. The RMA advocates complain that China's current military modernization is too slow and ought to be aimed instead at leapfrogging the other major powers. Since the mid-1980s, Local War advocates have been seeking to reduce ground forces and develop a better navy and air force. The advocates of continuing Chairman Mao's approach of Active Defense and People's War focus on ideological training, large, lightly armed infantry, and a national defense mobilization base.

There may be a tacit link among these three schools of thought and the debate about the future security environment. RMA advocates would prevail in a budget debate if forecasts of the future emphasized that China would face no local wars or major land invasions but would need to defend itself after two decades against a United States bent on dismembering China to prevent it from challenging U.S. hegemony. Local War advocates benefit from forecasts that China will indeed be challenged in the near term—such as by aggression on China's border with India or Vietnam, or in the South China Sea, or by a declaration of independence by Taiwan. People's War advocates benefit from forecasts that focus on the suspicious intentions of major powers (Japan or the United States) to invade or to dismember, justifying a 3-million-strong army and militia mobilization base.

Marxist Taboos

Some of the current strategic assessment was formulated secretly in the years between 1982 and 1985 through debate among the senior leadership in Beijing. The procedure, which can be seen as China's "assessment cycle," brought about publication of a set of premises that began to shift during the decline of Deng Xiaoping in the early 1990s. There is now a new component—the United States as a potential threat to China's rise. It is remarkable that 20 years ago China saw the United States as a potential military ally and source of advanced weapons, yet today portrays the United States as a future long-term rival and even potential military opponent. Many Chinese note, however, that such changes were routine in the Warring States era.

There remain untested ideological taboos. One cannot publicly forecast certain scenarios. No Chinese author can today openly argue that the United States will grow relatively stronger than other major powers; U.S. relations will improve with capitalist Europe or Japan; Japan will weaken or remain a quasi-pacifist nation under its Peace Constitution; "multipolarity" as defined in China is unlikely; or it is wrong to suspect the United States of being a greedy hegemon seeking to dismember China's Tibet or Taiwan, because it continues to receive 70 percent of China's exports, remains among the top three foreign investors in China, and pledges to reduce arms sales to Taiwan.

One taboo prohibits forecasts or debates about China's own future security role. In sharp contrast to widespread Western interest and writing about the consequences of the rise of China, this subject cannot be addressed by Chinese analysts beyond certain boilerplate phrases used by senior leaders in international fora. There is no discussion of alternative scenarios about the rise of China as a great power. Analysts only repeat platitudes that China will never be a superpower, never seek hegemony, and always be a force for peace and stability. Foreign commentary suggesting that China might behave as other great powers have done has been harshly criticized and punished. A top Chinese analyst agreed in 1987 with the prediction by the U.S. Commission on Integrated Long-Term Strategy that China will emerge by 2010 as the world's second economic power (after the United States and ahead of Japan and Russia). However, he warned that anyone who even considers unpleasant scenarios about China's future role, such as a "potential enemy," shows "a lack of sound strategic thinking."

Candid Chinese views of China's own possible future role as a great power either do not exist or are not available in open sources. This topic is avoided. Instead, daunting challenges are emphasized. China's leaders repeatedly warn that no one should be worried about China as a rising military power. Li Peng stated, "It will take more than 30 years for China to achieve modernization. Therefore, the China Threat Theory is not an objective view. It was spread by anti-China forces in Western countries with ulterior motives to contain China." Apparently, some authors fear that a growing trend in America and Japan will be to prevent China's rise as a future power. "Within the U.S. Congress and the Clinton administration (such as the Defense Department and the intelligence departments), there are a number of experts, strategists, and government officials who do not consider issues from the angle of political strife but instead focus on preserving the U.S. world hegemonist status and proceed from long-term geopolitical strategic awareness in holding that the rise of China will be an enduring challenge and even a threat to the United States. They call for maintaining strategic alertness and instituting strategic precautions against China. They fabricate and publish all kinds of 'reports,' and stir up all kinds of 'cases' for which there is no factual evidence, in order to create strategic opinion for the 'China threat,' 'alertness against China,' and 'precautions against China,' in a bid to attain their strategic and political goals in the world, Asia, and China (including Taiwan)." Chinese concern about the reaction of countries in the Asia-Pacific region to the development of its military force and a potential China Threat is one reason that a plan to build an aircraft carrier was postponed to the 2000-2005 Five-Year Plan. According to one officer, "We do not want our neighbors to misread the signals.. . but we need an aircraft carrier if we are to complete plans to modernize the navy. We have no plans to threaten anyone with an aircraft carrier."

No Self-Criticism

Chinese analysts have not engaged in public criticism about any aspects of China's foreign policy, in sharp contrast to the level of self-criticism in the USSR that Gorbachev permitted as early as 1987. No Chinese author has yet gone as far as Gorbachev's speech to the 19th Party Congress, which asserted, "It even happened that decisions of major importance were made by a narrow circle of persons.... This led to an inadequate reaction to international events and to the policies of other states and even to erroneous decisions." No Chinese author has yet agreed with Gorbachev's call for "de-ideologization of interstate relations," or with Deputy Foreign Minister Anatoli Adamshin's rhetorical question, "Why is injecting ideology into foreign policy so dangerous?... It is no less incorrect to suppose oneself the bearer of historical truth, the possessor of a patent on the future." Nor has any Chinese yet followed Gorbachev's speech on November 2, 1987, which challenged the Leninist view of international politics by suggesting that capitalist nations can do without militarism and neocolonialism. Allen Lynch concluded after this speech, "One may even speak of the emergence... of a new Soviet theory of international relations," while Sylvia Woodby referred to it as a "new world view." Not so in China.

China's commitment to its version of Marxism rules out the public use of purely Western international relations concepts to assess the future security environment. This ideology prohibits using certain concepts to assess the future. Deng's national security advisor on the State Council, Huan Xiang, wrote in 1987 that "bourgeois theories of international relations" were to serve the interests of imperialist foreign policies. One well-known Chinese analyst observed, "Differing from Western international relations theorists such as Hans Morgenthau, China's theory of international relations is based on dialectical and historical materialism." Textbooks of international relations in use in China, such as a recent book by Liang Shoude and Hong Yinxian, emphasize the interpretations of Marx, Lenin, Mao, and Deng Xiaoping. Liang asserts that the foreign policies of nations depend on whether the bourgeoisie or the proletariat is in power.

Capitalist Nations Trigger Wars

Chinese textbooks state that bourgeois states are greedy and constantly plot war and intervention; they are blocked from this course only by the socialist states, who desire peace and development. Students in China from high school on are examined on these principles. Liang Shoude headed the commission that drafted the national syllabus in international politics for all universities. Chinese have publicly rejected Western international relations theory, including the school of thought known as Realism or Neo-Realism, which began to be discussed in 1982 in China.

In contrast to Western research that suggests miscalculation and misperceptions may be the leading cause of war, Chinese analysts assert that "scrambling for resources" causes war. "Economic factors are... the most fundamental cause triggering war." This view may make it difficult for Chinese analysts to appreciate the role of miscalculations and misperceptions in causing war.

Chinese analysts often assert that signs of future trends appear in hidden in current events. For example, the Bosnia conflict is said to reveal a struggle between the United States and the European Union (EU) to dominate Europe and to re-divide the former Soviet sphere of influence. The hidden intent behind U.S. policies of NATO enlargement and revision of the U.S.-Japan defense guidelines is to challenge the spheres of Russia and China from both the east and west flanks.

Will another 25 years of Sino-American "strategic dialogue" and military-to-military exchanges eliminate the Chinese misperceptions identified in this study? American exchange programs have been effective and need to be increased in the future. However, China may not be willing to modify its most dearly held beliefs about traditional statecraft and the future.

PROLOGUE

Ancient Lessons

To reduce the potential for misunderstanding or mirror imaging discussed in the preface, this prologue draws together examples from nine authors in five key research institutes who draw upon concepts from ancient statecraft. Their comments about the future security environment would be difficult to understand without extensive knowledge of the metaphors of Chinese ancient statecraft. The Chinese language is rich in idioms from ancient statecraft. Moreover, Chinese writing about the future security environment describes the future in terms of the Warring States era in Chinese history. The age in which the classics of Chinese statecraft were produced was a time when a multistate competition to become "hegemon" featured stratagems, small wars, interstate conferences, treaties, and what Western scholars of international relations would label "anarchy." One set of "lessons" (among many) was how to become a hegemon; another was how to survive destruction at the hands of a predatory hegemon.

One specific Chinese premise from the ancient statecraft of the Warring States era seems to influence Chinese authors who write about the United States today—the concept of how to diagnose and deal with a powerful "hegemon" (*ba*) that seeks to dominate several other less powerful states. The way hegemons conducted themselves during the Warring States period of ancient China forms one of the sources of the classic lessons of Chinese statecraft. Unfortunately, lessons from Chinese statecraft about dealing with a predatory hegemon are little known in the West, and there is no guide for Westerners to the famous stories in Chinese traditional statecraft so well known to all our authors. According to interviews with Chinese military officers, these stories are embedded in Chinese culture just as the West has its own history, its own literature, and its own Bible stories. This prologue selects only one subject among many from the lessons of the Warring States—how China in the future should assess and deal with a powerful hegemon.

China's military authors have called the future multipolar world "amazingly" similar to the Warring States era and declare that China's future security environment resembles the Warring States era in several ways. A representative article by Colonel Liu Chungzi of the National Defense University Strategy Department states that Sun Zi's *The Art of War* was "the product of the multipolar world structure in China 2500 years ago," that "there are a surprising number of similarities between Sun Zi's time and the contemporary multipolar trend,"and that "in the 1990s, the world entered a multipolar era very similar to the time of Sun Zi." General Gao Rui, former Vice President of the Academy of Military Science (AMS), writes that the era is "extremely distant from modern times, but still shines with the glory of truth" and "the splendid military legacy created through the bloody struggles of our ancient ancestors... [today] has a radiance even more resplendent." Others claim that China should study "treasuries" of strategies from the Warring States. Many books have been published in the last 5 years as a revival of interest in ancient statecraft has been officially blessed by a large commission of China's generals. The director of research at the General Staff Department of the People's Liberation Army published six volumes of studies on ancient statecraft in 1996 that contained specific advice on how to comprehend the current and future security environment.

GEOPOLITICAL CALCULATIONS

n essential aspect of assessing the security environment is said to be determining the rank order of the power held by the various warring states. Although today's Chinese concept of Comprehensive National Power (CNP) was invented in the early 1980s, it originally stemmed from Chinese traditional military philosophy. Authors who currently assess the CNP of different nations can find precedents in the ancient classics. For example, Sun Zi identified "five things" and "seven stratagems" that govern the outcome of war, and Wu Zi wrote about six conditions in which, if the other side's strength was greater, war should be avoided. Colonel Wu Chunqiu of AMS writes that these six points "are relatively complete, they simply are the epitome of [today's concept of] Comprehensive National Power."

However, much like current times, Chinese ancient strategists also attempted to help their country achieve dominance through nonwarfare methods. According to Wu Chunqiu, calculating CNP can aid a nation not just for war but also to "coordinate a political and diplomatic offensive, to psychologically disintegrate the enemy forces and subdue them." Assessing one's own CNP can also aid a country in promoting development and growth.

Two studies by the late Herbert Goldhamer of the RAND Corporation sought to outline some of the content of Chinese statecraft and China's unique perceptions. One of Goldhamer's insights relevant to this study is his emphasis on how China's ancient statecraft demanded efforts to calculate the future. He points out that ancient China's first Minister was called "The Universal Calculator"; that the philosopher Han Feizi demanded that strategy be based on cost-benefit calculations; and that the philosopher Mozi persuaded an enemy general to surrender by showing he could calculate through a "seminar game" what the outcome of the battle would be.

The Warring States era had the equivalent of general staffs, which calculated the strengths and intentions of players in this multipolar world. Sun Zi warned that victory depended on calculations and estimates of enemy strength and weaknesses made in advance by advisers in the temple council; Mozi taught his students the future could be known. Two of ancient China's greatest advisers on statecraft, Lord Shang and Li Si, warned of the need for calculating the future in a multipolar strategic environment. Li Si wrote a famous memorandum to the ruler of Qin, the man who would unify China and become its first emperor, warning, "This is the one moment in ten thousand ages. If your Highness allows it to slip away... there will form an anti-Qin alliance."

With regard to calculating the future, Goldhamer suggests that political writings from ancient China contained "principled predictions," not just intuition or guess work. For example, Lord Shang, a famous adviser in Qin, warned that the price for neglecting quantitative calculations would be that even a state with a large population and a favorable geographical position "will become weaker and weaker, until it is dismembered....The early kings did not rely on their beliefs but on their figures." The subject of Chinese statecraft in a multipolar world explored by Goldhamer remains important to China's process of strategic assessment, especially judging by the sharp increase of Chinese military publications about the relevance of ancient statecraft in the last few years.

GEOPOLITICAL STRATEGY

Warring states that rose too fast suffered attack, dismemberment, and even complete extinction. In the final phase of the Warring States era, as every literate Chinese knows, a brilliant strategist formed a coalition that stood for several decades against the predatory hegemon Qin. Chinese authors today apparently believe the United States is this kind of hegemon, which, if provoked, will attack or "contain" China to preserve its hegemony.

The existence of a dangerous and predatory hegemon is the context of Deng Xiaoping's advice, which employs expressions from the Warring States and other ancient texts to guide future Chinese leaders on strategy. China must "*tao guang yang hui,*" which, literally translated, means "Hide brightness, nourish obscurity," or, as the official Beijing interpretation translates the four-character idiom, "Bide our time and build up our capabilities." China at present is too poor and weak and must avoid being dragged into local wars, conflicts about spheres of influence, or struggles over natural resources. Deng's much-quoted advice also is to "yield on small issues with the long term in mind."

How is Deng's advice about dealing in the future with a dangerous hegemon actually applied? Dr. Yan Xuetong, Director of the Center for Foreign Policy at the China Institute of Contemporary International Relations (CICIR), China's largest international research institute, warned in an article in 1997 that the probability of China's avoiding war for at least 10 more years will increase the more China avoids any confrontation not only with the current global hegemon but with at least two of the other major powers. Like his colleague at CASS, who warns about the dangerous decade from 2020 to 2030, when the U.S. leadership will finally realize that China's power is about to surpass America's, the CICIR center director warns that from ancient times, the hegemon will form a coalition to strangle to death (*e mo*) a rising power when he fears he is to be replaced. Deng Xiaoping's additional word of advice was *bu chu tou*—never be the leader or, literally translated, "Don't stick your head out."

President Jiang Zemin has issued traditional-style, poetic statements in sets of 16 Chinese characters that continue Deng's cautious advice about avoiding confrontation with the hegemon. Under Jiang Zemin, an additional set of writings (five books in 1996) has advocated that China's military programs be focused on the potential RMA rather than improving current weapons. According to these books, the potential RMA will not "mature" until at least 2030, by which time Chinese military authors calculate that China (or possibly Japan) will score highest in the world in CNP and be well positioned, as General Mi Zhenyu has written, to "get ahead of all the others."

Deng Xiaoping's call for caution is not the only lesson based on ancient statecraft. Other Chinese authors (called hotheads by their critics) want to take the initiative to form a coalition against the United States, Warring States style. This is the opposite of not sticking your head out, or biding your time. China's ultranationalist and well-connected author He Xin advocates that China, "under the banner of opposing the hegemon" should align with every anti-American nation in the world, explicitly citing the powerful precedent of the Warring States coalition. Critics of He Xin, especially authors from his former employer CASS, point out that the Warring States era ended when a more brilliant statesman adroitly broke up the coalition and became the founding emperor of China, which may be just what He Xin fears. He predicts that the future ambition of the United States is to impose world domination.

He Xin's critics, however, project a sharp decline in the global role of the United States, asserting that in two decades or so:

- The United States will inevitably decline to one of five powers.
- Japan, the European Union, Russia, and China will each equal the United States.
- The United States, Russia, and China will have nuclear equivalence.

From this viewpoint, dealing with the dangerous hegemon is only a temporary problem. Within two or three decades, or so, the problem will solve itself, as happened many times in the Warring States era.

Patience and caution are thus seen to be wiser than aggressive coalition building against the United States. Dr. Yan Xuetong, of CICIR, has cautioned that the ruling American hegemon can be kept from using force to contain China's rise as long as certain policy goals are maximized: annually increasing exports up to 9 percent and avoiding simultaneous confrontation with the United States and two other powerful nations. Using the following imaginative table of probabilities, Dr. Yan predicts that China can avoid war for at least 10 years by adopting these two policies. However, his table shows that as China's annual share of export markets declines and the number of powerful nations China confronts increases, the probability that China will become involved in war with the United States increases rather sharply.

Not all authors are as optimistic as Dr. Yan. Indeed, his fellow author at CICIR, Zhang Wenmu, presents a more pessimistic diagnosis also based on Warring States premises. The hegemon needs resources, and such a hegemon presents a set of dangers China will face because of America's desperate need for access to new oil and gas resources, especially in Central Asia. According to Zhang's assessment of U.S. future strategy, the United States has begun to interfere in the Tibet issue as part of a larger scheme involving the enlargement of NATO and the redefinition of the U.S.-Japan Defense Guidelines. Zhang believes U.S. strategy is always to "follow the oil." In World War II, the United States did not intervene until Japan changed its strategy and moved toward oil supplies. Similarly, before the Gulf War, the United States ignored Iraqi expansion toward the North and West and even "pretended" not to notice, but when Saudi and Kuwait oil was threatened, the United States went to war. Zhang writes that in 1998 the United States had a "two arms" strategy to contain both Russia (with NATO enlargement) and China (with the new Japan Defense Guidelines and promoting the China Threat Theory).

In addition, Zhang predicts that the United States wants to screen off both Chinese and Russian access to Central Asian oil and gas. To accomplish this strategic goal, the United States will promote the future independence of Tibet from China. If there is internal turmoil in Tibet or farther north in Muslim Xinjiang, Zhang predicts that the United States will try to set up an international no-fly zone as it did after the Gulf War. In a disguised manner, this would amount to "dismembering" Tibet and Xinjiang, the hub or pivot of China's geopolitical position. This is particularly dangerous because the Soviet collapse started with the independence of the Baltic states. A chain reaction from Tibet and Xinjiang would affect China's industrial southwest and cause the loss of the high plateau, which provides natural protection to the west. Zhang therefore recommends that China take the lead in settling the Afghan civil war (which he says the United States is prolonging through covert aid to the Taliban fundamentalists). At the same time, Zhang advocates more caution. China must get the Central Asia oil market oriented to China. It is better to place high priority on land transport of oil and gas, which China's superiority in ground forces can protect, rather than depend in the future on sealanes for oil supplies that the United States and Japan will threaten with their powerful navies. These recommendations had their counterparts in the Warring States era.

Zhang Wenmu and Dr. Yan Xuetong contrast sharply with the strategic diagnosis and recommendation based on the Warring States period offered by one of China's most colorful and controversial strategic authors, He Xin, who frequently uses analogies to the era. Reformers despise him and orthodox analysts tend to distance themselves from his outspoken nationalistic writings, which run against Deng Xiaoping's advice to "bide our time" and "never take the lead." Nevertheless, there is no better example of how statecraft from the Warring States era can affect China's assessments of the future. Among many other articles, He Xin has written a call for a Chinese-led coalition against today's hegemon before it is too late. He Xin cites the precedent of the Warring States era, because "the past can help us understand the present" and outlines key points:

- "The world situation, after the severe changes in the Soviet Union and Eastern Europe, in form actually appears amazingly similar to the situation in the latter period of the Warring States, where there were six powerful countries facing each other and one country dominating."
- The United States "will sacrifice different countries' national interests and independent sovereignty, take the entire world and change it into an American World Empire...[and] become the director, arbitrator, the final decider of all problems—the highest dictator of world economics and politics."
- "In the early period [of the Warring States era], the six countries 'joined horizontally,' and for a number of decades effectively resisted the powerful Qin threat. However, in the later period, one after another they accepted Qin

protection and were willing to become its satellite countries. The result was their collapse in 10 years. They were each destroyed by the Qin threat.... It is now necessary to form a modern strategy of 'joining horizontally.' "

- "China must pay close attention to those countries that are opposed to American interests, or are potential strategic enemies. It must be borne in mind that the enemies of enemies are one's own allies."
- "China should do all that it can to warn and help these countries, and prevent them from being destroyed by the United States as the Soviet Eastern European bloc was. It must bring together the world antihegemonism force under the flag of fighting hegemonism."
- "Know this: the more the United States encounters trouble in other places in the world, the more difficult it is for it to concentrate its power on dealing with China and the greater the opportunities for China's existence and development."
- "China must seek allies among all countries that could become America's potential opponents today or in the future. The following three regions are especially worth serious attention: Japan (America's future potential strategic opponent in the Asia-Pacific); Germany (America's future potential strategic opponent in Europe); and the South Asia peninsula (a border region that is of important strategic significance to China). I solemnly put forward a three-point plan, 'Join Japan, work with Germany, stabilize the South.' "

Somewhere between the cautionary advice of Deng Xiaoping, Dr. Yan, and Zhang Wenmu, and the bold demand of He Xin for anti-U.S. coalition building, lies the strategic advice offered by Liu Jinghua, of CASS. While less dramatic than He Xin's proposal for a global anti-U.S. coalition, his suggestion deals with the same problem of preventing the predatory, hegemonic United States from containing China's rise, or worse, and is also firmly in the tradition of Warring States statecraft. Liu warns that by 2020 to 2030, serious confrontations will begin among the major powers.

At present, it is wise to *tao guang yang hui* (conceal abilities and bide time), in order to eliminate the China Threat Theory, but by 2020 that policy will not be sufficient. The United States (and Europe, too) will by then begin seriously to attempt to contain China. Then, "once the flood begins, we must have a 'Great Wall' that cannot collapse." One part of this "Great Wall" must be a partnership with Russia to defeat Western containment of China, which will be attempted by restricting access to capital markets and technology, promoting Western values and using military power "as the core" against China. Implicit here, too, is that China has plenty of time and needs mainly not to provoke the hegemon in the intervening two decades until the Great Wall can be made ready.

Another diagnosis and recommendation project onto the United States the kind of knowledge from ancient statecraft that a true predatory hegemon ought to have. This is a kind of mirror image from the Warring States. According to General Li Jijun, one of China's most distinguished military authors and a former Vice President of AMS, the greater danger to a nation's survival is not warfare but *zhanlue wudao*—"strategic misdirection"—in the current multipolar world structure. General Li describes the United States as being particularly adept at this strategy, as powerful hegemons used to be.

According to Genera Li, the United States brought about the collapse of the Soviet Union with strategic misdirection. Washington deceptively stimulated the Soviets to increase their defense budget to great heights through various means, including the Strategic Defense Initiative ("Star Wars"), which the United States had no intention of deploying, Li writes. The United States also supported the opposition in Poland and Afghanistan, drove down the price of oil to cut off the main source of Soviet foreign exchange, and exacerbated the domestic Soviet political crisis. In 1990, Washington again used strategic misdirection against Saddam Hussein, in order to contain his rising power in the Gulf. As supposedly revealed by an American author, Washington deliberately lured Saddam into invading Kuwait, in part through deliberately deceptive comments to Saddam by the U.S. Ambassador in Baghdad, to the effect that the United States did not care if he invaded Kuwait. General Li, comparing the strategic cultures of all the major powers, concludes that the preferred "strategic cultural" approach of the United States is strategic misdirection.

Citing the lessons of history, General Li warns that "unconsciously accepting an opponent's strategic misdirection causes a nation to be defeated or collapse, and not know why."

General Li is not the only PLA officer to hold this view. Following the NATO bombing of the Chinese Embassy in Belgrade in spring 1999, a Chinese journal interviewed several PLA generals about the attack; they stated that one reason for the United States to bomb the embassy was strategic misdirection.

An article in the June issue of *Zhongguo Pinglun* concludes, "The Western forces are attempting to drag China into the mire of the arms race. The United States is planning to pursue a TMD [theatre missile defense] system... so that the Chinese will step into the shoes of the former Soviet Union. In an arms race with the United States, China will consume its national power, and collapse without a battle." A key strategy of the Warring States was to attempt to do just this to an opponent.

Having made the point that these nine authors from five key research institutes use lessons and metaphors from the Warring States era and ancient statecraft, the first chapter presents several debates underway among many authors about the exact nature of the future "multipolar" security environment China will face in the decades ahead.

CHINA DEBATES THE FUTURE SECURITY ENVIRONMENT

The multipolarity debate

THE VISIONS OF MORE THAN 30 AUTHORS are presented in this chapter about the geopolitical features of the future. They reveal debates between orthodox and reformist authors about which nations will be the most powerful by 2020, what kinds of international alignments will form, and the nature of the post-Cold War transitional pattern.

THE CURRENT ASSESSMENT, 1986-99

China's current assessment of the future security environment is based on the kind of calculations Sun Zi and the Warring States strategists would recognize. It was issued before the collapse of the Soviet Union and the end of the Cold War and can be dated to early 1986. The assessment characterizes the present world as being in a "new era" of transition that will last several decades. During this period, great rivalries will emerge among the powers, and many local wars will be fought (as large as Korea in 1950 or the Gulf War in 1991), as a "re-division of spheres of influence" and a struggle for world leadership takes place. Bosnia is one example of the strife that typifies the era, because the Bosnia conflict is frequently called a "struggle between the United States and the European Union for domination of Europe." NATO enlargement, which China opposes, is another example of this "struggle to re-divide spheres of influence." The outcome of this transitional period of "turbulence" will have the following eight features:

- After the transition period is complete, there will no longer be any "superpowers" but instead a "multipolar world" in which five major nations—China, the United States, Japan, Europe and Russia—will each have roughly equal Comprehensive National Power (CNP).
- The nations that will do "best" in competitive terms during the transitional period will pursue "peace and development" and enhance their economic competitiveness. By avoiding local wars, they can decrease defense expenditures and avoid the damage of warfare. Chinese authors frequently assert that the collapse of the Soviet Union and the decline of the United States are due in large part to extremely high defense spending and diminishing competitiveness in CNP.
- Today's "sole superpower" is in severe decline. The United States risks declining so extensively in contrast to the rise of other nations that it will fall to the level of a mere "common major nation." This continual weakening of U.S. strength in the decades ahead is an important feature of

the Chinese assessment, so this study provides more details on this subject than on China's views of other major powers.

- After the transition to the multipolar world, a new "world system" will emerge to govern international affairs, one that will probably resemble the current Chinese proposal of the "Five Principles of Peaceful Coexistence." Chinese authorities assert that world politics since the 1800s always has had a "system" or a "strategic pattern." Under those rules, there is a competition among powers that includes a global division of spheres of influence. Chinese historical textbooks discuss the "Vienna System" of 1815-70; an intermediate system when Germany and Italy each unified and Japan launched the Meiji Reform; the "Versailles System" of 1920-45; the "Yalta System" of 1945-89; and the present "transition era."
- The new Chinese-style world system of the Five Principles will be much better than systems of the past and present, because there will be harmony, no "power politics," and no more "hegemony." This harmonious world requires a transition away from capitalism in the major powers toward some type of "socialist market economy." Just as China has modified the doctrines of Marx, Engels, Lenin, and Stalin to produce what Deng Xiaoping called "Socialism with Chinese Characteristics," so will the United States, Germany, Japan, and Russia ultimately develop their own socialist characteristics.
- Some Chinese military authors believe that there is now underway a Revolution in Military Affairs (RMA) that will radically change future warfare. Several recent Chinese books assert that the United States may not exploit the RMA as well as other nations in the decades ahead. China's generals "plan to be better, to be ahead of everyone... and become latecomers who surpass the old-timers" in the new revolution.
- A major global nuclear war is highly unlikely for two decades. This official forecast is a sharp change from the forecasts of Chairman Mao that a global nuclear war was inevitable. Therefore, China claims to have cut its defense

spending from more than 6 percent of gross national product (GNP) in the 1960s and 1970s, to between 2 and 3 percent when the current assessment came into force by the mid-1980s, and down to about 1.5 percent of the GNP in the 1990s. This claim by China that it has drastically reduced defense spending, which included cutting the People's Liberation Army (PLA) from 7 to 3 million, is based on China's expectation that it can remain above the fray of local wars during the turbulent transition era ahead.

- There are many global forces at work for *luan* (turbulence, a word that also may be translated as chaos), including the potential for nationalist, militarist takeovers of Japan and India. The "main trend" in the world is toward "peace and development," but "potential hot spots exist which could lead to the involvement of major powers and regional powers in direct military confrontation." As suggested by one writer, this is true even in Asia: "Although the Asia-Pacific region has been relatively stable since the end of the Cold War, there are also many uncertainties there. If certain hot-spot problems are not handled properly, they may cause conflicts, confrontations, and even war in this region, thus wrecking the peace, stability, and prosperity of the region."

Within the framework of this strategic assessment, China's analysts discuss a number of subjects in their journals and books. For example, the question frequently arises about how current events fit into the framework. Some Chinese authors see the following examples of the "turbulent period of transition" as suggesting that former spheres of influence are being "re-divided." While not all Chinese authors included in this volume would agree with all these findings, the examples demonstrate how the framework of the assessment of the future is applied in practice:

- The United States is exploiting Russian weakness by enlarging NATO in order to increase its domination of its European NATO allies.
- The United States ("its hegemonistic ambitions further inflated") is forcing Japan to increase its financial support

for U.S. bases and forces in Japan under the guise of the Defense Guidelines.

- The United States arranged the Bosnian settlement at Dayton to dominate further its European NATO allies.
- Japan is seeking to embroil the Unites States and China in a struggle that will weaken both Washington and Beijing.
- Some in the United States are fearful of China and seek to contain or block China's gradually increasing influence by promoting the China Threat Theory. This is wrong because "China has neither the strength nor the will to compete with the United States and other big powers in global affairs."
- Central Asia may be the location of political struggles and wars among the big powers as the former Soviet sphere of influence is re-divided. For example, a recent article stated, "Following the Soviet Union's disintegration, the United States has cast its covetous eyes on Central Asia, the 'second Middle East of the next century,' with the goal of eventually controlling most of the energy resources in Central Asia." The article asserts that in 1998 "Russia and the United States continued their contention in Central Asia by covert and overt means. The basic situation is still that 'the United States is on the offensive while Russia is on the defensive.' What has changed is that Russia has switched its 'passive defense' to 'active defense.' " The author concludes that this change means the United States will "find it difficult to have a free rein in Central Asia."
- NATO airstrikes against Yugoslavia in spring 1999 were a part of a U.S. plan to gain control over Eurasia. "On the surface, the 'salvation' of the ethnic Albanians in Kosovo by NATO troops seems to be out of 'humanitarian considerations' but some important geostrategic interests are undoubtedly hidden behind this operation." An article entitled, "What are NATO's Motives in Bombing the Federal Republic of Yugoslavia," explained, "Kosovo is located in the middle of the Balkan Peninsula and the peninsula is at the meeting point of Europe, Asia, and Africa. It is an

important corridor joining the north, south, east, and west and leading to Asia and Africa.... The United States knows full well the importance of the Balkan region and has regarded it as a 'new priority for consideration'.... In this region, it can strengthen its security system in the Mediterranean and the North Atlantic to the west; can consolidate the 'southern wing of NATO' to the south through converging it with its Middle East strategy; can infiltrate and expand in the Black Sea and the Caspian Sea regions to the west, that is, the outer Caucasus and Central Asia regions, weakening and squeezing out Russian forces and influence, and taking a step further, can press on to China's northwestern boundary to coordinate from afar with its Asia-Pacific strategy; and finally, can exercise restraints on its European allies to the north, especially the NATO move southward. In this way, the United States will be able to properly fulfill its ambition of making Europe more important and practicing hegemony in the world."

MULTIPOLARITY PROCLAIMED IN 1986

Chinese analysts do not observe international scholarly standards by footnoting each other or providing bibliographical information. Most authors write as if they were the sole Chinese to ever deal with an issue, in sharp contrast to Western scholarly books and articles, where the author is expected to make clear his debt to earlier work and narrowly and modestly to describe his new contribution. Thus, no Chinese author writing in the 1990s refers to the origins of the current view of the future security environment. Interviews have established that it was Huan Xiang, Deng Xiaoping's national security adviser, who had both access to scholarly experts from Shanghai as well as experience as China's ambassador to Britain, who announced its features in early 1986, just after the U.S.-Soviet summit. Huan's speeches and articles in 1984 and 1985 described a world structure that was changing, but it was still unclear what actions the major players would take and its characteristics were not yet determined:

- "The two largest military powers are weakening and declining... militarily they are developing in the direction of multipolarization... if the Star Wars plan develops, multipolarization could develop toward bipolarization, and could again return to bipolarization. If secondary ranked countries want to carry out a Star Wars plan, it will be very difficult. The position of those countries will immediately decline."

- "The old world order has already disintegrated and the new world order is now taking shape, but up to now it still has not yet completely formed."
- "U.S. domination of the Asia-Pacific will end."
- "Japan knows what role it should take, but it still hesitates.... China must go through a long period of hard work... 30 to 50 years time will make it truly powerful."

Beginning in January 1986, the uncertainty about the future world structure had disappeared, and its transformation and transition had definite traits and stages. Huan explained, "Future international politics and economics are facing a new period."

- "In the confrontation between the two superpowers, changes that are deeper and more significant than those of the past have occurred."
- "Even though the two superpowers still are the two countries with the most solid actual strength,... the new stage of U.S.-Soviet relations will further weaken their ability to control and influence their respective allies. More and more of their allies will seek an even greater level of independence... within the two blocs, there are also increasingly developing trends of economic and political friction and being at odds with the leadership.... The world's political multipolarity trend will further develop."
- "The focal point of the competition has been raised from the past emphasis, which was solely on the struggle for military superiority... to a contest of entire economic, scientific and technological, military and political comprehensive strength. Thus for the next several years... strengthening Comprehensive National Power will be the main task."
- "The development toward multipolarity is divided into two steps. The first step is the big triangle... China, the

United States and the Soviet Union.... After China's national might and military prowess greatly developed during the Korean War and the Indo-China war, the world had to recognize that China is a very powerful nation. Currently, after revision of its domestic and international policy, its position in the three poles is definite. Western Europe and Japan also are regarded as poles, but they have not completely formed the power of a pole. To form a single pole force, it must be seen if they can be independent with the initiative in their own hands.... As the world moves toward a multipolar world, both in the first large triangle stage, and in the future as it moves toward a five pole world, when the United States and the Soviet Union are considering problems, they must think about the China factor, and also the other poles."

- "Militarily there still are two poles, the United States and the Soviet Union.... Economically, there currently are four centers: the United States, the Soviet Union, Japan, and Western Europe.... Politically, the Sino-U.S.-Soviet large triangular relationship is currently the major factor most able to influence the development of the international situation. In regional issues there are two squares. In the Far Eastern Asia-Pacific region, there is China, the United States, the Soviet Union and Japan... . In Europe the square is the United States, the Soviet Union, Eastern Europe, and Western Europe."
- "Japan considers the United States to be its main economic opponent, for deployment of its offensive and for making challenges. It not only wants to strive to be on equal footing with the United States economically and politically, but further, it is deliberately planning, when the time is ripe, to surpass the United States and replace America's world economic hegemony. Once it has economic hegemony, political, and military hegemony would not be too difficult."

China's national security analysts became very concerned about Bush administration proposals for a "new international order" and held a conference in 1991 to discuss their own views. The phrase "New World Order" was first used by then Soviet President Mikhail Gorbachev at the November 1990 Conference on Security and Cooperation in Europe (CSCE) Summit in Paris and at the U.N. General Assembly speech on December 7, 1988, when he announced severe reductions in Soviet military forces, including Soviet forces stationed in the Warsaw Pact countries, which, according to a congressional research study, may have stimulated the unraveling of support for the Communist parties in Eastern Europe and "the demise of the Warsaw Pact." Multipolarity in the 21st century was forecast by a senior scholar in 1991.

REVISIONIST MULTIPOLARITY

Challenging the Orthodox View

As mentioned, Chinese authors rarely refer to each other and almost never criticize other authors by name, but in 1997, two unusual articles broke this apparent taboo in two national journals. The episode began when Yang Dazhou, a well-known senior analyst at the Institute of American Studies of the Chinese Academy of Social Science (CASS), published a direct and detailed criticism of the orthodox assessment of the coming world of multipolarity. It is difficult for any foreign observer to know whether the article remained within the bounds of scientifically "seeking truth from facts" that Deng Xiaoping demanded in 1978, or whether it was a "poisonous weed" that threatened Communist Party doctrine, because Central Party documents, which authoritatively set the range of debate, are never made public. Some of those interviewed said the article tested the outer limits of Party orthodoxy about the future world.

The article met with a vigorous response from a senior general in military intelligence. In a departure from the tradition of merely stating a view without debating anyone else, the PLA general actually quoted long passages from the reformer's article. The general then wrote that these views were ridiculous, without foundation, and unsupportable and, worst of all, played into the hands of the United States.

Several Chinese authors commented in interviews on both the style and the issues of this unusual "debate." They acknowledged that the two articles reflect a difference among the senior leadership of China about *the pace* of the decline of the United States and *the rate* of the rise of "multipolarity." At least a few influential civilian analysts are said to have written sensitive internal studies for the senior leadership of China, concluding that the United States may remain a superpower for as long as 50 more years. However, analysts stated that no one is willing yet to openly publish the view because of resistance by the military and some civilians who cling to the conventional assessment. This "debate" may have been addressed at the 1997 traditional annual month-long meeting of China's most senior leaders. If so, it highlights the importance of these contradictory two articles on the future security environment.

In his article, Yang Dazhou heretically argues against each of the key features of the orthodox view of the future security environment, putting forward a reformist scenario:

- The United States will maintain its superpower status for at least three decades.
- The United States will maintain its alliances with Japan and Germany.
- There will not be a period of "uncertainty" in the next two or three decades.
- There will not be an extended transition period featuring a trend toward multipolarity.
- A "pluralistic" world structure of "one superpower and four powers" already exists.
- Only the United States is really a "pole" able to decide key issues in any region, as it did with the Dayton Accords. "The United States plays a leading role that no other nation can replace... the only country that is a 'pole.' "
- China "does not have sufficient qualifications to be a 'pole.'"
- For more than 20 years, no other nations, including those in the Third World, will emerge as major powers to challenge the five strongest, therefore the phrase used by many analysts "'one super many strong' is actually not appropriate."
- It is not likely large local wars will break out among nations.

The Orthodox Counterattack

According to an interview the author of this volume conducted in Beijing in May 1998, the editor of the PLA journal *International Strategic Studies* decided that an unsolicited article by General Huang Zhengji merited publication even though it was very "sharp" (hostile in tone) and "out of the ordinary" in style. General Huang quoted passages from Yang's article without directly citing it and reasserted the orthodox view on each of these points:

- U.S. decline is inevitable and continuing; U.S. global influence is already severely limited.
- Five-pole multipolarity is inevitable, especially as friction grows between the United States and Japan and Germany (as proved by the new summits between the European Union (EU) and Asia, which excluded the declining United States).
- The rise of the Third World has transformed world politics and will continue to restrain the United States.

Local wars are certain, even though "'peace and development' is the main trend" during the transitional period of uncertainty in the decades ahead.

According to interviews, the orthodox forecast of the future security environment continues to dominate in all Chinese international studies journals. It is as if the reformist views of Yang Dazhou's article had never appeared. Two methods reinforce the orthodox view. First, new developments are assembled to "prove" the orthodox view. For example, a typical review of 1997 supposedly provided clear evidence not only of the "acceleration" of the inevitable trend toward multipolarity, but also of America's declining international influence: the Association of South East Asian Nations (ASEAN) refusal of U.S. demands that Burma not be admitted as a member of ASEAN; Russian and European defiance of U.S. pressure not to trade with Iran; and Brazil's blocking of U.S. efforts for a free-trade zone in South America.

The second method to reinforce the orthodox and ignore the reform view is repetitive articles by senior officials. One novel example is the publication of a speech given at Harvard University in December 1997 by the Deputy Chief of the General Staff of the PLA, General Xiong Guangkai, that contained all the features of the orthodox view. According to interviews in Beijing, the use of Harvard as the location and a senior PLA policy maker as the "awesome" vehicle was an emphatic message to reformers. It is useful to quote at some length the words Xiong used to reinforce the orthodox view of the future:

- "Peace and development have become the main theme of the current epoch. However, we cannot but note that the world is still not tranquil."
- "Since the beginning of the 1990s, as many as 68 local wars or armed conflicts have broken out in all parts of the world."
- "Any efforts for seeking hegemony and world domination can only result in accumulating contradictions and fermenting war."
- "Only by facing up to and promoting such a trend as the co-existence of multipolarity can we bring about peace and prosperity."
- "The practice of resolving contradictions among countries by relying on augmenting military blocs, strengthening military alliances or engaging in military confrontation is not conducive to preserving peace and safeguarding security."
- "It is necessary to develop a new concept. I think the Five Principles of Peaceful Coexistence, which has been consistently initiated by the Chinese Government for years, shall constitute an important foundation for establishing a global security system in the 21st century."
- As to the extent of future local wars, Xiong states the death toll was 14 million in the First World War, 60 million in the Second World War, and as high as 24 million in the "40 years of the Cold War."

TECHNIQUES FOR SHOWING DISSENT

As stated, the orthodox and reform views rarely confront each other. Therefore, the open "debate" between Yang Dazhou and

Huang Zhengji was without precedent in dealing with such core issues as to whether:

- The United States is really declining
- Local wars will arise
- China is even a "pole"
- Nations other than the 5 strongest can become poles
- There continues to be any "transitional era" of uncertainty about the future.

This is not to say that there are no differences or variances in opinion about the above issues; merely, other authors do not mention anyone else's views, let alone criticize them. Sometimes a "neutral" author alludes to the existence of different points of view on an issue, or a journal will publish the comments of several scholars from a conference in a way that shows disagreements exist. For example, in *2000: Where is the World Going?*, Yang Zheng sets forth six different scenarios for the future world structure, but he only provides a scholar's name in one scenario, does not distinguish between the views of Chinese and foreign analysts, and does not examine or give his own opinion on the feasibility of these possible scenarios.

In 1997, a very senior analyst at CICIR, Li Zhongcheng, outlined three different views of the future world structure by analysts at CICIR and CASS. Although they are not described as being part of a debate, their conflicting arguments fall into the opposing sides of the Yang Dazhou-Huang Zhengji dispute. The first scenario is depicted in the writings of Xi Runchang of CASS, who, like Yang Dazhou, refers to the world pattern following the collapse of the Soviet Union as "one super, four strong," and believes that this pattern constitutes a world structure: "Currently there has already basically formed a new embryonic structure supported by the five powers... in the 21st century, this new structure will further form and be perfected."

The views of Yan Xuetong of CICIR are representative of the second scenario, "the theory on finalizing the basic design of multipolarity." He asserts, "The basic establishment of the great nations' strategic relations in 1996 caused the post-Cold War transition from a bipolar structure to a one super many strong structure to be completed." Finally, the writings of Song Baoxian and Yu Xiaoqiu of CICIR offer a third scenario, which is more similar to that of Huang Zhengji and the orthodox camp, that "multipolarity is forming" and that countries other than the five most powerful are growing in strength. They argue, "The development of the multipolarity trend is accelerating" and "A new group of powers will rise" that will have a "restricting role with regard to the five major powers, [and] will cause the multipolarity trend of the world structure to be even more attractive and varied." Li does not directly criticize any of the authors whose concepts he presents, although his own views appear to be much closer to those represented in the third scenario.

Authors sometimes resort to citing respected foreign experts in order to dissent. For example, in 1997 in a book published by CICIR, the three authors, who are presumably aware of the orthodox position that there can only be five poles, hinted that Henry Kissinger holds a reform view: "Kissinger predicted that the future world will have six poles—America, Japan, China, Russia, Europe, and India....[Today] India's military power is only fourth behind the United States, Russia and China, and India's Comprehensive National Power is continually increasing."

Another innovative technique to avoid debate of the orthodox view is to rise above it by inventing new definitions of orthodox terms. Yan Xuetong of CICIR writes, "The new international structure has some special characteristics, the most important of which is the replacement of 'poles' (*ji*) by 'units' (*yuan*). The nature of 'poles' is long-term stable confrontation, but the nature of 'units' is that the dominant position of key countries is determined by the nature of specific affairs." These definitions elude the orthodox line. Much of Yang Dazhou's article challenged the orthodox view by employing this very tactic of establishing and clarifying definitions for key words and phrases, such as "pole," "transition era," "pluralization" (*duoyuanhua*) versus "multipolarization" (*duojihua*), and "major nation" (*daguo*) versus "a power" (*qiangguo*).

For example, Yang defined what constitutes a "pole" based on the standards of the Cold War era, when the United States and the Soviet Union were the only two poles. The "four strong," consequently, are not poles because "when compared to the Soviet Union, there still is a great distance." Similarly, in his argument against those who claim that the world is in a transition era that will go on for an undetermined long period of time, Yang argues that by definition a transition is not indefinite. "Some people believe that the post-Cold War transition period could continue for 20, even 30 years. This type of argument is not appropriate; a 'transition period' always has an ending time. Suppose the 'transition period' goes on for 20 or 30 years, then this itself already constitutes a new structure different from that of the Cold War period."

DIFFERENCES WITHIN THE ORTHODOX CAMP

Differences of opinion clearly exist between the reform and orthodox camps over whether or not a world structure has already been established, but even among scholars who adhere to the orthodox line and believe that the world is in a transition period, various views can be found on how long it will last. No real consensus appears to exist on the subject. Many authors simply make vague predictions without giving a time frame of when multipolarity might emerge, other than "in the early 21st century." For example, He Feng of the State Council International Studies Center writes, "Because the replacement of the old world structure by a new one is taking place under peaceful conditions, this transition era certainly will be comparatively long," and he believes that it will "continue into the early part of the next century."

Chen Qimao, former president of the Shanghai Institute for International Studies (SIIS) breaks down the transition period into three stages, which the world will go through before a multipolar structure is established. The first stage was from 1989 to 1991, when the fall of communism in Eastern Europe and the Soviet Union brought about the end of the Cold War. Currently, according to Chen, the world is in the second phase, from the Soviet collapse to "the basic formation of the new multipolar structure." He writes that during this stage, where "the old structure has already ended, but the new structure has not yet formed,... a situation of 'one super (the United States) many strong (the European Union, Japan, Russia, China),' or the so called 1-2-3-5 layered structure has emerged—1 (one superpower, the United States), 2 (two military powers, the United States and Russia), 3 (three economic powers, the United States, Japan, and Europe), 5 (five political powers, the United States, Europe, Japan, Russia, and China)." He foresees the world will be "complex and changeable, turbulent and unstable" until "the beginning of the next century," when "the period of major changes will come to an end, and a new balance will be established." The world will then begin the last phase of the transition, "the formation and finalization of the foundation of the multipolar structure, a stage where a new international political and economic order suited to the requirements of the new structure will be established and adjusted." However, Chen does not predict when the final transition stage will end.

Some analysts have even revised their own estimates. In the early 1990s, Lieutenant General Li Jijun, Vice President of the Academy of Military Science (AMS), wrote, "Because of the fast development and globalization of science, technology and economics, the dispersion of world power will speed up." Therefore, the creation of a " world structure of multipolar coexistence... might take 10 or 20 years to take shape." However, a few years later, he extended the timetable for the transition period. "By the mid-21st century, I believe, the world will have gradually built a real multipolar structure and a mature security structure as well so that absolute hegemonism will have declined and this is likely to dictate a global trend in the second half of the 21st century."

Other differences of opinion exist about who will be a pole once the world has gone through its transition period and finally formed a multipolar structure. For example there is the issue of a European pole. Some authors, such as Gao Heng of CASS, believe that Germany as an independent nation will be one of the world's five poles, not the EU. The First Secretary at the Chinese Embassy in Germany, Shang Jin, regards unified Germany as "the biggest winner of the Cold War" and the future overlord of Europe's economy. Several authors assert that Germany is striving for domination of Europe in order to establish itself as a pole. However, it is running into opposition from Britain and France. According to Qi Deguang of CICIR, the struggles among the European powers are manifested through leadership conflicts, such as over how to proceed in the Bosnia crisis. He claims Germany supported the Bosnian Croats in order "seize the leadership of Europe," but France and Britain "would not bow out in favor of Germany." London and Paris therefore "invoked the provision in the German Constitution that forbids Germany from sending its troops abroad" and supported NATO instead. The French and British decision to send peace-keeping troops to Bosnia was also "meant to belittle Germany."

Other analysts argue that while Germany may be the strongest of the Western European nations, it still is no match for the United States; only Europe has that potential. In a study conducted by SIIS, Wang Houkang asserts that none of the Western European nations individually has the power to constitute a pole, but the joint strength of the European Union not only provides it with "pole" qualifications, but once its integration process has progressed and solidified, it will then be able to contend with the United States for global influence:

Each independent country in the European Union, including Germany, which is the most powerful, when viewed globally, is at most a regional power, but the European Union taken as a whole, is a force that can be completely equal to the United States... if Europe wants to surpass the United States and play the role of a future world leader,... the most important basic condition is European unity. This is to say, Europe must not only realize economic integration, but also political integration, and during this process establish a powerful military force. As of today, the European Community and the European Union still are alliances of sovereign nations.

While noting the difficulties in the integration process and predicting that it will be long in duration, Wang also believes that its eventual completion is inevitable: "The trend of European integration will not stop or reverse, this point is certain." Finally, Wang questions the potential for Europe to be the dominant world power in the future: "In the 18th and 19th centuries, Europe... was the acknowledged leader of the world for several hundred years.

In the 20th century it declined and the U.S. moved ahead of it. In the 21st century can it rise again? People can not eliminate this possibility." His view is shared by a Senior Research Fellow at CIISS, Shen Guoliang, who writes, "Today not a single country in Europe, including such European powers as Germany, France and Britain, can possibly be independent of European integration and cope with the complex and fierce challenges independently. Europe can only become one of the poles in the world by way of integration and playing a role in the multipolar order."

Whether or not Third World countries will play a significant role in the future multipolar world also is an issue where Chinese authors have differed. Like Yang Dazhou, Chen Qimao believes that the CNP of Third World countries will continue to grow in the early part of the next century but does not see their strength increasing fast enough to allow them to come close to the power of the five poles. Chen, however, predicts that they will rise somewhat more quickly than Yang, "The power of India, Brazil and ASEAN will greatly increase, but until the early 21st century (before 2010) there is no prospect for any of them to become one of the world's poles." In contrast, He Fang estimates that great changes involving Third World countries will have occurred in the world by the end of the next decade. He writes, "The rise of the developing countries shows even more so the irreversible trend of relative U.S. decline.... By 2010, seven of the world's ten economic powers will be developing countries.... Regional powers will be elevated to world powers and world powers will decline to regional ones."

POST-KOSOVO DEBATE

The NATO strikes on Yugoslavia and the NATO bombing of the Chinese Embassy in Belgrade in the spring of 1999 have given prominence to the debate concerning the future world structure. One of the biggest outgrowths of the Kosovo crisis and the bombing is that they led to reevaluation of previous assessments of the pace of U.S. decline and the rate at which the world is moving toward multipolarization. It appears that the reformist view, represented by Yang Dazhou, gained support as a result of U.S. and NATO actions in Yugoslavia. A clear post-Kosovo trend has been the number of Chinese authors admitting that the transition to multipolarity has been delayed: "An analysis of the situation at the present stage shows that... the deeds of the United States have slowed down the multipolarization process and made it more difficult for the international community to build a new political and economic order in the next century." A key element in the new assessment is the corresponding issue of why the time frame for the transition to the new world structure has been greatly extended—the United States remains powerful. Not only are some authors no longer focusing on current U.S. decline, but rather, they are predicting that its strength may even continue to increase:

The United States, as the sole superpower, occupies a relatively prominent, single, superpower position of domination, and it will for some time maintain the momentum of expansion....Right now multipolarization has lost its momentum for "accelerated development." Multipolarization in the course of history may be more complicated and tortuous than once thought. It would be more appropriate for us to describe today's world as "single-superpower pluralism" than "multiple powers with one superpower." The early part of the 21st century may see a situation characterized by "single superpower domination, and pluralistic disputes."

Chinese authors explain U.S. dominance as stemming from a number of factors. Current U.S. economic and technological superiority is at the top of their list. "The United States is at the peak of a financial monopoly of capital. Moreover, being propelled by a contemporary technological revolution, it is in the leading position in most high and new technological fields, in addition to enjoying relative superiority in the technological industry and economic strength." According to Xiao Lian of the North American Institute at CASS, future U.S. economic domination may last many decades because of the success of U.S. strategy. He gives several reasons. First, "no matter how the European economy is reorganized or integrated, Europe will be unable to control the Japanese and the Asia-Pacific economies unless the United States participates in this process. By the same token, no matter how the Asia-Pacific economic cooperation zone is built, Europe will be unable to play a significant role in the Asia-Pacific economy unless the United States takes part in this process." The second reason Xiao lists is that "United States has all along controlled the WTO [World Trade Organization], the World Bank, and has had a bigger say in the IMF [International Monetary Fund] to date.... United States has time and again succeeded in consolidating and enhancing its control over the world economy." This success includes "controlling and manipulating the foreign exchange markets the world over" in order to get "huge profits by virtue of its economic and financial strength and the special position of the U.S. dollar."

Another argument put forward by Chinese authors to explain the delay in multipolarization is that the other poles do not yet have the strength to independently stand up to the United States. For example, Shen Jiru, Director of the International Strategic Studies Office of the Institute of World Economics and Politics at CASS, describes the EU position in international activities rather negatively. He writes, "In world affairs, it has always remained a political shorty and a military dwarf....So far, the EU has yet to develop any independent defense strength which can be of some real use; and the EU still has to largely depend on NATO for its defense." Consequently, Chinese authors assert, the United States has taken advantage of the relative weakness of European countries and Japan to create some powerful alliances. These partnerships are an additional factor boosting current American dominance. One author stated, "Internationally, the United States has formed a collective hegemonist alliance, turning some international political, economic, and military organizations into U.S. tools for hegemony." Shen Jiru agrees, claiming that it is an "ill omen that the unipolar world dominance of the United States takes the form of a U.S.-Europe and a U.S.-Japanese joint hegemony." According to Shen, because the U.S. share of the world economy will drop in the future, "this means that its economy will be unable to provide adequate backing for its hegemonist practices," so it must rely on its allies to maintain its superiority. "In order to establish a unipolar global dominance, the United States needs a group of helpers no matter whether it is viewed from the political, economic, or military angle." However, Shen cautions, while "this group of helpers"— NATO and Japan—may "look like joint hegemony outwardly," it "is actually dominated by the United States in reality; in other words, a unipolar hegemony still dominated by the United States. Such a practice can considerably prolong the life of the U.S.-dominated unipolar hegemony and greatly put off the formation of a multipolar world setup."

Other Chinese analysts, while recognizing that the pace of the multipolarization process has decreased, and predicting further increases in U.S. power, also emphasize that the current trend does not mean that the U.S. will be able to establish a unipolar world. It is only a setback in the transition to a new world structure: "For the world to advance toward multipolarization is the inevitable trend of history. Although twists and turns and ups and downs may occur in the process of the development of this trend, no force can block the tide of development of multipolarization." Another author writes:

> A few years ago, people were over-optimistic about the "multipolar" trend. They thought that the "multipolar" trend would "move faster and faster." Some even thought that the multipolar world had already taken shape. After NATO use of force against Yugoslavia and its attack on the Chinese Embassy, some people went to the other extreme and believed that the 'unipolar' trend now reigned supreme and the world remained a unipolar world. Both views are rather biased. Judging from the present situation, the multipolar pattern has not yet taken shape, but the trend cannot be changed. Recent developments only serve to show that the trend of multipolarism is obviously slowing down and that the U.S. pole will be further strengthened, but the plots of the United States to build a "unipolar world" where it can dominate everything can never succeed.

The reason cited by most authors for the ultimate success of multipolarization is that the other poles will become more powerful and come into greater conflict with the United States: "The true essence and the vital point of the U.S. pursuit of hegemonism is to establish an international order under U.S. dominance, but the developing countries will not allow this, and even its allies will not allow it." Another author writes, "Although cooperation and coordination between Europe and the United States are obviously growing, conflicts and differences remain," and asserts that the same situation also applies to the U.S. relationship with Japan. Zhang Zhaozhong, Director of the Science and Technology Teaching and Research Section of NDU, concurs: "NATO is by no means totally united, and it is certain that splits will occur in the future, and multipolarization remains a trend. France will not follow the United States for ever, Germany has become stronger since reunification and it too is not willing to always follow the United States; since the Europeans have organized the euro, this will naturally match the dollar."

SHANGHAI'S ELABORATE STUDIES

The "orthodox" features of the future security environment can be found in many books and articles of the 1990s, but those from Shanghai frequently are very thorough and elaborate. According to interviews conducted by the author in Beijing, open-source assessments are based on internal Chinese Government documents approved by Deng Xiaoping in the mid-1980s. Several officials pointed out that President Jiang Zemin has endorsed all the features of Deng's assessment. SIIS has a close relationship with Jiang, developed while he was mayor of Shanghai. Perhaps because of this personal relationship (and because Shanghai is far from the rigid, official climate of Beijing), SIIS publications often provide extensive details about the future security environment. SIIS publications, particularly those by its President Chen Qimao, who has also written articles for *Qiu Shi*, the journal of the Central Committee of the Communist Party, are authoritative and add greater detail and background about the future security environment. It is possible that the view from Shanghai tends to be both orthodox and elaborate, because scholars there can draw more from Central Committee documents, or maybe because they helped draft these documents and therefore have been permitted leeway to present them.

An example of the extensive details of the future world structure provided by SIIS can be found in "The Roots of the Transitional Era," which focuses on turbulence and wars. Former SIIS President Chen Qimao states,

Historically speaking, the disintegration of an empire is a long and painful process. The Eastern Roman Empire began to decline at the end of the 12th century and was destroyed by the Ottoman Empire in 1461. The whole process took more than 200 years, during which class conflicts were intensifying, [and]. . . invasions from the outside constantly took place.

Chen then compares the decline of the Ottoman Empire to the collapse of the Soviet Union. Chen points out that the full process of the decline of the former Soviet Union is not complete. He notes that there are still 25 million Russians living in republics outside Russia and 20 million other nationalities in Russia. He forecasts, "Due to the rise of nationalism, this situation may lead to a great deal of explosive potential." The process of reform and the completion of the process of disintegration of the former Soviet Union, Chen argues, will "become one of the important causes of turbulence in the transitional era." He reminds us that the former Soviet Union was a superpower and in World War II it "utterly routed the imperial fascist Germany."

Chen draws on several episodes of Chinese history to illustrate how the process of the emergence of a new era can take many decades. He begins with the decline of the Eastern Han Dynasty (25 B.C.-220 A.D.) to the establishment of the Western Jin Dynasty (265-316 A.D.), a period of about 80 years during which the "war lords fought each other, the Three Kingdoms dominated their own territories, while the masses lived in dire poverty." China saw another long period of turbulence when the Tang Dynasty (618-907 A.D.) collapsed.

Looking to the several decades that lie ahead for the emergence of a post-Cold War world strategic pattern, Chen points to Central Eurasia as a conflict zone where "religious frictions and national disputes are interlocking, leading to a lot of historic grievances." This is also where two world wars were fought. This whole zone in the past century or more has been dominated by tsarist Russia, the Ottoman Empire, and the Austro-Hungarian Empires. According to Chen, contradictions among these three empires produced several wars. He states, "Territorial issues were always so sensitive that a little disturbance could have resulted in enormous turbulence, thus leading to the danger of another world war." Chen adheres to the concept put forth by many Chinese analysts that the Vienna System built upon the Anti-Napoleon War, the Versailles System established after World War I, and the Yalta System built upon World War II created new political maps and divided spheres of influence among the great powers relatively rapidly, because of the international conference agreements that these great powers were able to work out after the wars.

Without such a war or international conference to mark the end of the Cold War, Chen states that a new world system cannot be created by way of victorious powers' conferences, "nor can spheres of influence be divided quickly." Thus, Chen believes violence is ahead, and the "re-division of spheres of influence will be a long-term and tortuous process... the struggle among big powers for spheres of influence is under way." Russia wants to maintain as its sphere all its former Soviet boundaries, while "there is little doubt that Western nations want to have East European countries joining NATO and to put them under the protection of the West." Besides the struggle for redividing spheres of influence in Europe, Chen states that "struggles between the United States and Japan for the dominating role in the Asia-Pacific as well as struggles among Germany, France, and Britain for the dominating role in Europe have not yet surfaced, but they do demonstrate themselves through a series of signs." Such struggles involve re-division of influence spheres and "will become significant roots for the emergence of turbulence in the transitional world."

In Europe, Chen agrees with many Chinese analysts that Germany was the major winner of the Cold War and has the best prospects to become a great power in the new era. He traces the origins of the Bosnia Conflict to "Germany's support for the independence of Slovenia and Croatia, without taking into account American objections and other European allies' reservations. Germany also went together with Austria to supply a great deal of weapons to Slovenia and Croatia, quickening the pace of disintegration of the former Yugoslavia and aggravating the turbulence in the Balkan Peninsula." However, Chen goes on to use the Bosnia case study as an "indirect demonstration of the struggle between the United States and the European Union" over who will dominate the future of Europe.

Chen, like many Chinese analysts, directly attacks the concept that the United States is the sole superpower and that there is a unipolar strategic pattern. Will there be American hegemony? According to Chen, "Enormous facts emerging after the end of the Cold War have proved that kind of view wrong." He believes that many issues "demonstrate that America's ability to control its allies has decreased." However, "The Yalta System in the Asia-Pacific region was not so complete and solid as that in Europe." Chen argues that a looser, multipolar system has long existed in Asia because of the American failure in the Vietnam War and the Soviet failure in the Afghan War, which reduced the two superpowers' influence. He states, "Their capacity to control the region was already much less than that in Europe. Because of these developments, many contradictions and disputes in the Asia-Pacific region were not covered by the bipolar system." Of course, he acknowledges that the Asia-Pacific region has a number of uncertainties, such as territorial disputes, the Korean problem, the Taiwan issue, and the leadership succession in several countries. However, the region has actually become a place where "the centers not only are relatively independent but also in mutual check and balance" among the United States, Russia, Japan, China, and ASEAN.

Using the indicators of CNP, Chen believes that "the heyday when the United States dominated the Asia-Pacific region has gone forever." Thus, the multipolar structure has begun to take shape earlier in the Asia-Pacific than in other regions of the world, so that it's possible already to say that "no single power can have the final say in the Asia-Pacific region." This has been achieved without a Yalta, a Versailles, or a Vienna conference. The role of China has become a source of regional stability because of its rapid economic growth and its adherence to the Five Principles of Peaceful Coexistence. Chen believes China's role has been important in encouraging this transition to take shape in Asia first.

Chen's argument that the rise of China will bring peace and stability is strengthened by an article from another former SIIS President, Liang Yufan. Liang states that because China was the "prey of imperialist aggression for more than a century, the rivalry of great powers inside China was once a major cause of persistent instability and turmoil and wars in East Asia." The implication is that a strong, unified China eliminates the influence of foreign great powers (who caused wars), so Chinese stability will help to end the era of transition and bring the new era to East Asia first.

FIFTY-YEAR STRUCTURES

One of the important premises on which Chinese assessments about the future security environment are based is the concept of "world structures" (*zhanlue shijie geju*). This term is used to refer to the design of the world pattern, which, according to Chinese, generally exists for several decades before undergoing a major transformation. Each "world structure" is based on the organization and state of relations among the great nations in the world. The process by which one world strategic pattern gives away to another usually is a major war. One author writes, "A world pattern is the relatively stable international structure formed by the interrelations and interaction between the main forces in the world during a certain historical period.... The changes in the world pattern are based on the changes in the relations of the world's main contradictions, and they accompany international and social phenomena such as turbulence, division, alignment and crises, that result in conflicts and war." The basic Chinese catechism identifies four major "world strategic patterns" during the past 200 years. One scholar at CICIR has put together a grid illustrating characteristics of the world order in the 20th century.

The first world structure, called the "Vienna System" by the Chinese, lasted 40 to 50 years and was set up by the victorious nations who defeated Napoleon. These four powers (Russia, Austria, Prussia, and Britain) established a world structure that was centered entirely on Europe and characterized by mutual bargaining and the use of "spheres of influence" to preserve stability. The second structure, which also lasted 40 to 50 years, was created by internal events in Japan, Italy, Germany, and the United States that destroyed "the original proportions and distributions of strength" and in so doing broke out of the strategic configuration confined to Europe. Although still centered on Europe, this new pattern also expanded to North America and

Asia. Briefly, the major developments were the rapid advancement of capitalism in the United States after the Civil War, the Meiji Restoration in Japan, and the political unification of Italy, as well as the unification of Germany in 1870 and its defeat of France in the Franco-Prussian War in 1871.

The third world structure derived from the conduct of the powers that won World War I. In a manner similar to the creation of the Vienna System Pattern, the new Versailles System was established by the strong victorious powers (the United States, Britain, France, Italy, and Japan). As had occurred with the Vienna Conference after the Napoleonic Wars, the Paris Peace Conference of 1919 "redivided the world" and laid down the rules for the next "era." However, the October Revolution established the Soviet Union in this period and Moscow participated in the Versailles System, which "broke the pattern whereby imperialism ruled the whole world." When discussing this era, several Chinese authors refer to it as the Versailles-Washington System, arguing that the three major treaties signed at the Washington Conference of 1921 played a major role in shaping the world structure of the time.

The fourth world structure is known in China as the Yalta System, a name derived from the Yalta Summit involving the United States, Britain, and the Soviet Union in February 1945. Most Chinese claim this conference "carved out the spheres of influence in Europe and Asia for the United States and the Soviet Union." With respect to China, the Yalta Summit included Soviet recognition of "U.S. control over Japan," while the United States in turn "satisfied the Soviet Union's wishes to regain Sakhalin Island, enabled Outer Mongolia to become independent, and enlisted northeast China into the sphere of influence." The Chinese state that the decline of British strength reduced its sphere of influence, so that the Yalta System actually established a world structure of two poles, Washington and Moscow, whose relationship largely determined world politics. The Yalta System endured until 1991, nearly 50 years. Because the core of the Yalta Agreement was the division of Europe and Germany into two parts, Chinese date the end of the Yalta System to the reunification of Germany in 1991. Although the Chinese say the Yalta System has "basically disintegrated," they recognize it continues in Northeast Asia in the division between North Korea and South Korea and in the unresolved territorial dispute between Moscow and Tokyo over the northern territories. There have been some Chinese references to the unresolved problem of Taiwan's sovereignty also being a part of the Yalta System because Taiwan's legal status was not resolved either at Yalta or the 1951 San Francisco Peace Conference.

Within a world structure there is also what is known as a world order (*shijie zhixu*), or the ways and means by which nations interact and deal with each other:

A world structure refers to a relatively stable international framework and strategic situation formed on the foundation of a certain power balance. A world order then refers to, on the basis of the world structure, the mechanisms and rules of the motion of international relations (such as handling international affairs and international contact). The two have both generalities (both take the power balance as their base) and differences (they do not adapt to one another; if the old structure collapses, the old order probably continues to exist).

FUTURE WARS

Rivalries, Struggles, and Local Wars

The future world structure will depend on the outcomes of competitions in both military strength and CNP. The struggle for "peace and development" will shift the competitive rank orders of various nations according to their CNP, which is based on the economic and technology policies they pursue. At the same time, in the military domain there are different rules to the international competition, including the use of force and the competition for military superiority. This field has been addressed primarily by military authors in China, although a few civilian analysts have also written about the consequences of local war and the development of military technology.

The rivalries and struggles to achieve CNP and military superiority will greatly contribute to the turbulence that characterizes the transition period, say Chinese analysts. As a consequence, the "new era" will feature destabilizing factors and inevitable local wars that will last for several decades. In fact, many Chinese articles mention the current trend of "relaxation," and then warn that there are prospects for more wars in the future. Three NDU analysts write, "The overall situation is one in which frequent regional conflicts are the outcome of the changing strategic pattern and international political disorder."

The certainty of future local wars does not seem to be debated. On the contrary, all Chinese analysts expect frequent local wars in the decades ahead. Liao Yonghe of CASS writes, "With the further reduction of the danger of a global world war, regional armed conflicts and limited wars will become the main field of military conflict." In the available literature, the definition of local war includes the conflicts in Korea (1950-53), Vietnam (1964-69), and the Gulf War (1991). This is an important premise of Chinese views of the future security environment: international wars on at least the scale of Korea, Vietnam, and the Gulf War are virtually certain in the decades ahead. Furthermore, there are many explicit references to the level of destruction caused by each of these past local wars. Different measures of destructiveness have been used, including logistics. In 3 years of war in Korea, 600,000 bombs were used; Vietnam required twice that number; and the Gulf War consumed nearly 8 million tons of supplies. Chinese articles on the "revolution in science and technology" expect future wars to have still higher levels of destruction.

Not only have Chinese authors noted that the intensity and scope of local wars are escalating, but they cite another major trend in the accelerating frequency with which they have been occurring since the Cold War period. According to Li Zhongcheng of CICIR, "In the 40 years of the Cold War, there were 190 regional conflicts, an average of four per year. In the first 7 years after the end of the Cold War there were 193, an average of 28 per year, seven times that of the former year average." Other authors, in order to predict future trends, have tracked the specific number of conflicts per year, distinguishing between wars that are new and those that are continuations from the previous year. Li Qinggong, a Research Fellow at CIISS, writes.

Throughout the world in 1997 there were altogether 38 armed conflicts and local wars of various scales, an increase of 8 in comparison with the 30 that occurred in 1996, but a decrease of 8 from the 46 that took place in the peak year of 1995. Of all these local conflicts and wars, 8 new ones occurred in 1997, an increase of 2 in comparison with the number of 6 in 1996, but a decrease of 8 in comparison with the number of 16 at the peak time of 1993.... This shows that after the Cold War, conflicts and wars have passed the "frequently occurring period" and entered the "period of ups and downs," with the new feature of "sometimes many, sometimes few, sometimes rising, sometimes falling."

In contrast to Western nations, there appear to be few Chinese articles or books on the international security situation that express optimism about the future role of arms control or the United Nations in building international trust or reducing the probability of the use of force. Since 1980, China has entered global economic institutions like the World Bank and International Monetary Fund but has never accepted the jurisdiction of international security arrangements such as U.N. peacekeeping forces.

Chinese authors appear to assume other nations share their views about the future role of military force. Chinese assessments about future military competition suggest they see other countries preparing themselves for the era of regional wars. For example, an article by two PLA analysts claims that the United States thinks "a new threat surpassing the confrontation between the East and the West in the past 45 years" is emerging. With regard to Russia, they argue, "The Russian military thinks that the process of easing up does not have an irreversible nature and that the danger of war still exists in the world." Japan, they assert, "faces military threats and serious competitors. Therefore, Japan will continue to beef up military strength and improve weapons and equipment." Concerning India, the PLA analysts claim that India thinks "India's security situation in the 1990s is still very grim, therefore it will continue to improve overall military strength and strategic deterrence strength." During the transition era some PLA analysts thus conclude that various countries "view the use of military strength as an important means to support their international status and safeguard their national interests."

After the U.S. accidental bombing of the Chinese embassy in Belgrade, some authors seemed to question whether the main trend of the times still is peace and development. For example, Yang Chengxu, President of CIIS, writes, "Simply put, NATO will have the right to interfere anywhere in the world. As an ideological organization, it is laying down some hidden troubles for the outbreak of World War III. The world has become more turbulent." An article in *Zhongguo Pinglun*, which interviewed generals from several military research institutes, brought up a similar issue, warning that "China must be ready to fight a world war." It said, "after NATO attacked the Federal Republic of Yugoslavia, Chinese strategists believe that before peacetime truly comes, world war could erupt at any moment. China must be fully prepared for it." However, although the potential for a third world war was mentioned following U.S. and NATO actions in Yugoslavia, the majority of Chinese authors still claim that ultimately peace and development will prevail. Shen Jiru of CASS argues, "The military actions taken by NATO will hardly change the general trend of peace and development" for three reasons:

- "First, economic globalization is a powerful material force to restrict large-scale wars."
- "Second, the outcome of a war is determined by the balance between economic and military strength, public attitudes, and moral support of the two sides. We do not deny the great destructiveness of modern weapons, as well as the unprecedented cruelty of modern warfare. Nevertheless, it has been proven in history that wars are not necessarily won by military strength. France did not win the Algerian War with its advanced weapons nor did the United States win the Vietnam War with its advanced weapons. The more destructive a war, the more restrictive it is to the aggressors."
- "Third, peace and development are the common wishes of all people in the whole world....The will of the people is the fundamental safeguard for maintaining world peace and development. We firmly believe that world peace and development can be won by the joint struggle of all people in the world."

As before the Kosovo crisis, Chinese analysts maintain the seeming contradiction that regional wars will continue to exist even though peace and development are the main trend. "For the 21st century, peace and development will still be the theme of the times. We should not doubt or waver in this judgment.... However, limited war will be unavoidable since the roots of war will still be there."

Sources of Wars

What will be the causes of the regional wars that will occur throughout the transition period as the new world structure is in the process of replacing the old one? Where will they take place? Who will be involved? Chinese analysts explain the outbreak of local wars in the 1990s as having two major reasons: first, the ethnic, religious, historical, and territorial disputes previously covered up and restricted by the U.S.-Soviet confrontation were free to emerge following the end of the Cold War; and second, as the new world structure is forming, there is competition and contention for power, influence, and economic resources. As the transition period progresses, the hot spots where local wars are focused will not be static but are expected to shift as some conflicts come to an end and new ones emerge, and as relations between the powers develop. Former SIIS president Chen Qimao explains:

> These hot spots must go through a process, from breaking out, to intensifying, to relaxing, to resolution. Currently, their development still is not very even; some have already relaxed, some are intensifying, some have just broken out, some have not yet shown their heads; they still are in a stage where "as one falls another rises."... Internationally, following the end of the Cold War, the various forces have been re-dividing and uniting, and relations between the powers are very unstable, which also is a very significant source of the turbulence in the transformation period. Therefore, the current world still is not stable.

Consequently, the local wars will occur for a variety of reasons, with the participants ranging from small groups to major powers, and at locations worldwide.

Several Chinese authors have suggested that the fault lines of future war in the multipolar security environment will not be the same as during the bipolar Soviet-American confrontation. Following the end of the Cold War, the main area where local wars were focused was in Central and Eastern Europe and the former Soviet Union. However, most Chinese analysts, while not predicting protracted peace and stability, consider the region's turmoil and armed conflicts to have subsided to some extent and see the main local war hot spot as shifting to Africa. A *People's Daily* article reported that for 1997, "According to statistics, nearly half of all the local wars that took place worldwide this year happened in Africa.... Though these conflicts were of the nature of civil wars and were local, they have nevertheless posed a certain threat to peace and stability and have caused the concern of the international community." Chinese analysts do not foresee the problems in Africa disappearing any time in the near future and expect that there will continue to be frequent wars. For example, Li Zhongcheng of CICIR writes, "At the turn of the century, and the early part of next century, it is extremely possible that there will appear in the African Great Lake region a situation where as one racial or sectional conflict ends another begins." The Middle East is another area mentioned by Li and other authors as a current hot spot:

The Palestinian-Israeli peace process can only through repeated reversals slowly progress. At the same time, aside from the Palestinian-Israeli and Arab-Israeli contradictions, other Middle Eastern regional conflicts will gradually develop and intensify, becoming the sources of the Middle Eastern region's continued turbulence and intranquility, and its continued and frequent regional conflicts.

Many Chinese analysts point out that the proliferation of local ethnic, religious, and territorial wars has not meant that the major powers have not been involved in the conflicts. In fact, a number of analysts cite hegemonism and military interventionism as contributing to and exacerbating local wars. Wang Xuhe of the Strategy Department at AMS stated, "The factors threatening international security are pluralizing, becoming more complicated, and have more layers, but hegemonism and power politics will for a considerably long period still be the major threats to international security." With regard to the two current hot spots,

Africa and the Middle East, Chen Feng, a Senior Research Fellow at CIISS, writes,

The conflicts in Africa and the Middle East have their respective causes, e.g., the complicated ethnic or cultural contradictions, frontier resource disputes and internal struggles, etc. However, if analyzed from a deeper perspective, these conflicts reflect the struggle to control these regions between the great powers. Conflicts in these regions all have the intervention from those powers involved. The United States, making full use of the chance that France had adjusted its African policy, tried various means to create its own agents in Africa and to drive the French forces out of its sphere of influence. In the Middle East, because the U.S. policy is biased toward Israel, it has put the peace process in a stalemate, and its influence in the Arab world has declined.

Other examples of hegemonism and intervention on the part of the major powers are cited by another CIISS Research Fellow, Li Qinggong: the United States sending aircraft carriers to the Gulf when Iran crossed the "restricted airspace" to attack Iraq's Kurdish region; in Bosnia, "the U.S. peacekeeping forces clashing with local people and shooting a number of Serbian residents"; the United States "sending an 'expeditionary air force' to Bosnia to terrorize psychologically the Serbian people;" and France "continuously engaging in military intervention against the Republic of Central Africa."

Following NATO military strikes against Yugoslavia in spring 1999, there was a tremendous increase in criticism and alarm about U.S. hegemonism being a source of war. One author writes, "Hegemonism and power politics are still developing, and there will be no peace under heaven in the 21st century." Wang Jincun, a senior researcher at CASS portrays the United States as "striving to build a single-polar world and to strengthen its hegemony." After the U.S. accidental bombing of the Chinese embassy in Belgrade, Wang wrote that the United States is employing military methods as one means for achieving its goal: "What deserves more attention is that the United States, not yet satisfied with its Cold War achievements, seeks to gain more advances through military means. Therefore, there has appeared an even closer growing link between the new Cold War and 'hot war.' The military interference by the United States in Iraq, Somalia, Haiti, and Bosnia-Herzegovina, the bombing against Sudan and Afghanistan, and especially the ongoing air strikes against Yugoslavia, serve as prominent examples."

Chu Shulong of CICIR pointed out, "The number of times and the frequency with which the United States has used force in various parts of the world in just a few years have rarely been seen before in the history of U.S. foreign policy and in the history of international relations." An explanation offered by one author for the sudden increase in U.S. intervention is that it has a "Gulf War syndrome:" "The United States, the world's sole superpower, developed a 'Vietnam syndrome' on account of its defeat with heavy casualties in the Vietnam war, and became careful and cautious for a time about getting involved in overseas conflicts. Success in the 1991 Gulf War produced a 'Gulf War syndrome' in the United States and it became enthusiastic about military intervention activities." One article noted that, "Since 1990, the United States has dispatched troops more than 40 times, and 10 of them were strong military interventions." It concludes, "Given the large amount of indisputable evidence, the United States has become the world's major source of war by its arms expansion and implementation of hegemonism and power politics, and it has become a major threat to the world's peace. It is predictable that more countries will become test spots for the high- and new-technology weapons of the United States and the victims of its war machine."

For Chinese analysts, the question is not whether the U.S. will once again interfere overseas, but where. In its pursuit of global hegemony and a unipolar world order, U.S. military intervention is expected to continue to occur throughout the transition period. According to Colonel Zhang Zhaozhong of NDU, "Gangster logic is now emerging ever more prominently. We should realize from this that at the turn of the century we are in an extremely unstable strategic pattern, and the United States is also testing the water. At present it is in midstream, not knowing if it can get to the opposite bank and whether there will be any dangerous rocks or reefs. I believe that this testing of the water will go on for several years, and we need to observe whether Chechnya or the Korean peninsula will be next." An article in the *Liberation Army Daily*, after asserting that U.S. "gunboat policy will inevitably lead to endless wars and disorder all over the world," predicted that U.S. military interference may not be limited to smaller nations in the future. "The target today may be a small nation, but it could be a big country tomorrow! The target may be Kosovo today, but it could be any country that does not meet U.S. desires tomorrow.... War increasingly will become the major means adopted by the United States to establish a polarized pattern. Wars are not far away from us."

In addition to hegemonism and power politics and ethnic, religious, and territorial reasons, Chinese analysts see the struggle for economic resources as another major source contributing to local wars in the transition era. As Colonel Liu Mingde states, "The Marxists hold that the conflict of economic interests is the root of war." He explains that the Arab-Israeli dispute "has to do with Israel's heavy reliance on the Jordan River" and that the Iran-Iraq war and the Gulf War were about petroleum. Similarly, the civil war in Yugoslavia is a war between the "poor" Serbs and the "rich" Slovaks and Croats. Liu concludes, "Competition in Comprehensive National Power has aggravated the scrambling for resources among nations." An even bleaker forecast about the rivalry over economic resources is predicted by He Xin, who draws an analogy to the Warring States era of Chinese history:

The energy and natural resources crises of the early 21st century will unavoidably lead to the economic decline of industrial countries, and cause the intensification of economic and political wars as countries contend for natural resources and markets. In this situation, the world probably will enter a new "Cold War" (economic, political war), even a "Warring States era" with numerous local and regional hot wars emerging.

It is this struggle for economic resources that could lead to direct conflicts between the major powers. While many Chinese authors imply that there will not be a war among the five major powers, that they very likely will participate in the regional wars but probably not against each other, there is another viewpoint that believes the potential for conflict exists. Three analysts at the Strategy Institute at NDU write, "The majority of regional conflicts in the world are civil wars, social turmoil, and civil coups. Although there are influence and interference from some other countries, these interventions do not develop into military confrontations between large countries." However, they warn that, "Potential conflict areas do exist that may possibly involve direct military confrontations between large countries or regional powers. If large-scale armed conflicts and local wars happen in these regions, it can result in drastic changes in the world situation and harm the global strategic situation."

A likely area for future conflict among the powers will be Central Asia where "abundant natural resources will become the target of a struggle" between the major powers. Yang Shuheng from the U.S. Institute at CASS writes that the United States wants the region's energy resources, but Russia is unwilling to "drop to the status of a second-rank country" and will resist the United States. However, pursuing economic interests is not the only U.S. goal in the region—another is "squeezing Russia out." She explains, "The rivalry over the Caspian Sea region's oil and natural gas... is part of the U.S.-Russian rivalry over strategic interests and spheres of influence in the Eurasian hinterland." Yang predicts, "The number of countries involved will increase. The European Union also regards the Central Asian region as an energy resources base that can replace the Gulf in the future.... International forces covet the treasure chest that is Central Asia."

The NATO bombing of Yugoslavia was seen by a number of Chinese authors as part of the organization's efforts to gain influence and control in the region. Li Yonggang, a scholar at the Chinese Society for Strategy and Management, says geopolitical, economic, and energy interests were the motivations for NATO actions, for once NATO controlled the Balkans it had a direct path to Central Asia. He writes,

"From the angle of geopolitics, Kosovo is located in the middle of the Balkan Peninsula, which is situated among the three continents of Europe, Asia, and Africa; as such, Kosovo has a decisive strategic position. To NATO, with control over the Balkans, it can advance westward to the Mediterranean and North Atlantic, and southward, it can consolidate the 'southern wing of NATO,' offering a link to its strategy in the Middle East. Eastward in the region of Black Sea and Caspian Sea, that is, the region of outer Caucasus and Central Asia, NATO can infiltrate, expand, and weaken and push out the power and influence of Russia."

"Viewed from the angle of economic interests, NATO European powers have been quietly, secretly enthusiastic about getting through the Balkan corridor in the south to extend their sphere of economic influence to Central Asia and even further....

Although the European powers are still in line with the United States on several important issues, the building of a united, powerful, and eventually independent Europe to contend with the United States is still the long-term strategy of these countries.... Once the Euro has reached the bank of the Caspian Sea, it can enter the hinterland of Russia and can also come into contact with the five countries in Central Asia.

This will have an extremely far-reaching political, economic, and cultural significance. This is the general political, economic, and financial strategy of Europe."

- "What should also be noticed is that by putting the Balkans under control and moving westward, there is the possibility of manipulating a vast geographic area rich with oil and natural gas."

An additional source of instability in Central Asia has been pointed out by Gao Heng of CASS, who believes that "the development of Islamic resurgence activities" could lead to conflict. Moreover, Chen Feng of CIISS argues that the contention in Central Asia could be exacerbated by the military activities and exercises of foreign troops. For example, when the United States, "for the first time since the end of World War II, sent regular troops (more than 500 personnel of one battalion under the 82nd Airborne Division) to the region to take part in military maneuvers, it indicated that the struggle to control the region between the big powers has spread from economic and political fields to military and security fields."

Central Asia is one of two regions Chinese analysts predict will emerge as a new hot spot in the future; the other is the Asia-Pacific. There are, however, differing views concerning the potential for future wars in the latter region. While some authors are concerned about the possibility that major conflicts could erupt, others emphasize the recent greater stability in the Asia-Pacific as compared to other parts of the globe. Zhang Changtai, a Research Fellow at CIISS believes, "In a relatively stable security environment, the Asia-Pacific remains one of the regions in the world with fewer cases of armed conflicts and such a situation can still be maintained in the years to come." His views are backed up by the few number of local wars in the region. He writes:

For a long time, especially in the post-Cold War era, the Asia-Pacific has all along been a comparatively stable region. Statistics show that in 1991 prior to the end of the Cold War, 29 armed conflicts and local wars occurred in the world, out of which 6 were in the Asia-Pacific. In 1997 the total number of armed conflicts in the world increased to 38, while it was kept to 6 in the Asia-Pacific, namely the internal armed conflicts in Afghanistan, Sri Lanka, Cambodia, the Philippines and Myanmar, as well as that between India and Pakistan in Kashmir. The armed conflicts in the Asia-Pacific not only remain the least in the world, but also have decreased to some extent in intensity.

However, many authors argue that despite the low number of local wars and greater stability in the 1990s, there still is serious potential for the Asia-Pacific to become a hot spot.

Chen Peiyao, president of SIIS has pointed out, "During the Cold War, East Asia was the region where military conflicts and local wars were constantly seen. The end of the Cold War did not bring an end to all the regional problems." His argument is furthered by Shen Qurong of CICIR, who states, "The Cold War in the postwar Asia-Pacific was never 'cold' and peace in post-Cold War Asia-Pacific has been only lukewarm. The issue of regional peace awaits a fundamental solution. Beneath the surface of relative stability lie destabilizing factors.... In the 50 postwar years, the two largest local wars in the world both broke out in the Asia-Pacific region... the Asia-Pacific has now entered a stage of 'Cold Peace.' " According to Li Zhongcheng, of CICIR, major issues such as the Korean peninsula, Taiwan, the Nansha Islands, and the Diaoyu islands "make it clear that in the East Asia-Pacific region there exists the kindling for regional conflicts."

The Japanese parliament's adoption of the U.S.-Japan Security Guidelines, in spring 1999, also is considered to be a source of future conflicts. Not only does it signify the rise of militarism in Japan, considered by some to be a serious potential factor for instability in the region, but it also "increased the capacity of the U.S. military to intervene in the Asia-Pacific... [for] without Japan as a forward base, U.S. military forces would have to retreat east to Hawaii and south to Australia." Lu Guangye, a fellow at the Chinese National Defense Strategic Institute, claims that together with NATO, the U.S.-Japanese military alliance has become one of "the two black hands helping the tyrant to do evil." He sees NATO military strikes in Yugoslavia and the bombing of the Chinese embassy as omens of future U.S. and Japanese actions. "Everything that NATO does can be regarded as the most direct and most realistic mirror of what we understand as the substance of the Japanese-US military alliance and of how Japan and the United States will act in the Asia-Pacific region. The 'experiment' carried out in the Federal Republic of Yugoslavia by US-led NATO also provides a vivid example for the Asia-Pacific countries."

Another potential cause of war in the Asia-Pacific has to do with China's rise as a global power. Several authors have written about U.S. efforts in the next decade or two to contain China's development and prevent its rise in international affairs. Colonel Zhang Zhaozhong of NDU was asked in an interview why he considered "the next 10 to 15 years will be the most difficult and most important period in China's development." His reply was, "The United States has already realized that this is the best period for containing China, and so it produces stuff like the theory of the Chinese threat to suppress China. If the United States is unable to curb the momentum of China's development in the next 10 to 20 years, it will have wasted a lot of effort. During this period, therefore, the United States may devise all kinds of ways to cause trouble." However, Colonel Zhang does not foresee China and the

United States going to war in the near term. "Unless there are major changes over Taiwan or other issues, the United States at present does not have the gall to take the initiative in attacking China's territory. But we must be vigilant." Chu Shulong of CICIR also predicts that efforts to contain China could lead to problems, "Negative and extremist trends in U.S. domestic politics, external strategy, and diplomacy toward China are extremely dangerous for world peace and development and for the present and future of Sino-US relations." These views are echoed in the yearly *Study Reports on the International Situation—1997-1998*, published by the Chinese Society for Strategy and Management, where Yan Xuetong of CICIR warns of potential conflicts between China and the United States, as China's power increases and the "desperate" United States struggles to maintain its leading position:

In history, the rise of a new world power often leads to large-scale international wars, but these wars are not necessarily caused by the expansion of a rising power. Some of them resulted from the military policies of a hegemonic power in maintaining its hegemony. The U.S.-British War (1812-1814) is a typical example. In order to constrain the rise of the United States, Britain blocked American shipments to Europe... (just like) the case of the U.S. blocking Chinese ships, such as the Yinhe event of 1993.

The predictions of Yan and others tend to modify Deng Xiaoping's earlier assertion, discussed below, that China will never be a "source" of war. Yan and many authors are worried that the United States could somehow force a war upon China in order to contain its rise or dismember its territory.

Deng Xiaoping Thought

In the mid-1980s, Deng Xiaoping apparently described, in still-unreleased documents, four alternative scenarios, each of which was based on a different "basic contradiction" that would characterize the new era. He summarized a series of major conflicts in the world that might lead to war in four Chinese characters: "East, West, South, and North." The first set of conflicts, East-West, is posited as the conflict between the United States and the Soviet Union—that is, between socialism and capitalism; the second scenario suggests West-West conflicts between developed capitalist countries; in the third scenario South-North conflicts are between the developing Third World countries and the developed capitalist countries; and the fourth alternative view sees South-South conflicts as differences between Third World countries that can lead to warfare. In 1989 Deng predicted that two of these sets of conflicts could result in new Cold Wars. "I hope the Cold War will end, but I am disappointed. Perhaps when one cold war ends, two more cold wars have already started. One is directed against the south and the third world, the other against socialism."

A crucial part of Deng's formulation of the sources of future warfare is that China will never be a source of war, nor does China aspire to become a superpower, even though Chinese officials since 1988 have explicitly accepted the Iklé-Wohlstetter Commission estimate that China will have the world's largest economy around 2020. The one exception to these comments on the sources of war appears to be Taiwan; many authors echo the long-standing question of Taiwan's status as a national threat. According to Gao Heng of the usually moderate CASS,

If Taiwan (no matter what name or form it uses) publicly or officially flies a "Taiwan independence" flag, it will lead to a major crisis in relations between the two shores. On that occasion, if the United States, Japan, or other countries publicly intervene, it will lead to a serious armed conflict, or escalate to a local war. Its influence will go beyond the Asia-Pacific region, and have global and historical impact.

6

South Asia and the Security Dilemma

In recent years, experts have closely studied two main aspects of regarding South Asian nuclear issues. First, nuclear modernization in the region continues with the development of longer-range and more reliable delivery systems, as well as qualitative and quantitative increases in fissile material and warheads. Initiatives, such as the Indo-U.S. nuclear deal, have brought renewed focus on this issue due to its potential impact on proliferation in South Asia. Second, the A.Q. Khan network confirmed the entry of non-state actors into the realm of nuclear proliferation. Lingering questions regarding the network's activities suggest that its impact has not yet been fully assessed. There is still considerable demand for nuclear technology, both through horizontal proliferation from aspiring nuclear states such as Iran, and terrorist networks looking to augment their capabilities. This study will analyze these varied developments and investigate proliferation trends in the region.

Nuclear proliferation in South Asia is in part a consequence of the security dilemma existing in the subcontinent. Security dilemmas arise when a state's mechanisms for increasing its security negatively impact the security and threat perceptions of other states. As one expert stated, the South Asian nuclear security complex involves several security dilemmas, including Pakistan/India, India/China, and Russia/United States. A further security dilemma dyad is that of the United States and China, since it has an impact on attitudes in India and Pakistan, and helps shape their nuclear decisions.

It is helpful to analyze the security dilemma briefly through an example. From India's perspective, the threat from China is of prime importance, and therefore New Delhi's nuclear and missile development program is geared, in part, toward countering Beijing with a secure deterrent. However, Beijing's primary threat perception stems from the United States' role in the Asia-Pacific region. Consequently, one must consider the possibility that Beijing may conduct nuclear tests in the coming years if Washington goes ahead with plans to construct newer, more reliable warheads. In addition, analysts have predicted that Washington is likely to abandon the Strategic Arms Reduction Treaty-I (START-I) when it goes out of force in 2009. The abandonment of START-1 would remove all obstacles for U.S. plans to counter the strategic threat from China and other potential adversaries. To deal with this threat from the United States, Beijing has proceeded with its plan to strengthen its second strike capability through the development of mobile long-range ballistic missiles, both land-based and submarine-launched, according to a May 2007 Pentagon report.

However, China's desire to catch up with the United States would oblige India to prevent an adverse strategic balance. India's need for a reliable nuclear deterrent against China involves expanding New Delhi's nuclear weapons and delivery systems capabilities. Advanced capabilities include the development of a thermonuclear weapon and second strike capabilities through long-range ballistic missiles, such as the Agni-III or submarine launched ballistic missile capabilities, within the proposed nuclear submarine project and the Sagarika missile.

This impacts on the Indo-Pakistani equation because while New Delhi has a China focus for its expanding nuclear arsenal, it naturally increases its capability vis-à-vis Islamabad as well. It is widely accepted that since its inception, Pakistan's nuclear policy has been a constant response to the perceived threat from India. Therefore, in order to maintain the strategic balance or to at least prevent from the present imbalance from widening, Pakistan further expands its own nuclear capabilities. Furthermore, India on one side, and China and Pakistan on the other, are concerned over the extent of U.S. interactions with the other side, and the long-term impact this will have on the strategic balance in South Asia. This was evidenced in the immediate period after 9/11, when the U.S.-Pakistan counter-terrorism alliance was seen as detrimental to Indian interests.

The security dilemma in the South Asian subcontinent operates as a chain reaction that includes regional and extra-regional powers with competing interests. For countries like India and China, it is important to note that while the goals of nonproliferation (especially at a time of potential WMD-related terrorism) are extremely crucial, perceived national interests are a greater factor in shaping the eventual policy direction. With this motivational framework in mind, one must examine recent proliferation-related developments in South Asia, that are likely to have far reaching consequences both regionally and in terms of the global nonproliferation regime. They include the proposed Indo-U.S. nuclear cooperation, the significance of the A.Q. Khan network, and links between South Asian and Middle East proliferation dynamics. These developments reflect, partly or in whole, the need for the weaker protagonist to correct the perceived security imbalance against the stronger threat.

SECURITY DISPUTES, NUCLEAR DOCTRINES, AND PROLIFERATION TRENDS

To begin with, proliferation issues in South Asia must be understood in context of vertical and horizontal proliferation. Vertical proliferation takes place as nuclear states modernize their nuclear arsenals with more reliable delivery systems and warheads. Countries including the United States, China, India, and Pakistan, are in the process of modernizing their arsenals through actions such as proposals for "a reliable replacement warhead" (as in the case of the United States). In the context of South Asia, nuclear modernization is mainly a function of prevailing threat perceptions arising from security dilemmas. Modernization of arsenals includes the development and testing of longer-range missiles-such as the tests of the Agni-III by India, and the Shaheen-II by Pakistan in the first half of 2007.

Horizontal proliferation is the spread of nuclear weapons technology from nuclear states to other entities, including aspiring nuclear weapon states, as well as non-state actors such as terrorist groups. Horizontal proliferation generally involves a significant role for WMD supply networks that may or may not have a connection to official entities in a nuclear state. In the South Asian context, this variant of proliferation is especially pertinent, given the history of the A.Q. Khan network and its assistance to states such as North Korea and Iran. In addition, horizontal proliferation includes second-tier proliferation, where developing countries trade and barter nuclear technology with each other. While vertical and horizontal proliferation are variants of the proliferation dynamic, it is entirely possible that a nuclear state (such as Pakistan) could make use of non-state networks in the pursuit of nuclear modernization.

From the subcontinental perspective, one main question arises-given the lack of a comprehensive resolution of the disputes between India and Pakistan and India and China, how do nuclear doctrines in South Asia impact trends in the acquisition of nuclear and missile technology? The answer to this question links threat perceptions and nuclear doctrines with recent proliferation-related developments and requires a brief discussion of existing nuclear postures of India and Pakistan.

Subcontinental Rivalry

So what are the characteristics of the sub-continental rivalry that make nuclear proliferation in South Asia such a crucial security issue? Threat perceptions based on long-standing security disputes shape nuclear doctrines and proliferation dynamics. The intensity of disputes brings in security dilemmas that ensure continued dependence on nuclear weapons in South Asia.

South Asia is one of the most populated regions of the world, with India and Pakistan alone accounting for about 1.35 billion people. Both countries have been bitter rivals since partition of the subcontinent in 1947 that led to the creation of independent Pakistan and independence for India. The two countries have fought two wars over Kashmir (1947, 1965), one over East Pakistan/Bangladesh (1971), one limited war (Kargil, 1999) and the ongoing insurgency in Kashmir (since 1989). The 2001-2002 crisis further highlighted the dangers of terrorist violence provoking a conventional conflict that could lead to a nuclear crisis. Kashmir, which lies at the heart of the dispute, is more than a simple territorial problem. The province has a Muslim majority, and for India it is a symbol of its secular credentials as well as a repudiation of the partition, which was based on religion.

For Pakistan, Kashmir is crucial because it is seen as an unfinished agenda of partition, which was supposed to provide a homeland for the subcontinent's Muslim community. Thus, Kashmir is an integral part of both countries' perceived self-identities.

Since the 2001-2002 crisis, Islamabad and New Delhi have conducted several rounds of peace talks aimed at bringing a lasting settlement to the Kashmir issue. This peace process has involved several confidence-building measures such as strengthening of transport links between the two countries. The two sides also signed a crucial agreement on reducing the risk of nuclear accidents in February 2007. Nevertheless, the key dispute, Kashmir, is nowhere near resolution. This implies that both New Delhi and Islamabad are more inclined toward strengthening existing military capabilities, both conventional and non-conventional, to prevent an unfavorable scenario in a future standoff.

Apart from notions of sovereignty and nationhood, Kashmir is also of considerable strategic importance. Rivers originating in the Kashmir region provide crucial water supplies for food producing areas in the heartland. Furthermore, the Siachen glacier is also a region of military significance. The glacier, to the north of Kashmir, commands a strategic overlook of the small border between Pakistan and China and can potentially be used as a point of attack on India from northwest Kashmir. The glacier became a battle ground between the two armies in April 1984 and despite repeated talks, there has been no movement toward demilitarization. The complex rivalry between India and Pakistan involves territorial disputes based on notions of national identity as well as terrorist violence. Another integral element of the subcontinental security dyad is the role of China.

The China Factor

The role of China in South Asian security issues as well as in future conflict scenarios is crucial when considering two realities- (a) the historical animosity between India and China, and (b) the long standing 'all-weather' political and military alliance between Pakistan and China. Indian analysts often cite transfer of nuclear and missile technology from Beijing to Islamabad as evidence of an encircled threat to India. Through nuclear and missile technology transfers to Pakistan, Beijing restricts India to the South Asian strategic framework, and this constrains New Delhi's stated desire to seek a more global presence. From the Chinese political establishment's perspective, the concern is over India's defense expansion, its desire and movement toward a stronger regional and global role, and its increasing strategic connections with Washington.

Thus, any examination of the South Asian proliferation framework takes into account the Sino-Indian rivalry and dispute, the lowest point of which was the 1962 border war. In recent years, Indian and Chinese leaders and special representatives have met for regular talks on the border dispute issue; the most recent session (the 10th such round), took place in April 2007. In early rounds of these talks, China granted de facto recognition of Sikkim as a province of India, while India accepted Tibet as part of China. However, serious differences remain, and strategically important areas such as the state of Arunachal Pradesh have been claimed by China, while India has claimed Aksai Chin and certain parts of Kashmir handed over by Pakistan to China.

Despite periodic meetings, little progress has been made on these issues, and from time to time, controversial statements by each side threaten to derail talks. Whether a hardening of positions or a negotiating strategy, it demonstrates that the potential for friction is ever-present. Furthermore, there is also some dispute over an earlier agreement between the two sides to not insist on territorial exchanges of areas with settled populations, reflected in Beijing's recent demands that India cede Arunachal Pradesh, especially the Tawang tract. Therefore, in the absence of a permanent settlement, both India and China have adopted a hedging strategy to guard against any future strategic disadvantages.

A hedging strategy involves bolstering military-related capabilities in an ambiguous way that is not directly threatening to the adversary. At the same time, cooperative ties are encouraged without necessarily making any major concessions. In part, such an approach is chosen due to uncertainty over the adversary's future intentions and capabilities and as a way to safeguard against a downturn in future ties or in the regional or global strategic environment. Therefore, modernization of nuclear arsenals in South Asia has to be considered in this context.

Similarly, in the case of India and Pakistan, despite sustained peace talks and CBMs, the two sides continue a hedging strategy to guard against future uncertainty, such as another crisis situation like Operation Parakram in 2001-2002. This is done by developing more reliable nuclear delivery systems (especially longer range ballistic missiles), perfecting and increasing fissile material stock, and acquiring conventional weaponry in line with contemporary war-fighting doctrines.

Thus, in South Asia, underlying security disputes, based on territorial rivalry and terrorist violence, combined with a need to expand the nation's global and regional position encourages future uncertainties that shape the actors' nuclear policy decision-making. As mentioned earlier, apart from the Indo-Pakistan rivalry, strategic uncertainty, and suspicion in New Delhi is also generated by Pakistan's close military links with China. With China in the picture as a rival of India and a strategic ally of Pakistan, even if Delhi and Islamabad move towards a peaceful resolution of the Kashmir dispute, Beijing is likely to be the biggest factor in Indian threat calculations.

At the same time, the present threat perceptions between India and China are not the same as between India and Pakistan, which are more immediate and based on a 'hot' territorial dispute and state-sponsored terrorism. Nevertheless, analysts in New Delhi have long pointed to Chinese military modernization as a coercive threat to India. This modernization includes missile development, such as the current deployment of the DF-21 and DF-3 missiles in Qinghai and Yunnan provinces. Furthermore, there is some suspicion among Indian analysts that though Beijing's stated policy is that of minimum deterrence, the stationing of missiles such as DF-3 and DF-21 reflects a posture of nuclear coercion, and under some conditions, does not preclude a first strike against its neighbors. It is also possible that since 1998, Beijing may have deployed nuclear weapons on the Tibetan plateau in response to a perceived Indian conventional military advantage and the May 1998 nuclear tests. Thus, despite growing trade between the two sides, there is some degree of unease in India over China's long-term intentions, more so in light of predictions of increased competition between the two countries for global energy resources. The concern in New Delhi is that if bilateral relations take a negative turn at some point in the future, China's current military modernization will give Beijing a significant advantage.

The Sino-Indian security dilemma is also a function of China's desire to establish close relationships with other countries in the Indian Ocean region (most notably Myanmar), a policy that is seen as a potential threat by India and termed as "strategic containment." For India and China, the security dilemma also arises from threat perceptions based on consequences of future nationalistic tendencies. Both sides fear that a rise in nationalism in the other could lead to more hostile attitudes.

China's concerns over future expansions of the U.S. nuclear arsenal, missile defense and space dominance plans also lessen the possibility of any immediate restraint with respect to Beijing's nuclear plans. Therefore a chain reaction exists in South Asia where New Delhi, at the very least, wants to maintain its current relative capabilities vis-à-vis Beijing, if not actually improve them. The interconnected security dilemmas in the Asia-Pacific region shape defense policies and impact stability.

NON-STATE ACTORS AND SECURITY IN SOUTH ASIA

As aforementioned, nuclear weapons development and enhancement in South Asia are intricately related to long-standing rivalries between the concerned states. However, instability does not just stem from the risk of nuclear warfare between states in the region. Non-state actors also play a significant role in the nuclear security framework, aside from their role in facilitating nuclear proliferation. First, terrorist groups (such as Jaish-e-Mohammed and Lashkar-e-Toiba) that are connected to the Pakistani religious-political establishment can provoke tensions between India and Pakistan through mass casualty attacks. This was amply demonstrated following the December 2001 attack on the Indian Parliament by Jaish-e-Mohammed militants, which led to a ten-month stand-off between the two armies.

A second danger is through a Kargil-style episode in which militants, in cooperation with official Pakistani agencies and the military, occupy territory in Kashmir. As the July 2007 siege of the Lal Masjid (Red Mosque) complex in the heart of Islamabad showed, militant groups are steadily expanding their geographical area of influence, adversely affecting the stability of Pakistan. Although the nuclear weapon complex is under military control, there might be pockets within the military that are sympathetic to fundamentalist groups. At the very least, political and religious instability in Pakistan creates uncertainty in the minds of policymakers within and outside the region.

Finally, fears have been heightened since 9/11 over the possibility of nuclear weapons technology transfers from Pakistan to terrorist networks, especially after it was revealed that some senior Pakistani nuclear scientists met with the Al Qaeda leadership prior to 9/11. A related concern in the aftermath of 9/11 is that a fundamentalist Islamic group with Taliban/Al Qaeda links could take over Pakistan and with it, possession of the country's nuclear arsenal. Thus, Indian (as well as U.S.) threat perceptions include not just bilateral nuclear stability issues between India and Pakistan, but also the consequences of nuclear technology and materials falling into the hands of militant groups.

In general, the complex nuclear weapons scenario in South Asia is shaped by two main factors. First, the intense nature of the dispute between India and Pakistan strikes at the very core of their nationhood. It involves territorial disputes and terrorist violence, and is further complicated by the desire of some terrorist groups to acquire non-conventional technology. Second, South Asia is part of a broader nuclear weapons context that includes China and the United States. Military developments by either Washington or Beijing, which are perceived as a direct threat, also impact military policies (both conventional and non-conventional) in South Asia. At the same time, the continued strategic military collaboration between China and Pakistan (such as the joint development of the JF-17 fighter plane) is a factor that motivates India to continue nuclear and conventional modernization. Furthermore, while the territorial disputes between India and China are relatively dormant, there is no final resolution. As developments in 2006-2007 demonstrated, there is still a considerable gap between the two sides on the territorial issue. Due to this combination of factors, there are no clear incentives for either party to drastically reorient its nuclear policy.

NUCLEAR POLICIES IN SOUTH ASIA

Keeping the various security disputes and attitudes in mind, the next step is to consider the nuclear doctrines and policies of protagonists in the region. Both India and Pakistan strive for a minimum deterrent. The objective of India's nuclear strategy is credible minimum deterrence (CMD), meaning a secure and reliable second-strike capability after absorbing an adversary's first strike. The main potential targets of this projected deterrence capability are Pakistan and China. Pakistan's nuclear doctrine also seeks a credible deterrent, against India, and according to one senior nuclear weapons planner, its weapons are "aimed solely at India." In particular it seeks to deter New Delhi from launching a conventional military attack such as an offensive for limited war objectives, including destruction of terrorist training camps, as well as attacks on nuclear facilities.

For both India and Pakistan, key components of their attitudes in nuclear defense demonstrate the incompatibility between their mutual nuclear postures. India's offer of a no-first use pact has been rejected by Pakistan as nuclear weapons are an integral element of its (Islamabad's) defense doctrine. On the other hand, Islamabad has offered New Delhi a no-war pact, which ostensibly would reduce the prospect of full-scale conventional war and the risk of nuclear crises. However, such a proposal does not touch upon the proxy war waged by the Kashmiri militants and therefore has been rejected by New Delhi.

Thus, both India and Pakistan strive for a secure second-strike capability as an integral element of their credible minimum deterrent doctrines. Since neither side has constructed systems that are deemed completely satisfactory and reliable, nuclear modernization continues. For India, this means a survivable delivery mechanism that can conceivably strike major cities in China. At present the longest range deployed missile is believed to be the Agni-II with a range of 2,000-2,500 km, and can reach parts of western China. To have an increased range capability, the Indian Defense Research and Development Organization (DRDO) is developing the Agni III intermediate range ballistic missile, which was successfully tested for the first time in April 2007 and has a range of about 3,500 km.

Nevertheless, reports have stated that the Indian military is not altogether satisfied with the nuclear capable missiles that are in its arsenal-Prithvi I (short range ballistic missiles) and the Agni I & II. Thus, India's nuclear delivery systems are deemed far from adequate and for the time being. In the opinion of the Indian Air Force, there will be considerable reliance on fighter bombers such as the Mig 27, Jaguar, and Mirage-2000 for a nuclear delivery role.

This implies that for the foreseeable future, the Indian scientific-military establishment will reinforce their commitment to adequate delivery systems, especially the Agni III and the nuclear submarine project (the Advanced Technology Vessel or ATV) that could carry a sea-based deterrent in the form of a submarine-launched cruise missile (the Sagarika-currently under development). Reports in May 2007 stated that the ATV will be commissioned in 2011-2012 and that two Russian nuclear submarines might be leased before that.

As stated earlier, Pakistan's deployed missile systems can reach most parts of India. These deployed missiles include the Ghaznavi (Hatf-3, range 290 km), Shaheen-I (Hatf-4, range 600-800 km), and the Ghauri-I (Hatf-5, range 1,500 km). Development is also taking place on the Shaheen-II (Hatf-6, range 2,000-3,000 km), which was successfully tested in February 2007. These missile developments illustrate Pakistan's desire for a more secure deterrent, once the range issue had been dealt with. In addition, Pakistan is also seeking a more secure second-strike capability through the acquisition of the Agosta 90B class submarine in late 2007. This vessel, the second to be added to Pakistan's navy, can carry the nuclear capable Harpoon cruise missiles.

Both countries have also achieved considerable progress in manufacturing another delivery system-cruise missiles. India, in partnership with Russia, has developed the BrahMos, while Pakistan has the Babur. These missiles are meant to have land, sea, and air versions, and at least in the case of the BrahMos, will also have a variant for export. In the near future, Indian defense planners hope to introduce land attack cruise missiles with the capacity to carry a nuclear warhead over 1,500 km. In addition, submarine and air force versions of the BrahMos are due to be tested in 2007. The missile is also being installed on ships and IL-38D maritime reconnaissance aircraft to give "strategic relevance" to the Indian Navy. Similarly, Pakistan has successfully tested its nuclear capable Babur (Hatf VII) cruise missile (range 700 km), most recently in March 2007.

In sum, in order to strengthen their nuclear delivery capabilities both India and Pakistan are seeking to perfect their missile arsenals, both ballistic and cruise. The dynamic nature of the pursuit of more reliable deterrence capabilities is also affected by strategic developments involving extra-regional actors, especially China and the United States.

Fissile Material Accumulation

The final factor with an impact on nuclear acquisition dynamics is fissile material production. The renewed discussion on the Fissile Material Cutoff Treaty (FMCT) in 2006 focused attention on the attitudes of India and Pakistan (among other concerned states). The argument put forward by some is that capping the production of fissile material in South Asia would be an important step toward nuclear stability in the subcontinent. However, issues arising from the South Asian security dilemma play a role in stalled FMCT negotiations.

As some analysts have stated, a key motivation for Washington's support of the FMCT is to limit China's nuclear arsenal. Beijing is unlikely to agree to the FMCT under the current circumstances without amelioration of its concerns. If Beijing does not accept the treaty, there is little chance that New Delhi would accept it either resulting in Islamabad's refusal as well. While the Chinese government considers the FMCT to be crucial, its concern also lies in progress on a framework for the Prevention of an Arms Race in Outer Space (PAROS). Beijing has effectively linked progress on the FMCT to that on PAROS. Further, while Beijing is supposed to have stopped fissile material production, there is no official confirmation of this. In addition, theoretically the Chinese government can restart production of fissile material.

The lack of progress on PAROS is said to have been one of the reasons behind China's anti-satellite test in January 2007. Certain policymakers and analysts in the United States perceived the tests as symbolic of the potential military threat from China, a view that reinforces their arguments for the need for dominance in space. In response, China needs to counter a future U.S. national missile defense (NMD), possibly by increasing its quantity of warheads through increased fissile production. China's concern is that U.S. policies under the Bush administration, such as the withdrawal from the ABM Treaty and the reinforced focus on NMD, degrade Beijing's deterrent, which relies on about two dozen intercontinental ballistic missiles (ICBMs). Also, Washington's reluctance to consider a "no first use" policy increases the threat perception of the U.S. use of nuclear weapons in a Taiwan crisis.

From the Indian perspective, Beijing's anti-satellite test refocused the attention of analysts on the considerable gap between Indian and Chinese aerospace capabilities and its consequences for the strategic balance. Indian defense scientists have stated that India would take appropriate measures to deal with this expansion of Beijing's offensive capabilities, possibly through collaboration between the Defense Research and Development Organization (DRDO) and the Indian Space Research Organization (ISRO). The test came at a time when both India and China are pushing ahead with space-based projects (especially lunar missions) and this would be the sign of a new rivalry. Thus, security perceptions in

South Asia (including by extension China and the United States) contain a reinforced belief in the necessity of nuclear weapons and delivery systems development.

Even if China maintains its undeclared moratorium on fissile material production, it is unclear if India would consent to capping its fissile stock at a level much lower than that of China. This also strengthens the argument of Indian analysts who advocate more than just the minimum deterrent-related warheads stockpile and propose a thermonuclear arsenal. Furthermore, the Indian government also has a problem with the lack of verification measures in the existing FMCT proposals. Pakistan for its part has opposed any FMCT that would effectively perpetuate the fissile material asymmetry in the subcontinent, and wants negotiations to cover existing stocks as well. Pakistan's contention is that since its nuclear weapons program is a product of the threat from India, Islamabad would consent to a cap on fissile material production only as part of a bilateral moratorium.

However, since New Delhi's nuclear weapon expansion is driven by the need to construct a secure deterrent against Beijing, such a proposal is a non-starter in the present circumstances. Thus, while Pakistan may have reached the fissile material capacity to suit its credible minimum deterrent needs, this is not necessarily the case for India. Nevertheless, in the context of the proposed FMCT, some Indian analysts have stated that New Delhi has to decide whether its existing stocks are adequate for "strategic purposes," and if so, the FMCT could be beneficial for international stability.

In sum, from the South Asian perspective, there are no credible proliferation disincentives that would surmount security concerns driving India and Pakistan toward strengthening their nuclear capabilities. In essence, nuclear modernization, or vertical proliferation is likely to continue in South Asia. Next, we turn to the issue of horizontal proliferation in the South Asian context.

SOUTH ASIA AND HORIZONTAL PROLIFERATION

As a starting point, it is helpful to focus on cases of horizontal proliferation elsewhere that are connected to South Asia. This includes potential WMD supply routes as well as entities that might be involved, some of whom may be operating outside state control. In particular, the focus is on connections between entities in Pakistan and proliferation dynamics in other regions. Three major issues need to be addressed-(i) the North Korean nuclear program, and in particular the impact of the October 2006 nuclear test on South Asia; (ii) the current state of the A.Q. Khan network and its implications for WMD supply trends; and (iii) proliferation links between South Asia and the Middle East.

The North Korean Nuclear Test and South Asia

As expected, North Korea's nuclear test put renewed focus on the dangers of nuclear proliferation, and policymakers in India assumed it would lead to more stringent criticism of its nuclear agreement with the United States. Indian experts expected the North Korean test to impact especially on any nuclear test-related provisions of the nuclear agreement with the United States. Consequently, New Delhi swiftly condemned the test and indirectly highlighted Islamabad's contribution to Pyongyang's nuclear test. Some Indian officials even stated that Pyongyang's illegal acquisition of nuclear technology would actually spur reluctant supplier countries (such as Australia) to legitimately sell nuclear fuel to India, especially since it would be used for civilian purposes.

On the other hand, Islamabad refuted any suggestion that the activities of the A.Q. Khan network had contributed to Pyongyang's test, stating that North Korea's nuclear program is based on plutonium while Pakistan relies on uranium. In this manner, both India and Pakistan tried to ensure that proliferation in South Asia was not equated with proliferation in Northeast Asia. To a certain extent, the Bush administration obliged the subcontinental nuclear powers, as senior officials dismissed any parallels between North Korea's path to nuclear weapons to those of India and Pakistan. However, while Pakistan denied any links to the test, it did not help Islamabad's case when Japanese sources stated that days before Pyongyang's test, several Pakistani nuclear technicians arrived in North Korea through China. This augmented the suspicions that Pakistani agencies may have had some role in the test, perhaps through data sharing before or after the explosion.

The A.Q. Khan Network and Proliferation Dynamics

The A.Q. Khan network, which provided nuclear assistance to North Korea and Iran, has represented the most serious proliferation problem in recent years. Since Khan's public confession in February 2004, the Musharraf regime has consistently asserted that this network was the work of a rogue scientist and that the Pakistani government and its military leaders were not involved in these activities. However, it is not clear to what extent this assertion is accurate. Analysts and officials in Pakistan as well as in the United States have expressed skepticism over Khan's confession as well as the implicit professed innocence of the Pakistani political and military establishment. A highly publicized report released in April 2007 by the London-based International Institute for Strategic Studies, also stated that individuals and entities involved in the network could still be dormant and can conceivably be reactivated in the future.

So far, Islamabad has refused to allow foreign interrogators to question Khan even though the U.S. government has regularly expressed dissatisfaction over information released by Pakistan. > Furthermore, most individuals connected to the network are still at large, including important figures such as B.S.A. Tahir, while others, such as Henk Slebos, have been given light sentences. Moreover, the Khan claimed in a signed statement that successive army chiefs in the 1990s (Generals Mirza Aslam Beg and Jehangir Karamat) had authorized the sales of nuclear technology. While this could be taken as Khan's attempts to remove the burden of guilt, it is true that the military was closely associated with the nuclear and missile programs. In fact, in 1990, Gen. Beg warned U.S. government officials that Pakistan would be forced to provide nuclear technology to Tehran if Washington did not offer support to Pakistan.

Other circumstantial evidence, such as visits by the Pakistani military leadership to North Korea throughout the nineties, suggests that there was a barter deal between Pyongyang and Islamabad (uranium enrichment technology in exchange for missiles). Additionally, in August 2005, Gen. Musharraf conceded that Khan had transferred centrifuge machines to North Korea through which uranium hexafluoride (which was also transferred) can be enriched for eventual processing into civilian reactors fuel or for military purposes. Shipping out such large centrifuge machines without the military's knowledge would have been impossible. Therefore, it would have been highly unlikely that these activities were carried out without the military's acquiescence. On a side note, it is possible that Washington's attitude was colored by the need to retain Islamabad's support in the anti-Taliban/Al Qaeda campaign in Afghanistan.

Additionally, for a country to acquire a nuclear delivery system (such as the No Dong missiles transferred to Pakistan), the decision-making process incorporates several factors, as well as the opinions of numerous government agencies to ensure compatibility among the various systems. It is therefore not very plausible that a nuclear-missile barter deal with such serious and risky international consequences could have been approved without cooperation from senior levels of the political-military establishment in Pakistan. The issue of the Pakistani military-scientific establishment's involvement (or endorsement) in the Khan's network activities is crucial due to its implications for contemporary proliferation routes and processes. If these elements within and outside Pakistan (including non-Pakistani nationals) and their methods and routes remain undiscovered, it has two broad consequences for proliferation in South Asia.

First, it allows Islamabad to potentially procure missile and nuclear technology in the future, in an attempt to catch up with India. In this regard, a Pakistani national, Mohammed Aslam, working at the Tabani Corporation's Moscow office, was named by the Russian government in 2006 as having attempted to acquire dual-use technology and other materials for Pakistan's nuclear and missile development programs. This example demonstrates that elements of the network are still active, though it is unclear if they are directly connected to Pakistani nuclear and missile development programs. Given Islamabad's need to construct a secure deterrent against India (especially long-range missiles that can reach southern and eastern India), it is possible that the above case is an instance of continuing efforts to exploit non-state networks to procure prohibited equipment. As one analyst noted, due to Pakistan's apparent inability to acquire nuclear weapons components legally, it is encouraged to look toward illegal sources. Furthermore, according to some experts, apart from Pakistan, other countries can easily utilize the same supply networks. The Iranian government has made use of these networks for its nuclear and missile programs. As the previously mentioned IISS report states, Tehran controls a clandestine nuclear materials network comparable to the one run by Khan, and in the past has procured technology from some of the same suppliers used by Khan. In context of nuclear proliferation networks, a further concern is that if North Korea dismantles its nuclear weapons program, it will create a potential source of unwanted nuclear materials in the process. Such discarded, but nevertheless lethal technology, could be bought by illegal nuclear supply entities that may or may not have had any connection to the Khan network.

Second, the continued existence of the kind of middlemen that the network generated increases the possibility of nuclear technology leakage out of Pakistan in the event of a coup or widespread instability from radical groups. Since 9/11, there have been periodic fears of internal upheavals in Pakistan, especially from groups linked to the Taliban. Recent reports have also stated that two nuclear scientists from the Pakistan Atomic Energy Commission (PAEC) were kidnapped by the Taliban in late 2006, and as of March 2007 remained in captivity in the Waziristan area. > Soon after that kidnapping, there was an aborted attempt to capture six more PAEC officials in the North West Frontier Province of Pakistan in January 2007. While it is not clear if the officials and scientists were targeted specifically because of their links to Pakistan's nuclear program, these incidents demonstrate the potential danger of non-state actors' participation in the illegal market in nuclear technology.

In order to demonstrate to the international community that it is a responsible nuclear power, Islamabad has decided to set up a "Strategic Export Control Division" in its foreign ministry that will ostensibly prevent prohibited WMD-related technology from being exported. However, this does not necessarily address the problem of possible involvement of government entities and officials that have remained under the radar even after the network was uncovered. In general, the proliferation-related fear for U.S. policymakers is twofold-first, that nuclear technology could be transferred to a terrorist organization; and second, that the Musharraf regime could be overthrown, resulting in uncertainty for the counter-terrorism as well as nonproliferation campaigns.

The case of Pakistan demonstrates the difficulty that arises when nonproliferation goals collide with other strategic imperatives such as counter-terrorism. While the Khan network problem is one of the reasons why Washington has refused to offer a nuclear cooperation agreement to Pakistan, the perceived tilt toward India (through the Indo-U.S. nuclear agreement) can also be a reason why Washington has not pressured Islamabad any further on the A.Q. Khan issue. Nevertheless, in January 2007, in a proactive step, the U.S. Congress under the Democratic leadership passed the Nuclear Black Market Counter Terrorism Act, which authorizes the administration to implement "punitive actions" against states condoning or cooperating with entities actively engaged in nuclear proliferation.

SOUTH ASIA AND THE MIDDLE EAST: PROLIFERATION LINKS

While an analysis of proliferation in the Middle East is outside the scope of this study, it is necessary to highlight existing and potential links between the Middle East and South Asia, apart from the A.Q. Khan network mentioned above. Khan's network provided significant know-how to Iran in the late eighties and early nineties (including centrifuge technology), though the full extent of these transfers has still not been confirmed. While nuclear links between Iran and Pakistan have ended for now, Islamabad's nuclear connection to the Middle East remains, such as through possible collaboration with Saudi Arabia.

From the South Asian proliferation perspective, the close ties between Saudi Arabia and the development of Pakistan's nuclear program is a crucial development. News reports as well as official U.S. government analyses have claimed that Riyadh provided considerable financing for Pakistan's nuclear and missile program in the past, but some reports now suggest a more proactive role by Saudi Arabia-in terms of nuclear energy development itself. This is in line with the announcement in November 2006 by six Arab states-Saudi Arabia, Morocco, Egypt, Algeria, Tunisia, and the United Arab Emirates-that they would develop civilian nuclear programs. Earlier, in 2005, Saudi Arabia applied for and was granted exemption from nuclear inspections through the IAEA's 'small quantities protocol.' Before that, a widely quoted 2003 report in The Guardian stated that Riyadh was considering three nuclear options: (a) building a nuclear deterrent, (b) allying with a nuclear power, or (c) working toward a nuclear weapon free zone in the Middle East. Recent developments suggest that a combination of the first two options might be adopted given that it is highly unlikely that Iran and Israel relinquish their nuclear programs in the near future.

This is where Pakistan's role could be significant. German news reports stated in early 2006 that Pakistani scientists assisted Saudi efforts to develop a nuclear program and that this was done under the guise of pilgrimages to Saudi Arabia between 2003 and 2005. Several high-ranking Saudi royals as well as government officials are among the few non-Pakistanis who have toured Islamabad's nuclear facilities. These include defense minister Prince Sultan (now also crown prince) who visited the Kahuta uranium enrichment facility in 1999, and a son of the current Saudi ruler, King Abdullah, who attended a test of the nuclear-capable 950-mile range Ghauri missile in 1999. These developments suggest that if Riyadh decides to acquire nuclear weapons, the spotlight could be on Pakistan as one of the sources. A factor that could prompt Saudi Arabia to pursue nuclear weapons would be if Tehran unambiguously builds it own nuclear weapon, prompting Israel to shed the opacity over its arsenal.

While disincentives for Pakistan to go along this route are considerable (most notably, U.S. opposition), there are also incentives for Islamabad to aid the Saudis in their quest-cheap oil from Saudi Arabia, and a favorable endorsement for the Musharraf regime (or a successor regime) from powerful conservative Sunni religious and political groups within Pakistan. A 2003 news report quoted an anonymous Pakistani official who claimed that Riyadh and Islamabad had concluded a secret agreement under which Pakistan would receive subsidized oil in exchange for transferring nuclear technology. In 2004, Iranian government sources also claimed that they had information that confirmed this agreement, but there was no further corroboration of this from other sources. Therefore, even if there is no immediate possibility of such a transfer, Saudi Arabia could pursue this with Pakistan in the future to hedge against nuclear developments in the Middle East.

A key incentive for Pakistan could also be to use Saudi Arabia for strategic depth purposes. Islamabad's traditional geographic buffer against Indian military campaigns was Afghanistan, but that was lost after the fall of the Taliban in 2001. Ostensibly, Pakistan requires strategic depth to protect its forces (conventional and nuclear) from an armored offensive by the Indian military, which could cut off the country similar to the 1971 war. Saudi Arabia could provide a base for stationing Pakistani nuclear devices that would be safe from the reach of Indian missiles and give Islamabad a semblance of second-strike capability. This idea of looking towards the Middle East for strategic depth is not new. In the 1990s, former Prime Minister Benazir Bhutto, skeptical of the reliance on Afghanistan, recommended Iran as a more useful ally for purposes of strategic depth.

Apart from the Pakistan-Saudi Arabia link, concerns have also been expressed (especially in the U.S. Congress) over India's ties to Iran, at a time when the IAEA and western powers led by the United States are working toward controlling Tehran's uranium enrichment program. These concerns have arisen during the broader debate in Washington on the nuclear agreement with India. In particular, attention has focused on India's long-standing political and diplomatic relationship with Iran as well as the imposition of sanctions on two private Indian companies suspected of transferring chemicals meant for rocket fuel as well as chemical weapons. The Indian government claimed that both companies (Balaji Amines Ltd. & Prachi Poly Products) were doing legitimate business with Iranian firms. Balaji Amines insisted that they had been supplying products used for manufacturing life-saving drugs such as ampicillin and other antibiotics, but nevertheless, New Delhi ordered the company to stop all trade with Iran.

Both India and Pakistan have attempted to ensure that they are in compliance with the latest international regulations against Tehran's nuclear program. In February 2007, Pakistan froze assets of several individuals and other entities connected to Tehran's nuclear and missile projects in accordance with UN Security Council resolution 1737. In the same month, New Delhi banned exports of equipment and technologies to Iran that could be used in nuclear and missile development projects.

The Iran nuclear issue has been an important point of discussion in context of the Indo-U.S. nuclear agreement. The Hyde Act, passed by the U.S. Congress in December 2006, endorses nuclear cooperation between India and the United States, but it also states that New Delhi should assist the international community in clamping down on Iran's nuclear program. Furthermore, in May 2007, a group of U.S. senators sent a joint letter to Indian Prime Minister Manmohan Singh articulating their dissatisfaction over India's military ties with Iran, especially a 'joint defense working group' between the two countries. Nuclear ties between India and the United States are not limited to nuclear trade between the two, but also extends to discussions over restricting proliferation elsewhere.

Prime Minister Manmohan Singh has stated in the past that New Delhi does not favor another nuclear power in the neighborhood, and India voted against Iran at the IAEA in September 2005 and February 2006. However, two factors have restrained the Indian government from opposing Iran's nuclear weapons program more forcefully. First, the scramble for energy resources has made the Iran-Pakistan-India (IPI) natural gas pipeline a crucial economic issue for India. Stern Indian opposition to Iran's nuclear program would jeopardize the proposed IPI pipeline from Iran to India. The pipeline is considered to be of crucial importance to India in order to sustain high economic growth rates in the coming years. Thus, economic imperatives, specifically the need for energy sources, are an important factor in nonproliferation positions of countries such as India and China. In this context, New Delhi has reiterated that the construction of the pipeline will proceed in spite of pressures from Washington to cancel the project.

Second, for New Delhi, another variable is satisfying domestic political constituencies that are skeptical of the nuclear overtures from Washington that come at the cost of long-standing ties with Tehran. Since the Congress Party-led coalition government depends on parliamentary support from Communist parties, the government is obliged to periodically hold positions on contentious issues such as the Iranian nuclear program. The Manmohan Singh government has stated that it would be guided by India's national interest on the Iran nuclear issue, but this does not clarify to what extent India would be willing to go along with the United States on this issue. Some recent reports have also stated that New Delhi could play a more formal role in mediating the growing tensions over Iran's nuclear program in conjunction with the UN Security Council. However, it is unclear what form this would take.

In sum, nuclear issues in South Asia cannot be examined in isolation from developments elsewhere. Historically close political ties have existed between the South Asian subcontinent and the Middle East, and therefore, regional rivalries and bilateral relations play an important role in shaping decisions that impact broader nuclear issues, including horizontal proliferation.

INDO-U.S. NUCLEAR COOPERATION

Since July 2005, when the U.S. and Indian governments unveiled their nuclear cooperation agreement, a debate has risen over its impact on the global nonproliferation regime. This agreement will allow India to acquire nuclear technology and materials from the United States and other suppliers. In return, New Delhi will designate which of its nuclear facilities are for civilian use and which are for military use. The former list would be opened up for international inspections. Prior to implementation, New Delhi will have to conclude a safeguards agreement with the IAEA, while the Nuclear Suppliers Group (NSG) will have to effect changes in its rules to enable nuclear cooperation between its member states and India.

The Hyde Act passed by the U.S. Congress in December 2006, authorized the Bush administration to bring into place a nuclear cooperation mechanism with India, after concluding a bilateral agreement under Section 123 of the U.S. Atomic Energy Act. Negotiations on the '123' agreement began in early 2007, but as of early June, talks were stalled on a few contentious issues. The disagreement is over five main items; (i) the right to reprocess spent fuel, (ii) the conversion of a voluntary moratorium on nuclear testing into a legal commitment by India, (iii) the assured supply of fuel by the United States, (iv) the return of all equipment to the United States if India conducts a nuclear test, and (v) the level of inspections of Indian facilities.

The nuclear deal reflects an influential view in India that the nonproliferation regime embodied in the NPT is defective. According to Indian Prime Minister Manmohan Singh, the regime is ineffective and that the international community should introduce measures that restrict nuclear proliferation more effectively without suppressing peaceful uses of nuclear energy. At the same time, the contention is that India is a responsible nuclear state that has adhered to the guidelines of nonproliferation (without legally being part of the NPT regime) through strict export controls and denying nuclear assistance to other states, unlike the record of some nuclear weapon states.

A basic feature of this agreement is that by acquiring uranium from foreign sources (to free up domestic supplies) and by placing a set of nuclear facilities on the military list, India can increase its fissile material production for weaponization purposes. However, a different line of analysis examines the implications of increased uranium supplies in the context of India's fledgling nuclear submarine project. This perspective views that rather than increasing nuclear warhead production, New Delhi would use the expansion of its uranium supplies and enrichment capability to fuel its nuclear submarine project, a key element of India's desire to achieve a secure second strike capability under its credible minimum deterrence doctrine.

There are two separate lines of criticism of the deal; the first focuses on the nonproliferation objective, and the second on India's strategic needs. The first perspective is that the agreement will weaken the global nonproliferation regime by condoning India's nuclear weapons program. The argument is that by introducing India-specific changes to global as well as domestic U.S. nonproliferation laws, it will be more difficult to prevent nuclear transfers involving other countries such as China-Pakistan and Russia-Iran. A further objection is that even with 14 reactors under safeguards, 8 others will remain on the military list, free to manufacture plutonium for several nuclear weapons annually. Additionally, critics have stated that the agreement so far does not commit India to eschew nuclear testing formally, or to end fissile material production.

The second criticism comes most notably, from members of the nuclear scientific community in India, who contend that elements of the agreement would in effect cap India's nuclear program and constrain its thorium-based three stage nuclear project. They argue that while New Delhi has maintained a unilateral moratorium on nuclear testing, it does not want such a clause legalized in a bilateral treaty. The argument here is that India might have to reconsider its moratorium in the event that China or Pakistan conducts a nuclear test.

In addition, India's scientific community and government have insisted that it be explicitly granted the right to reprocess spent fuel for the three stage nuclear project that exploits the ample thorium reserves in the country (about 30% of the global supply). The Indian government wants to retain reprocessing rights as part of an advanced nuclear fuel cycle. This would involve recycling uranium oxide fuel while the consequent plutonium would be used with thorium in fast breeder reactors. However, some Indian scientific experts have stated that even if reprocessing rights and technology are not granted under the 123 agreement, it is likely that the initial reactors bought by New Delhi will come from Russia and France, rather than the United States. It is entirely possible that trade with these two countries, especially Russia, will involve reprocessing rights and sale of reactors and fuel. On the other hand, Indian analysts criticize the reported objective of the U.S. government of insuring that India's nuclear trade with other supplier states has equally rigorous conditions attached. Finally, Indian analysts have faulted the U.S. position of not allowing assurances of fuel supplies and of prohibiting India from stockpiling nuclear fuel.

Thus, the nuclear agreement between India and the United States has been criticized on the grounds of its potential impact on the global nonproliferation regime as well as its impact on India's strategic nuclear program. It must also be noted that since the bilateral 123 agreement between India and the United States is still under negotiation, it is too early to assume the eventual direction of the nuclear agreement framework. Even if the two countries conclude the 123 agreement satisfactorily (for both sides), India still must obtain approval for nuclear trade from the NSG and has to negotiate a safeguards agreement with the IAEA.

The China Issue

Several rationales have been offered as justification for the nuclear agreement (such as economics, strategic alliance, and nonproliferation benefits), but perhaps the most intriguing is one has been left largely unstated by the two governments-that of balancing China. Both India and the United States are concerned about the future direction of Chinese foreign and security policy. For the United States, aiding India through nuclear cooperation as well as a strategic partnership, Washington would be able to balance China more effectively in the region. In the process it would divert China from its main security issue-Taiwan. For India, the agreement is a significant diplomatic and strategic addition to its capabilities vis-à-vis China, with both the possible increase in fissile material production and a strengthened strategic partnership with the United States.

One argument supportive of the Indo-U.S. agreement stresses that China has built up Pakistan as a counter to India for several decades, a policy that involved transfers of nuclear and missile technology. It must also be noted that more than a year before the Indo-U.S. nuclear agreement was first announced in July 2005, there were reports in March 2004 that China was planning to provide Islamabad with a nuclear reactor. The implication is that that the Beijing-Islamabad nuclear partnership might have continued in any case. Nevertheless, it is important to consider the current pattern of nuclear cooperation between China and Pakistan in the light of the Indo-U.S. deal. Regardless of the pros and cons of the deal, it can be used by Beijing to lay the grounds for legitimizing continued nuclear collaboration with Pakistan. A sign of this has been China's argument that any changes in the NSG rules should be criteria-based rather than country specific.

In December 2005, China began construction of the 300 MW second phase of the Chashma Nuclear Power Plant (contracted in May 2004), subsequent to the commissioning of the first phase in September 2000. Parallel to the Indo-U.S. deal, China and Pakistan also reportedly agreed to a nuclear cooperation arrangement under which as many as six nuclear reactors of at least 600 MW capacity would be provided to Islamabad. As of now, no other details are available so it is not clear what kind of safeguards will be installed, though some sources have stated that this initiative is being opposed by the NSG.

Reports of a possible Beijing-Islamabad nuclear agreement gained ground ahead of Chinese President Hu Jintao's visit to Pakistan in November 2006. However, no such deal was announced during the visit, leading to a conclusion that Beijing is possibly waiting to see the final shape of the Indo-U.S. agreement to gauge its impact on China. However, one influential Pakistani analyst stated that the lack of a public nuclear cooperation agreement between Beijing and Islamabad does not mean that such an arrangement will not come about; China can supply Pakistan with the required nuclear technology at a more politically convenient time.

Pakistan's desire for a stronger and more public nuclear relationship with China is in part because Islamabad failed to obtain a similar arrangement with the United States. Some Pakistani commentators have in fact argued that their country needs nuclear cooperation with the United States (and other suppliers, for that matter) more than India because the gap between existing energy supplies and future energy requirements is far more serious for Pakistan that it is for India. A senior Pakistani official connected to the nuclear program, stated in October 2006 that Washington's nuclear policy should be guided by a "criteria-based" approach rather than one geared toward a single country. However, U.S. government officials have stated that they have no intention of considering a similar agreement with Pakistan. It is likely that this refusal has much to do with the activities of the A.Q. Khan network as well as Islamabad's reluctance to allow a full interrogation of Khan by U.S. experts that would shed light on some unanswered questions related to the network.

Islamabad has cited the fact that Washington declined to offer Pakistan a nuclear cooperation agreement as a motivation for increased self-reliance on nuclear energy, through indigenous fuel manufacturing capabilities. In this context, government officials in Pakistan stated in April 2007 that the country would set up an installation for fuel testing for use in nuclear plants in a quest for "complete technological capability."

As highlighted previously, Pakistan's overall agenda is to redress the perceived widening of the nuclear imbalance with India. Nevertheless, Pakistani experts have admitted that Islamabad's quest for increased nuclear capability is a result of the tacit rivalry between Beijing and New Delhi and the latter's desire to catch up with China. Apart from the impending nuclear technology transfers from Beijing, recent reports have also stated that the Musharraf regime has commenced construction of a 1,000 MW heavy water reactor that will potentially produce adequate plutonium for as many as 50 warheads per year. In addition, Islamabad is setting up a commercial scale nuclear reprocessing plant to allow production of weapons grade plutonium. Such activities would enable Islamabad to stockpile as much fissile material as possible before a future FMCT comes into force.

These developments suggest that Islamabad is attempting to diversify its nuclear weapons program through plutonium, as opposed to its traditional reliance on uranium as fissile material. Plutonium allows for more compact weapons and provides increased flexibility for the arsenal. For Islamabad, this is critical for developing a second strike capability against India. However, some Indian scientific experts have stated that even with the new Pakistani reactor, India will still be able to maintain an insurmountable lead in fissile material production through unsafeguarded reactors under the nuclear agreement.

Chinese support is key to Pakistan's quest for some strategic benefits vis-à-vis India, especially if the U.S.-India nuclear agreement reaches the implementation stage. In a possible attempt to reduce Chinese opposition to the nuclear deal with Washington, New Delhi has committed itself, in principle, to civilian nuclear cooperation with Beijing, a declaration announced during President Hu's visit to New Delhi in November 2006. This could be viewed as an incentive from Beijing to dissuade India from a potential anti-China partnership with Washington. Nuclear trade between India and China is not necessarily an empty proposal; it has a precedent. In 1995, India acquired low enriched uranium from China for the Tarapur nuclear reactors. The official Chinese position is opposition to any NSG amendments that would adversely effect the non-proliferation regime, and that they would consider viable arrangements at the NSG, and not bilaterally. Beijing's response reiterates its view that any exceptions should not be India-specific and should include other states.

Interestingly, Indian Foreign Minister Pranab Mukherjee stated in November 2006 that New Delhi does not have any problem with a similar nuclear agreement between Pakistan and China. If this attitude is indeed the Indian government's position, the implication could be that New Delhi is confident that the benefits it will accrue from the agreement with the United States far outweigh the possible increase in nuclear cooperation between China and Pakistan.

Commercial Issues

The Indo-U.S. nuclear agreement also demonstrates that changes in the nuclear supplier regimes will not be restricted only to bilateral nuclear trade between the United States and India. Nuclear energy firms from several countries other than India are already lining up to negotiate commercial nuclear deals with India. NSG member states such as Australia are considering approval of changes in the group's rules to permit nuclear cooperation with New Delhi. Even though Australia (a major uranium producer) has not yet agreed to revoke the prohibition of supply to India, Australian companies such as BHP Billiton are anticipating lucrative sales. Other important members of the NSG have also supported civilian nuclear cooperation with India, within the appropriate IAEA safeguards framework. French and Canadian companies have also contacted the Nuclear Power Corporation of India (one of the main government nuclear energy entities), in connection with the supply of light-water nuclear power related equipment.

Thus, nuclear energy companies are important players in the future of this agreement as well as the broader nonproliferation regime. Firms such as General Electric and Bechtel have lobbied the Bush administration in favor of the agreement. Besides deals in the nuclear energy sector, the expectation is also that such cooperation will facilitate contracts in the conventional military sector, especially with respect to the impending deal for 126 fighter aircraft for the Indian Air Force, a deal worth about $9 billion. Aerospace giants such as Lockheed Martin and Boeing are among the contenders for the contract. Therefore, the implication is that the incentives go well beyond the nuclear energy sector.

Finally, it is instructive to consider the scenario if the nuclear agreement between India and the United States is scrapped, either because of insurmountable differences over the 123 agreement or later in the implementation stage. In India, several members of the influential atomic energy scientific community have expressed reservations over the agreement as have the communist parties and the opposition Bharatiya Janata Party (BJP).

In the United States as well, there has been considerable opposition from nonproliferation experts as well as sections of the political establishment.

It is not certain if the reservations expressed by the Indian government towards certain clauses of the December 2006 Hyde Act will be rectified in New Delhi's favor in the bilateral 123 agreement, which again has to be approved by the U.S. Congress. Given these complicating factors, the implications of scrapping the agreement are immense; affecting broader bilateral ties between India and the United States, the nonproliferation regime in general, and the global nuclear energy market.

GLOBALIZATION IMPACT ON THREAT PERCEPTIONS IN INDIA, PAKISTAN AND CHINA

For the purpose of this book, South Asia has been taken to cover India, Afghanistan, Pakistan, Bangladesh, Sri Lanka, Nepal, Bhutan and the Maldives. Even though China is not considered a part of South Asia, it has common borders with some of the countries of the region and their threat perceptions are influenced by the China factor. There cannot, therefore, be any meaningful discussion on this subject without a reference to this factor. South Asia, as defined above, covers only about 10 per cent of the total land area of the Asian continent, but about 40 per cent of Asia's total population and between 45 and 50 per cent of Asia's Muslim population live in this area.

Many analysts in India, including this writer, make a distinction between the Indian sub-continent and South Asia. When they talk of the Indian sub-continent, they have in mind India, Pakistan, Bangladesh, Nepal and Bhutan. Of these, India, Pakistan and Bangladesh constituted one political entity before the British left the sub-continent in 1947. Pakistan was born in 1947 through the partition of the British India and Bangladesh was born in 1971 through the partition of Pakistan after a war of liberation waged by the Bengalis of the then East Pakistan, with Indian assistance.

Indian analysts, who talk of the Indian sub-continent, wish to keep in mind, in their analyses, the common historical, political, religious and cultural heritage of these three countries. The term sub-continent is used less and less in Pakistan and Bangladesh.

The political leadership and the policy-makers in these two countries do not wish to be reminded of this common heritage. Any highlighting of this common heritage by Indian analysts is viewed by them with suspicion— — as indicating a hidden desire to reverse history and undo the 1947 partition. They, therefore, talk only of South Asia and have, for all practical purposes, banished any reference to the sub-continent from their strategic discourse. This has to be kept in mind since complexes arising from sub-continental memories tend to influence their mind-set and threat perceptions and have stood in the way of the progress of globalization in this area. They view any Indian enthusiasm for globalization as a concealed attempt towards political and economic re-subcontinentalisation.

The threat perceptions of the countries of South Asia are influenced and will continue to be influenced in the short and medium terms by four factors:

- The India factor.
- The China factor.
- The Pakistan factor.
- The non-State actors factor.

The India Factor

The India factor has had an impact on the threat perceptions of all the countries of this region except Afghanistan and the Maldives. This arises due to the following reasons:

- Asymmetry in size, human and material resources and economic and military potential.
- Perceived Indian willingness/tendency to assert its national interests even if they be detrimental to those of the neighbours. Examples: India's role in the creation of Bangladesh, alleged Indian support to the Tamils of Sri Lanka.
- Perceived Indian encouragement of its political favourites in the countries of the region. Examples: India's alleged soft corner for the opposition Awami League in Bangladesh and for the democratic forces in Nepal.
- Continuing differences relating to territory (Kashmir with Pakistan) and utilization of water resources (Pakistan and Bangladesh).

The other countries, except Afghanistan and the Maldives, tend to guard themselves against these factors by avoiding too close economic linkages with India, which comes in the way of the region as a whole benefiting from the fruits of globalization, by developing economic and military linkages with China and by supporting Chinese aspirations for a role in regional organizations such as the SAARC as an observer.

Pakistan and Bangladesh embarked on a policy of liberalization of their economies before India. Despite this, their economic development has not been as satisfactory as they would have like it to be. Amongst the reasons, one could cite the bad internal security situation, which keeps foreign investors away despite a favourable policy framework; political instability due to periodic interventions by the Army in politics; inadequate investment in a modern education system due to the diversion of the limited resources to meet military and strategic needs; and failure to diversify the economy. Pakistan's economy continues to be largely a three-commodity (cotton and cotton textiles, leather goods and sports articles) and one-port (Karachi) economy. Bangladesh's economy continues to be largely textiles, jute and raw materials dependent.

Though India embarked on the liberalization of its economy only from 1991 onwards, its economy has made impressive progress freeing it from its past dependence on traditional goods such as textiles, tea etc. India's rapid diversification and development of its economy have been facilitated by the facts that democracy has taken firm roots in the country; that its internal security problems, though serious, are confined to areas in which the foreign investors are presently not interested; and that its founding fathers had shown foresight in investing heavily on a modern education system, including institutes of excellence in technology, which have significantly contributed to its emergence as a leading Information Technology (IT) power.

Complexes and concerns arising from the India factor continue to come in the way of the normalization of trade relations between Pakistan and India, the improvement in the trade relations between India and Bangladesh and progress towards the integration of the economies of the region through appropriate institutional and policy frameworks. Political factors continue to receive priority over economic and prejudices and fears continue to rule out pragmatism.

However, economic realities ultimately have a way of asserting themselves. One could already see a beginning of it in Pakistan. Its rulers and policy-makers have realized that a favourable policy frame-work and wide-ranging reforms alone will not attract foreign investors. They also need a market and consumers large enough to make their investments adequately profitable. Pakistan does not provide such a market and such a reservoir of consumers. Unless the foreign investors perceive the sub-continent as a whole as a single economic entity and market and are able to sell their products anywhere within this entity, they are reluctant to invest in Pakistan or Bangladesh alone, without guarantees of access to the Indian market.

The realization of this ground reality has already brought about a significant change in Pakistan's policy since Gen. Pervez Musharraf came to power in October, 1999. While continuing to oppose the normalization of economic relations with India till the differences over Jammu & Kashmir (J&K) are settled, he has made an exception in respect of energy supplies. He is prepared now to allow the foreign investors investing heavily in the construction of oil and gas pipelines to Pakistan from Iran or Turkmenistan to cater to the requirements of the Indian market too in order to make their investments adequately profitable. Significantly, even the religious fundamentalist parties, who continue to insist on a policy of "Kashmir first and the rest later", have not objected to what Gen. Musharraf describes as the stand-alone exception. If this exception materializes and if the benefits of it are felt by the Pakistani people, this will become more and more a rule than a mere exception.

Such a realization is yet to come about in Bangladesh. The trade relations between India and Bangladesh are not as restricted as those between India and Pakistan. There is a much, much freer flow of trade between the two countries. While encouraging a greater flow of trade with China, Bangladesh continues to prevent pragmatism, profitability and mutual benefits from having a free play to contribute to a rapid expansion of the bilateral economic relations with India.

Four examples could be cited as illustrations of the Bangladesh attitude:

- It refuses to sell its surplus gas to India on the ostensible ground that it wants to conserve it for its future use. At the same time, it has reportedly entered into negotiations with China for selling it through a pipeline to China via Myanmar.

- It refuses to grant transit rights to India to facilitate the movement of Indian goods to India's northeast.
- It has been reluctant to permit a pipeline to bring gas from the Arakan area of Myanmar to India pass through Bangladesh territory.
- During the period from July to December, 2005, the value of Chinese exports to Bangladesh amounted to US $ 1.03 billion and Chinese imports from Bangladesh only US $ 27.9 million. During the same period, the value of Indian exports to Bangladesh amounted to US $ 820 million and imports from Bangladesh to US $ 105 million. India's imports from Bangladesh are still small, but they are four times the value of Chinese imports from Bangladesh. Chinese exports to Bangladesh are nearly 25 per cent more than those of India. And yet, while Bangladesh nurses a grudge against India on the ground that it has allegedly been dumping its goods in Bangladesh and has not been buying enough from there, it does not voice a similar grievance against China.

Feelings of insecurity, an aggressive inferiority complex, and a Me-too syndrome continue to influence policy-making in Pakistan. What India does, it must do too. What India gets, it must get too. One saw an example of this syndrome in action during the recent visit of President George Bush to India and Pakistan, when, during Mr. Bush's talks in Islamabad, Gen. Musharraf reportedly pleaded with him to reach with Pakistan an agreement on co-operation in the development of civilian nuclear energy similar to the agreement offered to India. Mr. Bush had to point out to him that the needs and circumstances of the two countries are different.

These factors— —feelings of insecurity, the inferiority complex and the Me-too syndrome—will continue to influence the Pakistani mind-set and policy-making in the short and medium terms. Though there has been progress in the identification and implementation of confidence-building measures and in the promotion of people-to-people contacts, the relationship between the two countries will continue to be fragile and the exploitation of the opportunities for beneficial co-operation provided by globalization will be slow.

While Pakistan's longing for the acquisition of J&K and its painful memories of 1971 could explain its attitude to India, no convincing explanation is possible for the behaviour of Bangladesh. While there are differences between India and Bangladesh over the utilization of river waters, there are no major differences over territory compared to the Kashmir issue with Pakistan and Bangladesh has no negative memories of India's military might in action against it. The anti-Indian reflexes in Bangladesh are largely confined to the present ruling formation headed by Begum Khalida Zia and are not shared by the opposition headed by the Awami League, which was in the forefront of its independence struggle.

India-Bangladesh relations will continue to zigzag—— improving when the Awami League is in power and stagnating, if not declining, when the Bangladesh National Party comes to power. Globalization has not made any significant difference to this zigzag and is unlikely to do so in the short and medium terms.

THE CHINA FACTOR

China is not a South Asian power, but it has acquired a significant South Asian presence, by skilfully exploiting the complexes and reflexes of the countries of the region vis-a-vis India. Amongst the steps it has taken to make its presence felt in this region are:

- The clandestine supply of nuclear and missile technologies to Pakistan, which might one day fall into the hands of Al Qaeda and other jihadi terrorist organizations should the jihadis capture power in Pakistan.
- Strengthening Pakistan's military capability in the Army, the Air Force and the Navy in order to reduce its feeling of insecurity vis-a-vis India.
- Strengthening Pakistan's strategic infrastructure through projects such as the construction of the Gwadar port on the Baloch coast and the Mekran Highway connecting Gwadar with Karachi.
- Strengthening Pakistan's IT capability.

- Strengthening Bangladesh's military capability.
- Helping Bangladesh in the development of its energy resources.
- The reported offer of assistance to Bangladesh for setting up facilities for research into the peaceful uses of nuclear energy.
- Reported military supplies to the royal regime in Nepal at a time when India has cut down its military supplies in view of the suppression of democracy by the King.
- Reported assistance to Sri Lanka for the development of the Hambantota port.

These developments are viewed by many analysts, including this writer, as an attempt to strengthen China's strategic presence and influence in the South Asian region. However, these perceptions, not invalid, have not been allowed to resurrect feelings of animosity between India and China. The border dispute between the two countries continues to remain under negotiations without any visible forward movement. At the same time, there have been significant gestures— —such as the Chinese recognition of Sikkim as a part of India and the bilateral agreement to resume border trade through the Sikkim sector.

The presence of the Dalai Lama and a large number of Tibetan refugees in the Indian territory and their activities— —perceived by Beijing as political behind a religious facade— continue to be a matter of concern to China, but these concerns are no longer articulated in strong language.

China has shown signs of being comfortable with the idea of India emerging as an important power, but it does not seem to be comfortable with the prospect of India emerging as a power on par with China. This was evident from its strong opposition to India's aspirations of becoming a permanent member of the UN Security Council and its reticence on the question of the Nuclear Suppliers' Group (NSG) relaxing restrictions on the sale of civilian nuclear technology to India, despite India's initiative for separating its civilian nuclear establishments from its military and placing the former under international safeguards. It seems to be opposed to any unilateral concessions to India until such time when such concessions could be made applicable to Pakistan too. Despite these factors, the trust deficit between India and China has steadily declined. India has been noting with not-openly-articulated concern the steady modernization of the Chinese Armed Forces and the growing Chinese military and economic linkages with the countries of South Asia, but it has not allowed this to come in the way of the steady improvement in the bilateral relations. At the same time, one has also noted the moderating role played by China during the military conflict in 1999 between India and Pakistan following Pakistani military intrusions in the Kargil sector of India's Jammu and Kashmir.

The leaderships of India and China have shown great political maturity in not allowing the continuing differences over the border come in the way of economic and other linkages. Bilateral trade has boomed during the last 10 years—increasing from a total of about US $ two billion to 13 billion. However, it needs to be underlined that this boom has been considerably due to the requirements of raw materials for the rapidly expanding Chinese industries——particularly its steel industry.

Globalization and the consequent networking and interactions between the policy-makers and the business classes of the two countries have contributed to a remarkable resurgence of interest in each other and to a dilution of the mutual threat perceptions. Nobody in India, any longer, talks —at least openly—of China as a threat. In the past, China was viewed mainly as a worrisome power. Now its image is more positive. The remarkable change for the better in Indian threat perceptions of China is evident from the fact that the Indian intelligence and security establishment no longer opposes, as strongly as it used to do in the past, the presence of Chinese companies even in cities such as Bangalore, India's Silicon Valley, where many of India's sensitive defence and other strategic establishments are located.

The steady forward movement of India and China towards a common shared future of prosperity and mutual confidence can be endangered if the leaderships of the two countries do not skilfully manage the misgivings in China over the implications of the growing strategic partnership between the US and India to its aspired pre-eminence in Asia and the world and the likely tensions in Tibet, when the Dalai Lama ceases to be no more and the Chinese attempt to have their say, as they are bound to, in the selection of his successor. The continuously developing military, nuclear and other strategic linkages between China and Pakistan would remain a source of worry to Indian policy-makers and could stand in the way of the bilateral relations developing to their fullest potential.

THE PAKISTAN FACTOR

A reference has already been made to the Pakistan factor while discussing India-Pakistan relations. Two other aspects, which have not been touched upon earlier, need to be highlighted. The first relates to Pakistan's use of terrorism as a covert weapon to achieve its strategic objective of forcing a change in the status quo in Jammu and Kashmir. The second relates to its long-nourished objective of acquiring a strategic depth vis-a vis India by bringing Afghanistan under its control and by establishing military and strategic linkages with Iran.

It was these objectives, which led Pakistan to set up a clandestine infrastructure not only in its territory, but also in Afghan territory for training and arming terrorists for use against India. It was from this infrastructure that Al Qaeda, the Taliban and the various terrorist organizations, which are members of the International Islamic Front (IIF) of bin Laden came. This infrastructure continues to function undisturbed creating national security problems not only for India and Afghanistan, but also for other countries.

Pakistan's strategic relationship with Iran, the foundations for which were laid by the late Zulfiquar Ali Bhutto and the Shah of Iran, led to the flow of funds from Iran for Pakistan's military nuclear programme to produce what was described as the world's first Islamic atomic bomb. The recent enquiries by the International Atomic Energy Agency (IAEA) of Vienna into Iran's clandestine nuclear programme have brought out the covert role of Dr. A. Q. Khan, the so-called father of Pakistan's Islamic bomb, in assisting Iran to become the world's second Islamic military nuclear power.

Will the so-called Islamic bomb developed by Pakistan with funds not only from Iran, but also from Saudi Arabia and Libya and any similar bomb developed by Iran with Pakistani complicity fall into the hands of Al Qaeda, the IIF and organizations such as the Lashkar-e-Toiba (LET) and become the world's first jihadi atomic bomb? It is fears caused by the spectre of a jihadi bomb in the hands of the terrorists that should explain India's vote in the IAEA in favour of a continued role by the Agency to pre-empt this danger.

Afghanistan, a pre-2001 failed State, is yet to start benefiting from the fruits of globalization. India's efforts to develop trade links with Afghanistan and bring it into the global economic mainstream continue to be thwarted by Pakistan's refusal to grant Indian businessmen transit rights to Afghanistan through Pakistani territory.

The Non-state Actors

The US-orchestrated covert war against the Soviet troops in Afghanistan in the 1980s turned the region into a play ground for non-State actors of various hues, persuasions and motives— — — jihadi and sectarian terrorists, trans-national crime mafia groups, narcotics producers and smugglers and money-laundering gangs. These non-State actors turned Afghanistan into a failed State and almost caused the collapse of the Pakistani economy before 2001.

The anti-communist jihadi terrorism of the 1980s gave place to the anti-modernisation terrorism of the 1990s personified by the Taliban, which, in turn, has given way to the revanchist terrorism of the present decade personified by Al Qaeda and the International Islamic Front (IIF). The recently in a keynote addresss to an international conference on terrorism organized the Intelligence Summit of Washington DC from February 18 to 20, 2006, Al Qaeda and the IIF are revanchist in character, medieval in their objectives and frighteningly modern in their methods of operation.

Even more than four years after the so-called war on international terrorism was launched on October 7, 2001, the international community is not yet able to get the better of a determined, well-motivated and elusive enemy. Two of the four epicenters of international jihadi terrorism are located in this area. The first is in the Waziristan area of Pakistan, from where Al Qaeda, the Taliban, the Islamic Movement of Uzbekistan (IMU), the Jundullah (Army of Allah) and the other components of the IIF are making a determined bid to stage a come-back in Afghanistan and Osama bin Laden is planning another 9/11 in US territory. This is also the epicenter from which the continuing use of terrorism against India is fuelled.

The second epicenter is located in Bangladesh, which has become an alternate command and control for jihadi terrorists from the Harkat-ul-Jihad-al-Islami (HUJI) and the LET operating in Indian territory. The epicenter in Bangladesh has also serious implications for the future security and stability of Myanmar and Southern Thailand.

Narcotics production in Afghanistan has again increased significantly and the resulting cash flow has nullified any benefits to the war on terrorism from the campaign against terrorism funding mounted after 9/11 under the UN Security Council Resolution No.1373. There is no trust deficit coming in the way of networking and co-operation among the non-State actors. As a result, the non-State actors have benefited more than the State actors of the region from the fruits of networking, freer flow of human beings, the communications revolution and the innovations in science and technology. Al Qaeda and the IIF are making better use of the Internet than the State actors.

Globalization has given rise to two parallel trends towards a radicalization of sections of the youth of South Asia. The first trend is a radicalization of sections of the youth of all communities due to continuing economic and social disparities despite the growing economic prosperity. Uneven distribution of the newly-created wealth and opportunities is a major cause of this trend. There are more haves than in the past, but the number of have-nots is still very high and is more than the total population of many countries of the world. For example, in India, about 260 million people are still below the poverty line.

There has been an aggravation of the divide between the privileged and the under-privileged and of the feelings of relative deprivation among different layers of the society. The result: Ideology, which, according to conventional wisdom, should have become increasingly irrelevant in pragmatism-driven economies, has assumed a new relevance. One sees this in the resurgence and aggravation of ideological terrorism. Example—the Maoists of India and Nepal. The second trend is the growing radicalization of sections of the Muslim youth, more due to religious than economic reasons. Anger against the non-Muslims, who are projected as the enemies of Islam for allegedly committing various wrongs against the Muslims, has given rise to a new kind of terrorism personified by Al Qaeda and the International Islamic Front (IIF). Innovations in science and technology, knowledge of Information Technology and modern means of communication are sought to be used by the revanchist terrorist elements not as forces of creation, but of destruction, not to integrate, but to disintegrate.

The tensions caused by the old divide between the developed and the developing or the under-developed have been reduced, but the attempts by these elements to create a new divide between Islam and the rest have brought in new threats to peace, security and prosperity.

As a result of these trends, dealing with threats to internal security has become an over-riding preoccupation of the states of the region, consuming a considerable proportion of their resources, time and attention. Linkages between sources of internal and external threats to security are stronger in the South Asian region than in any other region of Asia. Exploitation of internal tensions by external actors—State as well as non-State—for strategic reasons has come in the way of the region reaping the full benefits of the process of integration and globalization.

The result: Greater progress towards integration with the societies and economies of countries outside the region than of countries in the region. Example: the countries of the region moving closer to those of Southeast Asia, bilaterally as well as multilaterally, than to each other.

There has been a positive change in the relations of the countries of the region with countries outside the region such as the US,

China, Japan etc., but there has been little change in their relations with each other. Countries outside the region such as the USA, China and Japan are viewed with decreasing suspicion and increasing comfort. There is consequently a greater comfort level in the relations of the countries of this region with such powers outside the region.

However, there are incipient positive trends, which are having an impact on inter as well as intra-regional relationships, despite continuing inter-regional sources of discord. Example: Energy requirements driving India and Pakistan on the one side and India and China on the other towards solutions based on co-operation rather than competition in their energy quest.

The likelihood of threats to regional and global trade has been driving the countries of Asia towards a search for co-operative counter-terrorism and maritime security initiatives and mechanisms. However, the persistence of traditional distrustful mindsets in the South Asian region makes the search for such co-operative security mechanisms fractional rather than well-integrated. Example: Pakistan's attempts to keep India out of the co-operative mechanisms in the Gulf area despite India's support for the association of Pakistan with the ASEAN Regional Forum.

The trust deficit, which is a defining characteristic of the threat perceptions in the South Asian region, will continue to make the progress towards inter-regional integration slow and halting in the short and medium terms, but it is bound to acquire the needed momentum as the compulsions of economics acquire predominance over traditional sources of mistrust and discord.

7

Security Challenges in South Asia

South Asia is often described — quite rightly — as the most dangerous place on earth. South Asia urgently needs to overcome the bitter legacies of the past in order to create an enabling environment for peace and security, which is critical to unleash the synergies necessary for economic progress.

The twin phenomena of strategic peril and economic promise pose a daunting challenge, one that must be met for South Asia to be in sync with the great global transformation of our times. There can be little doubt about the economic and trade benefits that would accrue to the global economy from a peaceful and stable South Asia, as indeed a promising peace dividend for the people of the region.

Since the nuclear tests by India and then Pakistan in May1998, the focus on this region has been almost exclusively on the nuclear dimension of the confrontation between the two states. In reality, security in South Asia is challenged by an interplay of several factors operating at three different levels: domestic; regional or bilateral; and global.

There is, in fact, a symbiotic relationship between these factors and regional security.

INTERNAL FACTORS

Over half a century after independence, the nations of South Asia remain mired in a vicious cycle of poverty, deprivation, and underdevelopment. South Asian countries are at the very bottom of the world league in social and human development indicators. Very few have access to clean drinking water, and fewer have a permanent roof over their heads. Education is available only to the most fortunate. Life in these conditions is nasty, brutish, and short.

Economic deprivation, illiteracy, and unemployment provide a fertile ground for intolerance and extremism, which in turn promotes conflict and violence within our societies. Our region has been racked by intolerance of virtually every kind — ethnic, communal, religious, and sectarian. Consequently, tensions abound within and between our peoples and frequently reinforce tensions between our countries. As a result, the inherited legacy of conflict persists, constraining each government's ability to fulfil the social contract with its people.

Currently negotiating one of the most critical transitions in its history. Pakistan sees national security — and by extension regional economic security — in the broader sense, encompassing economic and social security. Pakistan regards this broader perspective to be an indispensable component of peace and stability within and outside its borders.

REGIONAL FACTORS

At the regional level, the pursuit of domination by one state over its neighbours is a recipe for insecurity and instability. The prevailing asymmetry — with regard to both strategic objectives and the relationship between military forces — between the largest country in South Asia, India, and its smaller neighbours is a built-in factor for instability and has been exacerbated by India's desire to dominate. Certainly attempts at domination cannot but be destabilizing and thus highly dangerous.

The pursuit of domination underscores the second asymmetry in South Asia, that between the military force levels of India, which maintains the fourth largest military in the world, and its neighbours. Its nuclear explosions in May 1998 were primarily status-driven. In response, Pakistan has been forced to maintain a credible nuclear deterrent of its own to ensure its security against India's nuclear and conventional capabilities.

If the past is any guide, the future is fraught with risk. Within a year of its nuclear explosions, India unveiled an ambitious nuclear doctrine. The fact that it also increased its massive defence budget by 28 percent — an increase larger than Pakistan's entire defence budget — to fuel its indigenous strategic and conventional defence programmes as well as its foreign military acquisitions, demonstrates that New Delhi is already working to implement this strategic doctrine.

While ostensibly aimed at acquiring a minimum nuclear deterrent, the Indian nuclear doctrine advocates a triad of land, air, and sea-based delivery systems. The large arsenal is justified on the basis of the need to maintain a second-strike capability, which in turn is justified by India's so-called no-first use declaration. The international community should share Pakistan's deep concern about India's nuclear plans.

An ambitious Indian nuclear programme, coupled with augmentation and an upgrade of its conventional capability, evokes concern and negative reactions throughout the region. While Indian efforts proceed apace, Pakistan's modest efforts to replace and modernize its exhausted conventional weapons inventory have been seriously affected by US sanctions, as the United States has historically been the traditional source of Pakistan's arms supply. In view of this growing asymmetry, Pakistan is increasingly forced to rely on its strategic capabilities.

Meanwhile, the Kashmir dispute remains a flash-point of tension between the world's newest nuclear powers. Pakistani and Indian troops continue to confront each other on the Line of Control (LoC) in Kashmir and along the Siachen glacier. Repression in occupied Kashmir continues to provoke violence and retribution. Both sides recognize the dangers of nuclear confrontation arising from the Kashmir dispute, but the risks of escalation through accident or miscalculation cannot be discounted.

The Kargil crisis of 1999 was but the latest example of escalatory exchange along the LoC, which began with the Indian occupation of the Siachen glacier in the mid-1980s and has continued with New Delhi's incursions into border areas such as Qamar, Chorbat-la, and the Neelam Valley. The Kargil crisis followed nuclear saber-rattling over Kashmir by senior Indian leaders who, immediately after the nuclear tests, demanded that Pakistan accept "new realities" in Kashmir. One lesson of Kargil is that nuclear deterrence ultimately compelled restraint, de-escalation, and disengagement on both sides.

However, another lesson is that there is little reason to be sanguine about the future in a nuclearized environment characterized not by a cold peace, but by a "hot front" in South Asia's long running cold war. This danger is dramatized by persistent Indian pronouncements about a limited conventional war – a possibility voiced by none other than India's army chief. Such statements and the current Indian military buildup are dangerous brinkmanship: how a spiral of escalation could be controlled if hostilities erupt remains an unanswered question.

This uncertainty underscores the urgency of finding a peaceful resolution to the Kashmir conflict, where no military solution is possible. The Indian approach to a dialogue with Pakistan on Kashmir has been aimed at formalizing the status quo, instead of ascertaining the wishes of the Kashmiri people. The status quo is the problem; therefore, it cannot be the solution. Moreover, any solution based on the status quo will not be durable, as it must be acceptable to the Kashmiri people. The Kashmiri struggle cannot be designated as a terrorist movement, as India has sought to portray it. On the contrary, the Kashmiris are engaged in a legitimate freedom struggle to exercise the right of self-determination promised to them by resolutions of the UN Security Council. They have the right to defend themselves against Indian repression.

INTERNATIONAL FACTORS

The state of play in South Asia, described above, has an obvious bearing on the international environment, including security in adjacent regions. The reverse also holds true. The pursuit of a lopsided approach in South Asia by the world's primary power, the United States, could undermine security and compound regional tension. For instance, the suggestion made by some to build up India as a counterweight to China could prove to be destabilizing and counterproductive for the region, and indeed for US interests globally. Instead of pursuing an outdated balance of power approach, American interests would be better served by a partnership with South Asia as a whole.

A new challenge is posed by decisions being made in Washington about the development and deployment of ballistic missile defence (BMD) and theatre missile defence (TMD) systems. A ricochet effect on South Asia will become apparent if such systems spark a renewed nuclear and missile race between the major powers. It would also justify and perhaps encourage India's ambition to acquire a large nuclear and missile arsenal in accordance with its nuclear doctrine. This, in turn, would evoke a response by Pakistan. Such developments at the international level could, therefore, further complicate and exacerbate the security environment in South Asia, while undermining any effort to contain the nuclear arms race and build a regional restraint regime.

Another dynamic affecting South Asian security is determined by the interaction of the regional states with external powers or adjacent regions. In this regard, three factors are important:

- Afghanistan. Stabilizing Afghanistan should be seen to be in the long-term economic and strategic interest of both Pakistan and India, as it provides the best route for access to Central Asia's energy, along with other resources and markets for exports.
- Persian Gulf/Middle East region. Regional stability in South Asia and the success of modernist and moderate forces in Pakistan is of vital importance for the adjacent Gulf/Middle East region, which is once again facing a period of turbulence and violence.
- Sino-Indian relations. China and India are seeking to normalize relations, but any setback in this process could greatly destabilize the security environment in South Asia and indirectly accelerate the nuclear and conventional arms race between India and Pakistan.

A NEW SECURITY ARCHITECTURE FOR SOUTH ASIA

Pakistan has a vision of a security architecture for South Asia that seeks to address the sources of insecurity at all three interdependent levels that have been identified above. This proposed security architecture consists of four main pillars:

1. nuclear and missile restraint by Pakistan and India;
2. an agreement for conventional arms control in South Asia;
3. peaceful resolution of all outstanding disputes and sources of tension, especially Kashmir; and
4. economic and social revival of South Asia through regional cooperation and global integration, in order to address problems of poverty and deprivation.

A STRATEGIC RESTRAINT REGIME

While the acquisition of nuclear capabilities by Pakistan and India cannot be reversed, it is imperative to ensure stable and credible deterrence at the lowest possible level. Accordingly, in October 1998, Pakistan proposed to India the development of a strategic restraint regime. Even though New Delhi rejected this proposal, Pakistan remains committed to it as the best guarantor of security in South Asia. Pakistan's proposal for a strategic restraint regime in South Asia is not only relevant to, but also essential for, nuclear stability in the region. Indeed, India and Pakistan do not need massive nuclear arsenals, since even "existential deterrence" effectively worked between the two countries before May 1998. Both states are publicly committed to keep their respective nuclear deterrents at the minimum possible level. This commitment should be formalized in a strategic restraint regime, the purpose of which would be three fold:

- to prevent the use of nuclear weapons by accident, miscalculation, or design;
- to ensure the lowest possible level — both qualitative and quantitative — of nuclear weapon arsenals and delivery systems; and
- to ensure that the capabilities for nuclear weapons and their delivery systems do not spread from India or Pakistan to other states.

To promote these objectives, Pakistan believes that the following five measures, if pursued by both India and Pakistan, would be worthwhile:

- A commitment to observe a moratorium on nuclear testing. India is known to be considering the development and construction of thermonuclear weapons, in order to implement its ambitious nuclear doctrine. The promise to observe a moratorium on further nuclear testing or to sign a regional test ban treaty, as proposed by Pakistan in 1987, would remove apprehensions surrounding India's nuclear programme. This would also assuage international concerns over Pakistan's and India's nuclear programmes and help them move forward on the question of adherence to the Comprehensive Test Ban Treaty (CTBT).
- Implementation of a non-weaponization/non-deployment agreement. Before May 1998, "existential deterrence" was maintained between the two countries; therefore, weaponization and deployment of nuclear weapons seems unnecessary. Additionally, the deployment of nuclear weapons would require elaborate command and control structures to prevent unauthorized or accidental use. At this stage, both India and Pakistan lack the technological capabilities and experience to put in place such structures. Thus, by undertaking not to weaponize or deploy nuclear weapons, the two countries will ensure that they do not increase the danger of nuclear use and that they avoid the heavy expenditures involved in nuclear weapons deployment, including the development of elaborate command and control structures.
- A moratorium on operational deployment of nuclear capable missiles. Even if missiles are not overtly equipped with nuclear warheads, the perceived threat of a preemptive strike can be best addressed by an agreement prohibiting missile deployment. Such an agreement would entail the following: (1) a declaration of "non-deployment" of nuclear-capable missiles; (2) a declaration of the numbers and operating status of aircraft capable of delivering nuclear weapons; and (3) possible verification measures.
- A moratorium on the development, deployment, and acquisition of ballistic missile defence (BMD) systems. As

has been argued in the context of US plans for BMD and TMD, the acquisition and deployment of BMD in South Asia is also likely to enhance fears that an offensive preemptive strike, nuclear or conventional, could be undertaken behind the "shield" of BMD. One consequence of such a development would be an increase in the incentive to multiply the numbers of offensive missiles, and also to enhance operational readiness to avoid the destruction of these assets in a preemptive strike. Thus, the acquisition or deployment of BMD systems such as the S-300 and S-400 — reportedly being procured by India from the Russian Federation — would be entirely incompatible with the concept of minimum nuclear deterrence, which both India and Pakistan have declared to be their nuclear posture. Moreover, foregoing the acquisition, development, or deployment of BMD could avoid costly expenditures that both sides would incur in acquiring the systems and/or by enlarging offensive nuclear capabilities.

- Implementation of confidence-building and risk-reduction measures. These measures could build upon the steps envisaged in the Memorandum of Understanding (MoU) signed in Lahore, Pakistan, in February 1999. As a first step, Pakistan and India could finalize an agreement to provide prior and adequate notification of missile flight tests. Some degree of information sharing (transparency) on aspects of the deployment status of strategic assets may also enhance mutual confidence. However, in case India moves ahead with deployment, Pakistan will be obliged to follow suit. In that event, risk reduction mechanisms will be required to prevent unauthorized or accidental use of nuclear weapons. Such measures could involve setting up a nuclear command authority, nuclear risk reduction centres, and a host of other steps, some of which were envisaged in the Lahore MoU.

These five specific measures to promote nuclear restraint offer more effective ways to prevent any possible use of nuclear weapons than a mere declaration of no first-use, which has only rhetorical or propagandist value and can be revoked anytime. Nuclear restraint agreements between India and Pakistan could be accompanied by other confidence-building measures (CBMs) as well. Bilateral or technical arrangements could be devised to ensure the credibility and confirmation of mutual nuclear restraint measures, including agreed monitoring mechanisms. Such arrangements could also include enhancing the effectiveness of the command and control systems in each state as well as establishing round-the-clock communications between designated authorities, with a view to crisis stability and management.

CONVENTIONAL ARMS CONTROL IN SOUTH ASIA

Conventional arms control is also essential to preserving the stability of nuclear deterrence in South Asia and reducing wasteful defence expenditures. Pakistan has made specific proposals to promote these objectives, including: (1) a mutually agreed ratio of forces between India and Pakistan; (2) measures to increase mutual confidence; and (3) measures to eliminate the threat of surprise or preemptive strikes by either country. These proposals seek to promote regional stability and should be considered by India and Pakistan in the context of bilateral talks or in multilateral mechanisms created to explore a new security framework for South Asia.

It is, however, unfortunate that India, Instead of responding to the needs of stability in nuclear South Asia, is further compounding the security environment in the region. During the last three years, India has increased its defence budget by more than 55 percent, spending on an average of $15 billion per year: It maintains the fourth largest army in the world and continues to purchase all types of conventional weaponry, ranging from main battle tanks to fighter aircraft procured from different foreign sources, particularly the Russian Federation. India seeks to justify its huge defence outlays by invoking its long borders; but this argument is misleading. The fact is that virtually all of India's military assets are deployed against Pakistan.

Pakistan's conventional capabilities, on the other hand have seriously eroded owing to unjustified and discriminatory sanctions.

One ineluctable consequence of this growing conventional imbalance is Pakistan's increasing reliance on non-conventional means. This "asymmetric deterrence" raises the need for Pakistan to increase numbers of missiles and enhance operational readiness. Such a hair-trigger environment, in turn, diminishes the possibilities for the resolution of Kashmir and other disputes, thus perpetually locking the two states in a conflictual relationship. Consequently, each will be compelled to continue incurring huge defence expenditures from meagre resources, eroding the economic goals of Pakistan and perhaps those of India as well. Given India's limited oil and gas resources, and the fact that it is facing a severe shortage of energy to power its economy, the possibilities of an Indian threat to neighbouring regions, especially the oil-rich Persian Gulf, will grow accordingly.

Peaceful Resolution of Outstanding Disputes

The third pillar of the proposed security architecture is the peaceful resolution of outstanding disputes. To attain this objective, Pakistan's President, General Pervez Musharraf, proposed a "No War Pact" at the UN Millennium Summit in October 2000 and offered to engage in dialogue with India "any time, at any level and any place." Pakistan is committed to an eight point agenda for dialogue with India, aimed at addressing all outstanding issues between the two countries.

Unless India and Pakistan resume a genuine dialogue, it is simply not feasible to pick up from where the two left off in Lahore. From Pakistan's perspective, the involvement of a third party — be it the United Nations or the United States — would be preferable, with a view to achieving concrete results. Nevertheless, Pakistan is prepared to approach dialogue with an open mind. It is important, however, that all bilateral arrangements related to security be adequately verifiable. In this regard, it is relevant to recall that, while both India and Pakistan committed not to produce chemical weapons under a joint declaration in August 1992, India continued to manufacture chemical weapons in violation of this declaration. This was disclosed only in early 1997, months after India's ratification of the Chemical Weapons Convention (CWC) in September 1996. The two countries should aim to immediately resume foreign secretary-level talks, following which a bilateral standing committee of experts could be set up to explore further steps and measures towards stabilizing the nuclear environment in South Asia.

Economic Progress as a Means to Achieve Peace

The realization of durable peace will not be possible without simultaneous and sustained economic progress. The persistence of economic and social deprivation serves only to intensify the forces of chauvinism, religious extremism, and ethnic particularism in South Asia. It is important that Pakistan and India create an environment that facilitates mutually beneficial economic and trade relations. Only through shared economic and social development will we be able to address the domestic sources of tension and instability in our countries, and at the same time address our long-standing differences.

Pakistan has repeatedly called for cooperation among the countries of South Asia on matters relating to economic development and social progress, particularly through the South Asian Association for Regional Cooperation (SAARC). Economic expansion and liberalization of our economies can be mutually beneficial, especially if SAARC, becomes a genuinely free trading area, and the South Asian economies are linked to those of Central and West Asia.

The possibilities for economic growth and prosperity in South Asia can be enhanced by innovative measures of support from the international community. These could include:

- Effective poverty reduction strategies for South Asian countries, sponsored and supported by the International Monetary Fund (IMF), World Bank and the OECD countries.
- Trade and transit arrangements, to be concluded and implemented without delay, linking Central and South Asia by a five dimensional corridor (oil, gas, electricity, roads, and railways) through Afghanistan and Pakistan. This process should be pursued simultaneously with an Afghan nation-building and economic reconstruction process; and

- The conclusion of preferential trading arrangements between SAARC and the European Union, the North American Free Trade Association, and Japan. Such arrangements would neutralize the disadvantages South Asian countries currently suffer due to their exclusion from all present regional trading arrangements. A preferential trading relationship between China and SAARC could be pursued especially now that the latter has joined the World Trade Organization.

A Role for the United States

In Pakistan's view, US relations with our region should not be characterized by a zero-sum outlook. At the same time, these relations ought not to be pursued or built with one state at the expense of another. The improvement in relations between Washington and New Delhi can be instrumental in encouraging responsible Indian behaviour and in constructing an effective security architecture in the region.

The United States can assist the region by broadening and balancing the scope of its economic engagement with all South Asian countries, in order to promote overall economic growth and prosperity in the entire region. With regard to Pakistan, such engagement can ensure the success of its ongoing critical efforts for economic revival and national reconstruction. This, in turn, would enhance Islamabad's ability to construct a viable and durable security architecture to promote future security in South Asia as well as to overcome its domestic difficulties.

The Bush administration should take a longer term strategic view of American interests in South Asia and its adjacent regions. Both US national security and economic and trade interests are dependent primarily on promoting and preserving structures of peace and stability at the global and regional levels. The Bush administration can and should play an active role in promoting durable peace and stability in the world's major crisis areas, including South Asia. In doing so, it could move the past approach of crisis management to effective and timely preventive diplomacy. A new US policy paradigm towards Pakistan should be evolved within the framework of broad US objectives and priorities, not only in South Asia but also Central Asia and the Persian Gulf — three regions in which Pakistan can play an influential role given its geopolitical location.

The nub of the matter is that peace and stability in South Asia will remain elusive unless addressed comprehensively. India and Pakistan must develop some sort of strategic restraint regime, eliminate the conventional imbalance, and resolve the core conflict over Kashmir. Economic and trade innovations will work to solidify progress in these areas.

ARMED CLASH IN THE SOUTH CHINA SEA

The risk of conflict in the South China Sea is significant. China, Taiwan, Vietnam, Malaysia, Brunei, and the Philippines have competing territorial and jurisdictional claims, particularly over rights to exploit the region's possibly extensive reserves of oil and gas. Freedom of navigation in the region is also a contentious issue, especially between the United States and China over the right of U.S. military vessels to operate in China's two-hundred-mile exclusive economic zone (EEZ). These tensions are shaping—and being shaped by—rising apprehensions about the growth of China's military power and its regional intentions. China has embarked on a substantial modernization of its maritime paramilitary forces as well as naval capabilities to enforce its sovereignty and jurisdiction claims by force if necessary. At the same time, it is developing capabilities that would put U.S. forces in the region at risk in a conflict, thus potentially denying access to the U.S. Navy in the western Pacific.

Given the growing importance of the U.S.-China relationship, and the Asia-Pacific region more generally, to the global economy, the United States has a major interest in preventing any one of the various disputes in the South China Sea from escalating militarily.

THE CONTINGENCIES

Of the many conceivable contingencies involving an armed clash in the South China Sea, three especially threaten U.S. interests and could potentially prompt the United States to use force.

The most likely and dangerous contingency is a clash stemming from U.S. military operations within China's EEZ that provokes an armed Chinese response. The United States holds that nothing in the United Nations Convention on the Law of the Sea (UNCLOS) or state practice negates the right of military forces of all nations to conduct military activities in EEZs without coastal state notice or consent. China insists that reconnaissance activities undertaken without prior notification and without permission of the coastal state violate Chinese domestic law and international law. China routinely intercepts U.S. reconnaissance flights conducted in its EEZ and periodically does so in aggressive ways that increase the risk of an accident similar to the April 2001 collision of a U.S. EP-3 reconnaissance plane and a Chinese F-8 fighter jet near Hainan Island. A comparable maritime incident could be triggered by Chinese vessels harassing a U.S. Navy surveillance ship operating in its EEZ, such as occurred in the 2009 incidents involving the USNS *Impeccable* and the USNS *Victorious*. The large growth of Chinese submarines has also increased the danger of an incident, such as when a Chinese submarine collided with a U.S. destroyer's towed sonar array in June 2009. Since neither U.S. reconnaissance aircraft nor ocean surveillance vessels are armed, the United States might respond to dangerous behavior by Chinese planes or ships by dispatching armed escorts. A miscalculation or misunderstanding could then result in a deadly exchange of fire, leading to further military escalation and precipitating a major political crisis. Rising U.S.-China mistrust and intensifying bilateral strategic competition would likely make managing such a crisis more difficult.

A second contingency involves conflict between China and the Philippines over natural gas deposits, especially in the disputed area of Reed Bank, located eighty nautical miles from Palawan. Oil survey ships operating in Reed Bank under contract have increasingly been harassed by Chinese vessels. Reportedly, the United Kingdom-based Forum Energy plans to start drilling for gas in Reed Bank this year, which could provoke an aggressive Chinese response. Forum Energy is only one of fifteen exploration contracts that Manila intends to offer over the next few years for offshore exploration near Palawan Island. Reed Bank is a red line for the Philippines, so this contingency could quickly escalate to violence if China intervened to halt the drilling.

The United States could be drawn into a China-Philippines conflict because of its 1951 Mutual Defense Treaty with the Philippines. The treaty states, "Each Party recognizes that an armed attack in the Pacific Area on either of the Parties would be dangerous to its own peace and safety and declares that it would act to meet the common dangers in accordance with its constitutional processes." American officials insist that Washington does not take sides in the territorial dispute in the South China Sea and refuse to comment on how the United States might respond to Chinese aggression in contested waters. Nevertheless, an apparent gap exists between American views of U.S. obligations and Manila's expectations. In mid-June 2011, a Filipino presidential spokesperson stated that in the event of armed conflict with China, Manila expected the United States would come to its aid. Statements by senior U.S. officials may have inadvertently led Manila to conclude that the United States would provide military assistance if China attacked Filipino forces in the disputed Spratly Islands.

With improving political and military ties between Manila and Washington, including a pending agreement to expand U.S. access to Filipino ports and airfields to refuel and service its warships and planes, the United States would have a great deal at stake in a China-Philippines contingency. Failure to respond would not only set back U.S. relations with the Philippines but would also potentially undermine U.S. credibility in the region with its allies and partners more broadly. A U.S. decision to dispatch naval ships to the area, however, would risk a U.S.-China naval confrontation.

Disputes between China and Vietnam over seismic surveys or drilling for oil and gas could also trigger an armed clash for a third contingency. China has harassed PetroVietnam oil survey ships in the past that were searching for oil and gas deposits in Vietnam's EEZ. In 2011, Hanoi accused China of deliberately severing the cables of an oil and gas survey vessel in two separate instances. Although the Vietnamese did not respond with force, they did not back down and Hanoi pledged to continue its efforts to exploit new fields despite warnings from Beijing. Budding U.S.-Vietnam relations could embolden Hanoi to be more confrontational with China on the South China Sea issue.

The United States could be drawn into a conflict between China and Vietnam, though that is less likely than a clash between China and the Philippines. In a scenario of Chinese provocation, the United States might opt to dispatch naval vessels to the area to signal its interest in regional peace and stability. Vietnam, and possibly other nations, could also request U.S. assistance in such circumstances. Should the United States become involved, subsequent actions by China or a miscalculation among the forces present could result in exchange of fire. In another possible scenario, an attack by China on vessels or rigs operated by an American company exploring or drilling for hydrocarbons could quickly involve the United States, especially if American lives were endangered or lost. ExxonMobil has plans to conduct exploratory drilling off Vietnam, making this an existential danger. In the short term, however, the likelihood of this third contingency occurring is relatively low given the recent thaw in Sino-Vietnamese relations. In October 2011, China and Vietnam signed an agreement outlining principles for resolving maritime issues. The effectiveness of this agreement remains to be seen, but for now tensions appear to be defused.

WARNING INDICATORS

Strategic warning signals that indicate heightened risk of conflict include political decisions and statements by senior officials, official and unofficial media reports, and logistical changes and equipment modifications. In the contingencies described above, strategic warning indicators could include heightened rhetoric from all or some disputants regarding their territorial and strategic interests. For example, China may explicitly refer to the South China Sea as a core interest; in 2010 Beijing hinted this was the case but subsequently backed away from the assertion. Beijing might also warn that it cannot "stand idly by" as countries nibble away at Chinese territory, a formulation that in the past has often signaled willingness to use force. Commentaries and editorials in authoritative media outlets expressing China's bottom line and issuing ultimatums could also be a warning indicator. Tough language could also be used by senior People's Liberation Army (PLA) officers in meetings with their American counterparts. An increase in nationalistic rhetoric in nonauthoritative media and in Chinese blogs, even if not representing official Chinese policy, would nevertheless signal pressure on the Chinese leadership to defend Chinese interests. Similar warning indicators should be tracked in Vietnam and the Philippines that might signal a hardening of those countries' positions.

Tactical warning signals that indicate heightened risk of a potential clash in a specific time and place include commercial notices and preparations, diplomatic and/or military statements warning another claimant to cease provocative activities or suffer the consequences, military exercises designed to intimidate another claimant, and ship movements to disputed areas. As for an impending incident regarding U.S. surveillance activities, statements and unusual preparations by the PLA might suggest a greater willingness to employ more aggressive means to intercept U.S. ships and aircraft.

IMPLICATIONS FOR U.S. INTERESTS

The United States has significant political, security, and economic interests at stake if one of the contingencies should occur.

- *Global rules and norms.* The United States has important interests in the peaceful resolution of South China Sea disputes according to international law. With the exception of China, all the claimants of the South China Sea have attempted to justify their claims based on their coastlines and the provisions of UNCLOS. China, however, relies on a mix of historic rights and legal claims, while remaining deliberately ambiguous about the meaning of the "nine-dashed line" around the sea that is drawn on Chinese maps. Failure to uphold international law and norms could harm U.S. interests elsewhere in the region and beyond. Ensuring freedom of navigation is another critical interest of the United States and other regional states. Although China claims that it supports freedom of navigation, its insistence that foreign militaries seek advance permission to sail in its two-hundred-mile EEZ casts doubt on its stance. China's development of capabilities to deny American naval access to those waters in a conflict provides evidence of possible Chinese intentions to block freedom of navigation in specific contingencies.

- *Alliance security and regional stability.* U.S. allies and friends around the South China Sea look to the United States to maintain free trade, safe and secure sea lines of communication (SLOCs), and overall peace and stability in the region. Claimants and nonclaimants to land features and maritime waters in the South China Sea view the U.S. military presence as necessary to allow decision-making free of intimidation. If nations in the South China Sea lose confidence in the United States to serve as the principal regional security guarantor, they could embark on costly and potentially destabilizing arms buildups to compensate or, alternatively, become more accommodating to the demands of a powerful China. Neither would be in the U.S. interest. Failure to reassure allies of U.S. commitments in the region could also undermine U.S. security guarantees in the broader Asia-Pacific region, especially with Japan and South Korea. At the same time, however, the United States must avoid getting drawn into the territorial dispute—and possibly into a conflict—by regional nations who seek U.S. backing to legitimize their claims.
- *Economic interests.* Each year, $5.3 trillion of trade passes through the South China Sea; U.S. trade accounts for $1.2 trillion of this total. Should a crisis occur, the diversion of cargo ships to other routes would harm regional economies as a result of an increase in insurance rates and longer transits. Conflict of any scale in the South China Sea would hamper the claimants from benefiting from the South China's Sea's proven and potential riches.
- *Cooperative relationship with China.* The stakes and implications of any U.S.-China incident are far greater than in other scenarios. The United States has an abiding interest in preserving stability in the U.S.-China relationship so that it can continue to secure Beijing's cooperation on an expanding list of regional and global issues and more

tightly integrate China into the prevailing international system.

PREVENTIVE OPTIONS

Efforts should continue to resolve the disputes over territorial sovereignty of the South China Sea's land features, rightful jurisdiction over the waters and seabed, and the legality of conducting military operations within a country's EEZ, but the likelihood of a breakthrough in any of these areas is slim in the near term. In the meantime, the United States should focus on lowering the risk of potential armed clashes arising from either miscalculation or unintended escalation of a dispute. There are several preventive options available to policymakers—in the United States and other nations—to avert a crisis and conflict in the South China Sea. These options are not mutually exclusive.

Support U.S.-China Risk-reduction Measures

Operational safety measures and expanded naval cooperation between the United States and China can help to reduce the risk of an accident between ships and aircraft. The creation of the Military Maritime Consultative Agreement (MMCA) in 1988 was intended to establish "rules of the road" at sea similar to the U.S.-Soviet Incidents at Sea Agreement (INCSEA), but it has not been successful. Communication mechanisms can provide a means to defuse tensions in a crisis and prevent escalation. Political and military hotlines have been set up, though U.S. officials have low confidence that they would be utilized by their Chinese counterparts during a crisis. An additional hotline to manage maritime emergencies should be established at an operational level, along with a signed political agreement committing both sides to answer the phone in a crisis. Joint naval exercises to enhance the ability of the two sides to cooperate in counter-piracy, humanitarian assistance, and disaster relief operations could increase cooperation and help prevent a U.S.-China conflict.

Bolster Capabilities of Regional Actors

Steps could be taken to further enhance the capability of the Philippines military to defend its territorial and maritime claims and improve its indigenous domain awareness, which might deter China from taking aggressive action. Similarly, the United States could boost the maritime surveillance capabilities of Vietnam, enabling its military to more effectively pursue an anti-access and area-denial strategy. Such measures run the risk of emboldening the Philippines and Vietnam to more assertively challenge China and could raise those countries' expectations of U.S. assistance in a crisis.

Encourage Settlement of the Sovereignty Dispute

The United States could push for submission of territorial disputes to the International Court of Justice or the International Tribunal for the Law of the Sea for settlement, or encourage an outside organization or mediator to be called upon to resolve the dispute. However, the prospect for success in these cases is slim given China's likely opposition to such options. Other options exist to resolve the sovereignty dispute that would be difficult, but not impossible, to negotiate. One such proposal, originally made by Mark Valencia, Jon Van Dyke, and Noel Ludwig in *Sharing the Resources of the South China Sea,* would establish "regional sovereignty" over the islands in the South China Sea among the six claimants, allowing them to collectively manage the islands, territorial seas, and airspace. Another option put forward by Peter Dutton of the Naval War College would emulate the resolution of the dispute over Svalbard, an island located between Norway and Greenland. The Treaty of Spitsbergen, signed in 1920, awarded primary sovereignty over Svarlbard to Norway but assigned resource-related rights to all signatories. This solution avoided conflict over resources and enabled advancement of scientific research. Applying this model to the South China Sea would likely entail giving sovereignty to China while permitting other countries to benefit from the resources. In the near term, at least, such a solution is unlikely to be accepted by the other claimants.

Promote Regional Risk-reduction Measures

The Association of Southeast Asian Nations (ASEAN) and China agreed upon multilateral risk-reduction and confidence-building measures in the 2002 Declaration on the Conduct of Parties in the South China Sea (DOC), but have neither adhered to its provisions (for example, to resolve territorial and jurisdictional disputes without resorting to the threat or use of force) nor implemented its proposals to undertake cooperative trust-building activities. The resumption of negotiations between China and ASEAN after a hiatus of a decade holds out promise for reinvigorating cooperative activities under the DOC.

Multilaterally, existing mechanisms and procedures already exist to promote operational safety among regional navies; a new arrangement is unnecessary. The United States, China, and all ASEAN members with the exception of Laos and Burma are members of the Western Pacific Naval Symposium (WPNS). Founded in 1988, WPNS brings regional naval leaders together biennially to discuss maritime security. In 2000, it produced the Code for Unalerted Encounters at Sea (CUES), which includes safety measures and procedures and means to facilitate communication when ships and aircraft make contact. There are also other mechanisms available such as the International Maritime Organization's Regulations for Preventing Collisions at Sea (COLREGS) and the International Civil Aviation Organization's rules of the air. In addition, regional navies could cooperate in sea environment protection, scientific research at sea, search and rescue activities, and mitigation of damage caused by natural calamities.

The creation of new dialogue mechanisms may also be worth consideration. A South China Sea Coast Guard Forum, modeled after the North Pacific Coast Guard Forum, which cooperates on a multitude of maritime security and legal issues, could enhance cooperation through information sharing and knowledge of best practices. The creation of a South China Sea information-sharing center would also provide a platform to improve awareness and communication between relevant parties. The information-sharing center could also serve as an accountability mechanism if states are required to document any incidents and present them to the center.

Advocate Joint Development/Multilateral Economic Cooperation

Resource cooperation is another preventive option that is underutilized by claimants in the South China Sea. Joint development of petroleum resources, for example, could reduce tensions between China and Vietnam, and between China and the Philippines, on issues related to energy security and access to hydrocarbon resources. Such development could be modeled on one of the many joint development arrangements that exist in the South and East China seas. Parties could also cooperate on increasing the use of alternative energy sources in order to reduce reliance on hydrocarbons.

Shared concerns about declining fish stocks in the South China Sea suggest the utility of cooperation to promote conservation and sustainable development. Establishing a joint fisheries committee among claimants could prove useful. Fishing agreements between China and its neighbors are already in place that could be expanded into disputed areas to encourage greater cooperation.

Clearly Convey U.S. Commitments

The United States should avoid inadvertently encouraging the claimants to engage in confrontational behavior. For example, Secretary of State Hillary Clinton's reference in November 2011 to the South China Sea as the West Philippine Sea could have unintended consequences such as emboldening Manila to antagonize China rather than it seeking to peacefully settle their differences.

MITIGATING OPTIONS

If preventive options fail to avert a crisis from developing, policymakers have several options available to mitigate the potential negative effects.

Defusing a U.S.-China Incident

The history of crisis management in U.S.-China relations suggests that leaders in both countries go to great lengths to prevent a crisis from escalating to military conflict. Nevertheless, pre-crisis steps could be taken to limit the harmful consequences of a confrontation. Political agreements could be reached that would increase the possibility that communication mechanisms in place would be employed in a crisis. Steps should be taken to enhance operational safety at sea between U.S. and Chinese ships.

Confidence-building measures should also be implemented to build trust and promote cooperation.

Mitigating a Regional Crisis with China

Dispatching air and naval forces to the immediate vicinity of an armed clash to defend U.S. interests and deter further escalation should always be considered an option. Such actions, however, must be balanced against the possibility that they will produce the opposite effect, encouraging an even stronger response from China and causing further escalation of a confrontation. A less risky option would be to threaten nonmilitary consequences—diplomatic and economic sanctions—to force China to back off and deter further military action. But here again such measures may only inflame hostilities and escalate the crisis. It is also doubtful in any case whether such measures would be supported by many in the region given China's economic importance.

Several less provocative responses might contain a budding crisis while avoiding further escalation. One option for the United States would be to encourage a mediated dialogue between involved parties. However, while Southeast Asian states may welcome a neutral mediator, China would probably oppose it. Thus, such an effort would likely fail.

Direct communication between military officials can be effective in de-escalating a crisis. States involved should establish communication mechanisms, include provisions for both scheduled and short-notice emergency meetings, and mandate consultation during a crisis. Emergency meetings would focus on addressing the specific provocative action that brought about the crisis. Operational hotlines, including phone lines and radio frequencies with clear protocols and points of contact, should also be set up. To be effective, hotlines should be set up and used prior to a crisis, though even then there is no guarantee that they will be used by both sides if a crisis erupts. China and Vietnam have already agreed to establish a hotline; this could be a model for other states in the region and China. The goal would not be to resolve underlying issues, but to contain tensions in the event of a minor skirmish and prevent escalation.

RECOMMENDATIONS

Against the background of rebalancing U.S. assets and attention toward the Asia-Pacific region, the United States should takes steps to prevent a conflict in the South China Sea and to defuse a crisis should one take place. Although the possibility of a major military conflict is low, the potential for a violent clash in the South China Sea in the near future is high, given past behavior of states in the region and the growing stakes. Therefore, both U.S. and regional policymakers should seek to create mechanisms to build trust, prevent conflict, and avoid escalation.

First, the United States should ratify UNCLOS; though it voluntarily adheres to its principles and the Obama administration has made a commitment to ratify the convention, the fact that the United States has not yet ratified the treaty lends credence to the perception that it only abides by international conventions when doing so aligns with its national interests. Ratifying UNCLOS would put this speculation to rest. It would also bolster the U.S. position in favor of rules-based behavior, give the United States a seat at the table when UNCLOS signatories discuss such issues as EEZ rights, and generally advance U.S. economic and strategic interests.

Second, nations with navies active in the South China Sea—including the United States, China, Vietnam, and the Philippines—should better utilize the CUES safety measures and procedures to mitigate uncertainty and improve communication in the event of a maritime incident. Under current arrangements, observing CUES procedures is voluntary. Participating countries should consider making compliance compulsory in order to guarantee standardized procedures. Countries should also engage in multilateral and bilateral maritime exercises to practice these procedures in a controlled environment before a contingency unfolds.

Third, the United States should make clear its support for risk-reduction measures and confidence-building measures among claimants in the South China Sea. The United States should continue to voice its support for full implementation of the China-ASEAN DOC and subsequent agreement on a binding code of conduct.

Beijing needs a favorable regional security environment and therefore has important incentives to work out a modus vivendi with its neighbors, but will not likely do so absent pressure. Agreement on a binding code of conduct will require unity among all members of ASEAN and strong backing from the United States. In the meantime, cooperation should be further developed through expanded ship visits, bilateral and multilateral exercise, and enhanced counter-piracy cooperation. In addition, cooperation on energy and fisheries should be further promoted.

Fourth, the creation of new dialogue mechanisms—such as a South China Sea Coast Guard Forum, an information-sharing center, and a joint fisheries committee—would provide greater opportunity for affected parties to communicate directly and offer opportunities for greater coordination.

Fifth, the United States should review its surveillance and reconnaissance activities in the air and waters bordering China's twelve-mile territorial sea and assess the feasibility of reducing their frequency or conducting the operations at a greater distance. Any modification of U.S. close-in surveillance and reconnaissance activities requires assessment of whether those sources are uniquely valuable or other intelligence collection platforms can provide sufficient information about Chinese military developments. The United States should not take such a step unilaterally; it should seek to obtain a concession from Beijing in return lest China interpret the action as evidence of U.S. decline and weakness.

Sixth, the Military Maritime Consultative Agreement process should be made effective or abandoned. There is a pressing need for the United States and China to agree on operational safety rules to minimize the possibility of a conflict in the years ahead. A more formal "incidents at sea" agreement should be considered.

Seventh, Washington should clarify in its respective dialogues with Manila and Hanoi the extent of the United States' obligations and commitments as well as the limits of likely U.S. involvement in future disputes. Clarity is necessary both to avoid a scenario in which regional actors are emboldened to aggressively confront China and to avert a setback to U.S. relations with regional nations due to perceptions of unfulfilled expectations.

8

Cooperative Security Work in South Asia

The concept of national security has been broadened in recent years. Besides traditional military issues and issues pertaining to state sovereignty, the concept now includes many new dimensions. In his *1992 Agenda for Peace*, then-United Nations Secretary General Boutros Boutros-Ghali identified "new risks for stability: ecological damage, disruption of family and community life, greater intrusion into the lives and rights of the individual..." The 2004 report of the Kofi Annan-appointed High Panel focused on human rights issues and endorsed the controversial concept of "right to protect" in cases of genocide and gross human rights violations in a country.

Dealing with the wide range of security issues requires a new approach. The conceptual shift that has occurred after the end of the Cold War is that security can be dealt with through cooperation rather than confrontation. The concept of cooperation to deal with security is not new. The Helsinki Declaration of the early 1970s led to détente and the formation of OSCE – an attempt to deal with the security issues of the time through cooperation. But that approach was bound to fail because the underlying idea of détente remained confrontation and cooperation was employed only to minimise the risk of confrontation and not remove it altogether.

Some key features of the cooperative security approach are as follows:

- Globalisation has led to contradictory trends of integration of finances and trade but also fragmentation of communities and societies as a result of which the danger of state failure has heightened. The existential threat of climate change has given rise to many new security worries. No country is in a position to resolve these security problems by itself. It will require the cooperation of others.

- Cooperative security depends upon mutual trust, transparency, attention to global norms and eschewing zero-sum approach to security. It requires a broader look at the concept of national interest.
- Dialogue, transparency, information sharing, capacity building, confidence building measures and asymmetric reciprocity are at the heart of the cooperative security approach.
- Institution building is important for the success of the cooperative security approach. Institutional platforms are required at the national, regional and international levels. At the same time, broad participation of governmental, non-governmental and civil society stakeholders in these institutions is important. Track-2 dialogues serve a useful purpose in this regard.

Several examples of the cooperative security approach can be cited. In South Asia, SAARC is trying to deal with critical issues like climate change, food security, trade, health, terrorism, etc. in a cooperative spirit. Other regional organisations like the East Asia Summit, ASEAN, OAS, AU, SCO, OSCE are also dealing with cooperative security issues. In some cases, conflict resolution is given high priority. In South Asia, due to insufficient trust, conflict resolution has not been discussed at the regional level.

Despite the promise, there are several barriers to success through cooperative security. It takes time to build trust among participants, particularly between those who might be involved in long term conflicts. The capacities required may be insufficient. Perceptions of countries on the nature and scope of threats might differ significantly. Hidden agendas may spoil the show. Thus, there is no guarantee that the cooperative security approach may deliver lasting solutions. However, such an approach may lessen tensions.

COOPERATIVE SECURITY IN SOUTH ASIA

South Asia has numerous, long standing conflicts left over from history. In the last few years several other issues have been added to the portfolio of security issues. Economic development in South Asia is being threatened by burgeoning human security issues. Many security issues such as demography, economic security, environmental security, terrorism, etc., are issues requiring cooperation among countries of the region. Most states in South Asia are vulnerable to non-traditional security threats. South Asia lacks capabilities and mechanisms to deal with these issues. Is South Asia ready to adopt a cooperative security approach to address some of these issues?

The cooperative security approach to conflict resolution has not succeeded in South Asia. India, thanks to its bitter experience with the UNSC on Kashmir, has categorically ruled out any third-party mediation in Kashmir. Its experience with Russian mediation after the 1965 war (Tashkent Declaration) was none too happy either. The UN's recent involvement in Nepal and the Norwegian involvement in Sri Lanka's ethnic conflict were also not successful. India has for long advocated regional resolution of the Afghan problem but Pakistan is opposed to Indian involvement in such a solution. The Afghan problem remains unresolved despite the massive involvement of the international community. Thus, a cooperative security approach to conflict resolution in South Asia has not been successful.

The cooperative security approach might work in South Asia when it comes to resolving human security related issues. South Asian countries are routinely ravaged by floods, famines, hurricanes, pandemics and many other forms of natural and man-made disasters that take a heavy human toll. Floods in Pakistan in 2010, earthquake in India in 2011, Tsunami in India, Sri Lanka and Maldives in 2004, Hurricane Sidr in Bangladesh and Myanmar took thousands of lives. Yet, South Asian countries do not have a mechanism for dealing with natural disasters and human relief. They lack cooperative mechanisms to deal with these problems.

South Asia, despite its high population and common culture is one of the most poorly connected regions in the world. This is because mutual mistrust has prevented countries of the region from giving priority to build multiple connectivities. Intra-regional trade and tourism is at a low level. Building these connectivities will go a long way in mitigating some of the human security challenges in South Asia.

The countries of the region can also cooperate in tacking the challenges of food, water and energy security. South Asia faces the huge challenge of feeding its billions over the next decades. Agriculture, fishing and forestry are the mainstays of food security. South Asian countries are suffering from energy deficits and the picture is becoming increasingly grim by the day. Climate change poses a major threat to South Asia. Yet, there is no mechanism among the countries of the region to come up with coordinated actions. SAARC provides a forum for discussing these problems and indeed many of these problems have been discussed there. But no credible action plan exists. Although SAARC has been around since 1983, the progress in regional cooperation has been excruciatingly slow. But there are signs of activity. The 17th SAARC summit, held in Addu, Maldives in November 2011, came up with some significant initiatives which might potentially address the human security challenges of the region by strengthening regional cooperation in critical areas.

The SAARC summit declaration emphasised the importance of bridging differences and strengthening the institutions of regional cooperation. The event was notable because concurrently with the summit, the first summit of SAARC Forum was also held. This opens up the opportunity in the future to discuss some sensitive issues which might not be discussed at the formal summits. The summit directed the South Asia Forum to continue to work towards the development of the "Vision Statement" for South Asia on the goal and elements of a South Asian Economic Union.

The summit declaration highlighted a number of issues with significant potential for regional cooperation. These include:

- Reduction in Sensitive Lists as well as early resolution of non-tariff barriers, harmonizing standards and customs procedures.

- Ensuring greater flow of financial capital and intra-regional long-term investment.
- To conclude the Regional Railways Agreement, the Motor Vehicles Agreement, etc. before the next Session of the Council of Ministers.
- To complete the preparatory work on the Indian Ocean Cargo and Passenger Ferry Service.
- To implement the Thimpu Statement on Climate Change.
- To expedite the work on Inter-governmental Framework Agreement for Energy Cooperation, the Regional Power Exchange Concept, SAARC Market for Electricity.
- To resolve the operational issues related to the SAARC Food Bank.
- To initiate work towards combating maritime piracy in the region.
- To direct the finalization of the work on the elaboration of the SAARC Regional Convention on Preventing and Combating Trafficking in Women and Children for Prostitution.
- To undertake a comprehensive review of all matters relating to SAARC's engagement with Observers, including the question of dialogue partnership.

The above list shows that South Asian leaders are aware of the problems that need resolution through regional cooperation. But, the bane of SAARC has been its inability to convert promises into actions. In the future SAARC members need to show political will and urgency to deal with sustainable problems that confront the region. The setting up of a SAARC Forum and the likelihood of dialogue partners are precisely the innovations that SAARC requires to give boost to the cooperative security approach in the region.

South Asian countries need a bolder approach to cooperative security than has been the case so far. For instance, they can initiate a regular mechanism to discuss security issues in the regions like ARF, CSCAP, etc. Disaster management authorities, finance ministers, health misters, environment ministers can meet regularly to discuss the ways and means to meet the common challenges of disaster mitigation, economic cooperation, public health issues and environmental security. India, which has borders with most SAARC countries, can set up cooperative mechanisms for better regulation of orders. Defence cooperation can also be an excellent way of building confidence and reducing tensions. Maritime security and coastal security should be given higher priority. What is required is political will to implement a cooperative security approach.

GLOBAL FOOD SECURITY UNDER CLIMATE CHANGE

The Food and Agriculture Organization (FAO) defines food security as a "situation that exists when all people, at all times, have physical, social, and economic access to sufficient, safe, and nutritious food that meets their dietary needs and food preferences for an active and healthy life" (1). This definition comprises four key dimensions of food supplies: availability, stability, access, and utilization. The first dimension relates to the availability of sufficient food, i.e., to the overall ability of the agricultural system to meet food demand. Its subdimensions include the agro-climatic fundamentals of crop and pasture production (2) and the entire range of socio-economic and cultural factors that determine where and how farmers perform in response to markets. The second dimension, stability, relates to individuals who are at high risk of temporarily or permanently losing their access to the resources needed to consume adequate food, either because these individuals cannot ensure *ex ante* against income shocks or they lack enough "reserves" to smooth consumption *ex post* or both. An important cause of unstable access is climate variability, e.g., landless agricultural laborers, who almost wholly depend on agricultural wages in a region of erratic rainfall and have few savings, would be at high risk of losing their access to food. However, there can be individuals with unstable access to food even in agricultural communities where there is no climate variability, e.g., landless agricultural laborers who fall sick and cannot earn their daily wages would lack stable access to food if, for example, they cannot take out insurance against illness. The third dimension, access, covers access by individuals to adequate resources (entitlements) to acquire appropriate foods for a nutritious diet. Entitlements are defined as the set of all those commodity bundles over which a person can establish command given the legal, political, economic, and social arrangements of the community of which he or she is a member. Thus a key element is the purchasing power of consumers and the evolution of real incomes and food prices. However, these resources need not be exclusively monetary but may also include traditional rights, e.g., to a share of common resources. Finally, utilization encompasses all food safety and quality aspects of nutrition; its subdimensions are therefore related to health, including the sanitary conditions across the entire food chain. It is not enough that someone is getting what appears to be an adequate quantity of food if that person is unable to make use of the food because he or she is always falling sick.

Agriculture is not only a source of the commodity food but, equally importantly, also a source of income. In a world where trade is possible at reasonably low cost, the crucial issue for food security is not whether food is "available," but whether the monetary and nonmonetary resources at the disposal of the population are sufficient to allow everyone access to adequate quantities of food. An important corollary to this is that national self-sufficiency is neither necessary nor sufficient to guarantee food security at the individual level. Note that Hong Kong and Singapore are not self-sufficient (agriculture is nonexistent) but their populations are food-secure, whereas India is self-sufficient but a large part of its population is not food-secure.

Numerous measures are used to quantify the overall status and the regional distribution of global hunger. None of these measures covers all dimensions and facets of food insecurity described above. This also holds for the FAO indicator of undernourishment (1), the measure that was used in essentially all studies reviewed in this article. The FAO measure, however, has a number of advantages. First, it covers two dimensions of food security, availability and access; second, the underlying methodology is straightforward and transparent; and third, the parameters and data needed for the FAO indicator are readily available for past estimates and can be derived without major difficulties for the future.

This article reviews recent studies that have quantified the impacts of climate change on global food security. It starts with an overview of the principal aspects of climate change and their impacts on the four dimensions of food security. It then reviews model-based results and discusses the main findings that have arisen from these assessments. Finally, limitations of the current modeling systems are discussed; this final section includes a discussion of potential surprises and some suggestions to improve future assessments to enhance their overall robustness and their relevance for policy makers.

CLIMATE CHANGE AND FOOD SECURITY

Impacts on Food Production and Availability

Climate change affects agriculture and food production in complex ways. It affects food production directly through changes in agro-ecological conditions and indirectly by affecting growth and distribution of incomes, and thus demand for agricultural produce. Impacts have been quantified in numerous studies and under various sets of assumptions. A selection of these results is presented in *Quantifying the Impacts on Food Security*. Here it is useful to summarize the main alterations in the agro-ecological environment that are associated with climate change.

Changes in temperature and precipitation associated with continued emissions of greenhouse gases will bring changes in land suitability and crop yields. In particular, the Intergovernmental Panel on Climate Change (IPCC) considers four families of socio-economic development and associated emission scenarios, known as Special Report on Emissions Scenarios (SRES) A2, B2, A1, and B1. Of relevance to this review, of the SRES scenarios, A1, the "business-as-usual scenario," corresponds to the highest emissions, and B1 corresponds to the lowest. The other scenarios are intermediate between these two. Importantly for agriculture and world food supply, SRES A2 assumes the highest projected population growth of the four (United Nations high projection) and is thus associated to the highest food demand. Depending on the SRES emission scenario and climate models considered, global mean surface temperature is projected to rise in a range from 1.8°C (with a range from 1.1°C to 2.9°C for SRES B1) to 4.0°C (with a range from 2.4°C to 6.4°C for A1) by 2100. In temperate latitudes, higher temperatures are expected to bring predominantly benefits to agriculture: the areas potentially suitable for cropping will expand, the length of the growing period will increase, and crop yields may rise. A moderate incremental warming in some humid and temperate grasslands may increase pasture productivity and reduce the need for housing and for compound feed. These gains have to be set against an increased frequency of extreme events, for instance, heat waves and droughts in the Mediterranean region or increased heavy precipitation events and flooding in temperate regions, including the possibility of increased coastal storms; they also have to be set against the fact that semiarid and arid pastures are likely to see reduced livestock productivity and increased livestock mortality. In drier areas, climate models predict increased evapotranspiration and lower soil moisture levels. As a result, some cultivated areas may become unsuitable for cropping and some tropical grassland may become increasingly arid. Temperature rise will also expand the range of many agricultural pests and increase the ability of pest populations to survive the winter and attack spring crops.

Another important change for agriculture is the increase in atmospheric carbon dioxide (CO_2) concentrations. Depending on the SRES emission scenario, the atmospheric CO_2 concentration is projected to increase from ≤379 ppm today to >550 ppm by 2100 in SRES B1 to >800 ppm in SRES A1FI. Higher CO_2 concentrations will have a positive effect on many crops, enhancing biomass accumulation and final yield. However, the magnitude of this effect is less clear, with important differences depending on management type (e.g., irrigation and fertilization regimes) and crop type. Experimental yield response to elevated CO_2 show that under optimal growth conditions, crop yields increase at 550 ppm CO_2 in the range of 10% to 20% for C_3 crops (such as wheat, rice, and soybean), and only 0–10% for C_4 crops such as maize and sorghum. Yet the nutritional quality of agricultural produce may not increase in line with higher yields. Some cereal and forage crops, for example, show lower protein concentrations under elevated CO_2 conditions.

Finally, a number of recent studies have estimated the likely changes in land suitability, potential yields, and agricultural production on the current suite of crops and cultivars available today. Therefore, these estimates implicitly include adaptation using available management techniques and crops, but excluding new cultivars from breeding or biotechnology.

For instance, total land and total prime land would remain virtually unchanged at the current levels of 2,600 million and 2,000 million hectares (ha), respectively. The same study also showed, however, more pronounced regional shifts, with a considerable increase in suitable cropland at higher latitudes (developed countries +160 million ha) and a corresponding decline of potential cropland at lower latitudes (developing countries –110 million ha). An even more pronounced shift within the quality of cropland is predicted in developing countries. The net decline of 110 million ha is the result of a massive decline in agricultural prime land of H"135 million ha, which is offset by an increase in moderately suitable land of >20 million ha. This quality shift is also reflected in the shift in land suitable for multiple cropping. In sub-Saharan Africa alone, land for double cropping would decline by between 10 million and 20 million ha, and land suitable for triple copping would decline by 5 million to 10 million ha. At a regional level, similar approaches indicate that under climate change, the biggest losses in suitable cropland are likely to be in Africa, whereas the largest expansion of suitable cropland is in the Russian Federation and Central Asia.

Impacts on the Stability of Food Supplies

Global and regional weather conditions are also expected to become more variable than at present, with increases in the frequency and severity of extreme events such as cyclones, floods, hailstorms, and droughts. By bringing greater fluctuations in crop yields and local food supplies and higher risks of landslides and erosion damage, they can adversely affect the stability of food supplies and thus food security.

Neither climate change nor short-term climate variability and associated adaptation are new phenomena in agriculture, of course. As shown, for instance, some important agricultural areas of the world like the Midwest of the United States, the northeast of Argentina, southern Africa, or southeast Australia have traditionally experienced higher climate variability than other regions such as central Africa or Europe. They also show that the extent of short-term fluctuations has changed over longer periods of time. In developed countries, for instance, short-term climate variability increased from 1931 to 1960 as compared with 1901 to 1930, but decreased strongly in the period from 1961 to 1990. What is new, however, is the fact that the areas subject to high climate variability are likely to expand, whereas the extent of short-term climate variability is likely to increase across all regions. Furthermore, the rates and levels of projected warming may exceed in some regions the historical experience.

If climate fluctuations become more pronounced and more widespread, droughts and floods, the dominant causes of short-term fluctuations in food production in semiarid and subhumid areas, will become more severe and more frequent. In semiarid areas, droughts can dramatically reduce crop yields and livestock numbers and productivity. Again, most of this land is in sub-Saharan Africa and parts of South Asia, meaning that the poorest regions with the highest level of chronic undernourishment will also be exposed to the highest degree of instability in food production. How strongly these impacts will be felt will crucially depend on whether such fluctuations can be countered by investments in irrigation, better storage facilities, or higher food imports. In addition, a policy environment that fosters freer trade and promotes investments in transportation, communications, and irrigation infrastructure can help address these challenges early on.

Impacts of Climate Change on Food Utilization

Climate change will also affect the ability of individuals to use food effectively by altering the conditions for food safety and changing the disease pressure from vector, water, and food-borne diseases. The IPPC Working Group II provides a detailed account of the health impacts of climate change. It examines how the various forms of diseases, including vector-borne diseases such as malaria, are likely to spread or recede with climate change. This article focuses on a narrow selection of diseases that affect food safety directly, i.e., food and water-borne diseases.

The main concern about climate change and food security is that changing climatic conditions can initiate a vicious circle where infectious disease causes or compounds hunger, which, in turn, makes the affected populations more susceptible to infectious disease. The result can be a substantial decline in labor productivity and an increase in poverty and even mortality. Essentially all manifestations of climate change, be they drought, higher temperatures, or heavy rainfalls have an impact on the disease pressure, and there is growing evidence that these changes affect food safety and food security.

The recent IPCC report also emphasizes that increases in daily temperatures will increase the frequency of food poisoning, particularly in temperate regions. Warmer seas may contribute to increased cases of human shellfish and reef-fish poisoning (ciguatera) in tropical regions and a poleward expansion of the disease. However, there is little new evidence that climate change significantly alters the prevalence of these diseases. Several studies have confirmed and quantified the effects of temperature on common forms of food poisoning, such as salmonellosis. These studies show an approximately linear increase in reported cases for each degree increase in weekly temperature. Moreover, there is evidence that temperature variability affects the incidence of diarrhoeal disease. A number of studies found that rising temperatures were strongly associated with increased episodes of diarrhoeal disease in adults and children. These findings have been corroborated by analyses based on monthly temperature observations. Several studies report a strong correlation between monthly temperature and diarrhoeal episodes on the Pacific Islands, Australia, and Israel.

Extreme rainfall events can increase the risk of outbreaks of water-borne diseases particularly where traditional water management systems are insufficient to handle the new extremes. Likewise, the impacts of flooding will be felt most strongly in environmentally degraded areas, and where basic public infrastructure, including sanitation and hygiene, is lacking. This will raise the number of people exposed to water-borne diseases (e.g., cholera) and thus lower their capacity to effectively use food.

Impacts of Climate Change on Access to Food

Access to food refers to the ability of individuals, communities, and countries to purchase sufficient quantities and qualities of food. Over the last 30 years, falling real prices for food and rising real incomes have led to substantial improvements in access to food in many developing countries. Increased purchasing power has allowed a growing number of people to purchase not only more food but also more nutritious food with more protein, micronutrients, and vitamins. East Asia and to a lesser extent the Near-East/North African region have particularly benefited from a combination of lower real food prices and robust income growth. From 1970 to 2001, the prevalence of hunger in these regions, as measured by FAO's indicator of undernourishment, has declined from 24% to 10.1% and 44% to 10.2% respectively. In East Asia, it was endogenous income growth that provided the basis for the boost in demand for food, which was largely produced in the region; in the Near-East North African region demand was spurred by exogenous revenues from oil and gas exports, and additional food supply came largely from imports. But in both regions, improvements in access to food have been crucial in reducing hunger and malnutrition.

FAO's longer-term outlook to 2050 suggests that the importance of improved demand side conditions will even become more important over the next 50 years. The regions that will see the strongest reductions in the prevalence of undernourishment are those that are expected to see the highest rates of income growth. South Asia stands to benefit the most. Spurred by high income growth the region is expected to reduce the prevalence of undernourishment from >22% currently to 12% by 2015 and just 4% by 2050. Progress is also expected for sub-Saharan Africa, but improvements will be less pronounced and are expected to set in later. Over the next 15 years, for instance, the prevalence of undernourishment will decline less than in other regions, from H"33% to a still worrisome 21%, as significant constraints (soil nutrients, water, infrastructure, etc.) will limit the ability to further increase food production locally, while continuing low levels of income rule out the option of importing food. In the long run, however, sub-Saharan Africa is expected to see a more substantial decline in hunger; by 2050, <6% of its total population are expected to suffer from chronic hunger. It is important to note that these FAO projections do not take into account the effects of climate change.

By coupling agro-ecologic and economic models, others have gauged the impact of climate change on agricultural gross domestic product (GDP) and prices. At the global level, the impacts of climate change are likely to be very small; under a range of SRES and associated climate-change scenarios, the estimates range from a decline of –1.5% to an increase of +2.6% by 2080. At the regional level, the importance of agriculture as a source of income can be much more important. In these regions, the economic output from agriculture itself (over and above subsistence food production) will be an important contributor to food security. The strongest impact of climate change on the economic output of agriculture is expected for sub-Saharan Africa, which means that the poorest and already most food-insecure region is also expected to suffer the largest contraction of agricultural incomes. For the region, the losses in agricultural GDP, compared with no climate change, range from 2% to 8% for the Hadley Centre Coupled Model, version 3 and 7–9% for the Commonwealth Scientific and Industrial Research Organisation projections.

Impacts on Food Prices

Essentially all SRES development paths describe a world of robust economic growth and rapidly shrinking importance of agriculture in the long run and thus a continuation of a trend that has been underway for decades in many developing regions. SRES scenarios describe a world where income growth will allow the largest part of the world's population to address possible local production shortfalls through imports and, at the same time, find ways to cope with safety and stability issues of food supplies. It is also a world where real incomes rise more rapidly than real food prices, which suggests that the share of income spent on food should decline and that even high food prices are unlikely to create a major dent in the food expenditures of the poor. However, not all parts of the world perform equally well in the various development paths and not all development paths are equally benign for growth. Where income levels are low and shares of food expenditures are high, higher prices for food may still create or exacerbate a possible food security problem.

There are a number of studies that have ventured to measure the likely impacts of climate change on food prices. The basic messages that emerge from these studies are: first, on average, prices for food are expected to rise moderately in line with moderate increases of temperature (until 2050); some studies even foresee a mild decline in real prices until 2050. Second, after 2050 and with further increases in temperatures, prices are expected to increase more substantially. In some studies and for some commodities (rice and sugar) prices are forecast to increase by as much as 80% above their reference levels without climate change. Third, price changes expected from the effects of global warming are, on average, much smaller than price changes from socio-economic development paths. For instance, the SRES A2 scenario would imply a price increase in real cereal prices by ≤170%. The (additional) price increase caused by climate change would only be 14.4%. Overall, this appears to be the sharpest price increase reported and it is not surprising that this scenario would imply a stubbornly high number of undernourished people until 2080. However, it is also needless to say that a constant absolute number of undernourished people would still imply a sharp decline in the prevalence of hunger, and, given the high population assumptions in the SRES A2 world (>13.6 billion people globally and >11.6 billion in the developing world) this would imply a particularly sharp drop in the prevalence from currently 17% to –7% by 2080.

QUANTIFYING THE IMPACTS ON FOOD SECURITY

A number of studies have recently quantified the impacts of climate change on food security. In terms of quantifying agronomic yield change projections, these studies are either based on the AEZ tools developed by the IIASA analysis or the Decision Support System for Agrotechnology Transfer suite of crop models; all use the IIASA-Basic Linked System (BLS) economic model for assessing economic impacts. These tools, with some modifications relating to how crop yield changes are simulated, have also been used by others to undertake similar assessments and provide sensitivity analyses across a range of SRES and general circulation model (GCM) projections. Many other simulations have also examined the effects of climate change with and without adaptation (induced technological progress, domestic policy change, international trade liberalization, etc.), with and without mitigation (e.g., CO_2 stabilization, variants for temperature, rainfall change and distribution) or provide impact assessments for different speeds of climate change. This section focuses on the quantitative results for food security, trying to illuminate some of the differences and extract the main messages that emerge from the various studies. Unless indicated, all simulation results discussed below include the combined effects of climate change and elevated CO_2 on crops. The key messages can be summarized as follows:

First, it is very likely that climate change is likely to increase the number of people at risk of hunger compared with reference scenarios with no climate change; the exact impacts will, however, strongly depend on the projected socio-economic developments. For instance, it is estimated that climate change would increase the number of undernourished in 2080 by 5–26%, compared with no climate change or by between 5 million and 10 million (B1 SRES) and 120 million to 170 million people (A2 SRES), with within-SRES ranges depending on GCM climate projections. Using only one GCM scenario, others (10, 11) projected small reductions by 2080, i.e., – 5%, or –10 million (B1) to –30 million (A2) people, and slight increases of +13%–26%, or ≤10 million (B2) to 30 million (A1) people.

Second, it is likely that the magnitude of these climate impacts will be small compared with the impact of socio-economic development. As evident and within the limitations of socio-economic forecasts, these studies suggest that robust economic growth and a decline in population growth projected for the 21st century will, in all but one scenario (SRES A2), significantly reduce the number of people at risk of hunger in 2080. At any rate, the prevalence of undernourishment will decline as all scenarios assume that world population will continue to grow to 2080, albeit at lower rates. Compared with FAO estimates of 820 million undernourished in developing countries today, several studies estimate reductions of >75% by 2080, or H"560 million to 700 million people, projecting 100 million to 240 million undernourished by 2080 (A1, B1, and B2). As mentioned, the only exception is scenario A2, where the number of the hungry is forecast to decrease only slightly by 2080; but the higher population growth rates in A2 compared with other scenarios mean that the prevalence of undernourishment will decline drastically. However, these analyses also confirm that the progress will be unevenly distributed over the developing world, and more importantly progress will be slow during the first decades of the outlook. With or without climate change, the millennium development goal of halving the prevalence of hunger by 2015 is unlikely to be realized before 2020–2030.

In addition to socio-economic pressures considered within the IPCC SRES scenarios, food production may increasingly compete with bio-energy in coming decades; studies addressing possible consequences for world food supply have only started to surface, providing both positive and negative views. Importantly, none of the major world food models discussed herein have yet considered such competition.

Third, sub-Saharan Africa is likely to surpass Asia as the most food-insecure region. However, this is largely independent of climate change and is mostly the result of the socio-economic development paths assumed for the different developing regions in the SRES scenarios. Throughout most SRES and climate-change scenarios sub-Saharan Africa accounts for 40–50% of global hunger by 2080, compared with ≤24% today; in some simulations sub-Saharan Africa even accounts for 70–75% of global undernourishment by 2080. These high estimates have emerged from slower growth variants of the A2 and B2 scenarios; also an A2 variant with slower population growth yields a sharper concentration of hunger in sub-Saharan Africa. For regions other than sub-Saharan Africa, results largely depend on GCM scenarios and therefore are highly uncertain.

Fourth, although there is significant uncertainty on the effects of elevated CO_2 on crop yields, this uncertainty is carried to a much lesser extent on food security. This result emerges from a comparison of climate change simulations with and without CO_2 fertilization effects on crop yields. CO_2 fertilization would not greatly affect global projections of hunger. In view of the fact that essentially all SRES worlds are characterized by much higher real incomes, much improved transportation and communication options, and still sufficient global food production, the somewhat smaller supplies will not be able to make a dent in global food security outcomes.

Many studies find that climate change without CO_2 fertilization would reduce the number of undernourished people by 2080 only by some 20 million to 140 million (120 million to 380 million for SRES A1, B1, and B2 without, compared with 100 million to 240 million with CO_2 fertilization effect). The exception again in these studies is SRES A2, under which the assumption of no CO_2 fertilization results in a projected range of 950 million to 1,300 million people undernourished in 2080, compared with 740 million to 850 million projected under climate change, but with CO_2 effects on crops.

Finally, recent research suggests large positive effects of climate stabilization for the agricultural sector. However, as the stabilizing effects of mitigation measures can take several decades to be realized from the moment of implementation, the benefits for crop production may be realized only in the second half of this century. Importantly, even in the presence of robust global long-term benefits, regional and temporal patterns of winners and losers that can be projected with current tools are highly uncertain and depend critically on the underlying GCM projections.

UNCERTAINTIES AND LIMITATIONS

The finding that socio-economic development paths have an important bearing on future food security and that they are likely to top the effects of climate change should not, or at least not only, be interpreted as a probability-based forecast. This is because SRES scenarios offer a range of possible outcomes "without any sense of likelihood". Yet SRES scenarios, like all scenarios, do not overcome the inability to accurately project future changes in economic activity, emissions, and climate.

Second, the existing global assessments of climate change and food security have only been able to focus on the impacts on food availability and access to food, without quantification of the likely important climate change effects on food safety and vulnerability (stability). This means that these assessments neither include potential problems arising from additional impacts due to extreme events such as drought and floods nor do they quantify the potential impacts of changes in the prevalence of food-borne diseases (positive as well as negative) or the interaction of nutrition and health effects through changes in the proliferation of vector-borne diseases such as malaria. On the food availability side, they also exclude the impacts of a possible sea-level rise for agricultural production or those that are associated with possible reductions of marine or freshwater fish production.

Third, it is important to note that even in terms of food availability, all current assessments of world food supply have focused only on the impacts of mean climate change, i.e., they have not considered the possibility of significant shifts in the frequency of extreme events on regional production potential, nor have they considered scenarios of abrupt climate or socio-economic change; any of these scenario variants is likely to increase the already negative projected impacts of climate change on world food supply. Models that take into account the specific biophysical, technological, and market responses necessary to simulate realistic adaptation to such events are not yet available.

Fourth, this review finds that recent global assessments of climate change and food security rest essentially on a single modeling framework, the IIASA system, which combines the FAO/IIASA AEZ model with various GCM models and the IIASA BLS system, or on close variants of the IIASA system. This has important implications for uncertainty, given that the robustness of all these assessments strongly depends on the performance of the underlying models. There is, therefore, a clear need for continued and enhanced validation efforts of both the agro-climatological and food trade tools developed at IIASA and widely used in the literature.

Finally, we note that assessments that do not only provide scenarios, but also attach probabilities for particular outcomes to come true could provide an important element for improved or at least better-informed policy decisions. A number of possibilities are offered to address the related modeling challenges. One option would be to produce such estimates with probability-based estimates of the (key) model parameters. Alternatively, the various scenarios could be constructed so that they reflect expert judgements on a particular issue. It would be desirable to attach probabilities to existing scenarios. Information on how likely the suggested outcomes are would contribute greatly to their usefulness for policy makers and help justify (or otherwise) policy measures to adapt to or mitigate the impacts of climate change on food security.

9

Peace, Security, Development, and the Environment

Among the dangers facing the environment, the possibility of nuclear war, or military conflict of a lesser scale involving weapons of mass destruction, is undoubtedly the gravest. Certain aspects of the issues of peace and security bear directly upon the concept of sustainable development. Indeed, they are central to it.

Environmental stress is both a cause and an effect of political tension and military conflict. Nations have often fought to assert or resist control over raw materials, energy supplies, land, river basins, sea passages, and other key environmental resources. Such conflicts are likely to increase as these resources become scarcer and competition for them increases.

The environmental consequences of armed conflict would be most devastating in the case of thermo-nuclear war. But there are damaging effects too from conventional, biological, and chemical weapons, as well as from the disruption of economic production and social organization in the wake of warfare and mass migration of refugees. But even where war is prevented, and where conflict is contained, a state of 'peace' might well entail the diversion into armament production of vast resources that could, at least in part, be used to promote sustainable forms of development.

A number of factors affect the connection between environmental stress, poverty, and security, such as inadequate development policies, adverse trends in the international economy, inequities in multi-racial and multi-ethnic societies, and pressures of population growth. These linkages among environment, development, and conflict are complex and, in many cases, poorly understood. But a comprehensive approach to international and national security must transcend the traditional emphasis on military power and armed competition The real sources of insecurity also encompass unsustainable development, and its effects can become intertwined with traditional forms of conflict in a manner that can extend and deepen the latter.

ENVIRONMENTAL STRESS AS A SOURCE OF CONFLICT

Environmental stress is seldom the only cause of major conflicts within or among nations. Nevertheless, they can arise from the marginalization of sectors of the population and from ensuing violence. This occurs when political processes are unable to handle the effects of environmental stress resulting, for example, from erosion and desertification. Environmental stress can thus be an important part of the web of causality associated with any conflict and can in some cases be catalytic.

Poverty, injustice, environmental degradation, and conflict interact in complex and potent ways. One manifestation of growing concern to the international community is the phenomenon of 'environmental refugees'. The immediate cause of any mass movement of refugees may appear to be political upheaval and military violence. But the underlying causes often include the deterioration of the natural resource base and its capacity to support the population.

Events in the Horn of Africa are a case in point. In the early 1970s, drought and famine struck the nation of Ethiopia. Yet it has been found that the hunger and human misery were caused more by years of overuse of soils in the Ethiopian highlands and the resulting severe erosion than by drought. A report commissioned by the Ethiopian Relief and Rehabilitation Commission found: 'The primary cause of the famine was not drought of unprecedented severity, but a combination of long-continued bad land use and steadily increased human and stock populations over decades'. Wars have always compelled people to leave their homes and their lands, to become refugees. Also, the wars in our time have forced large numbers of people to leave their homelands. In addition, we now have the phenomenon of environmental refugees. In 1984-85, some 10 million Africans fled their homes, accounting for two-thirds of all refugees worldwide. Their flight was not surprising in a region where 35 million suffered from famine. Many of them swarmed into cities. But many others moved across national boundaries, heightening interstate tensions. Cote d'Ivoire, Ghana, and Nigeria have been generous in welcoming refugees from the desertified Sahel. Tanzania, Zambia, and Zimbabwe have also been receiving large numbers of refugees. Yet, the Cote d'Ivoire, for instance, which depends for much of its export revenues on timber, is suffering rapid deforestation caused in part by land hunger, and one-third of landless people are immigrants. Agriculture destroys 4.5 times as much forestland in the Cote d'Ivoire as logging does.

Almost 1 million Haitian 'boat people', one-sixth of the entire populace, have fled that island nation, an exodus fuelled in large part by environmental degradation. Haiti suffers some of the world's most severe erosion, down to bedrock over large parts of some regions, so that even farmers with reasonable amounts of land cannot make a living. According to a US Agency for International Development (USAID) report, 'The social and economic effects of environmental degradation are great, and contribute to the growing outflow from rural areas. Thousands of rural Haitians leave their homes each year for Port au Prince, other Caribbean islands and the United States in search of employment and better living conditions. El Salvador, one of the most troubled nations of Central America, is also one of the most environmentally impoverished, with some of the worst erosion rates in the region. The fundamental causes of the present conflict are as much environmental as political, stemming from problems of resource distribution in an overcrowded land, according to a draft USAID environmental profile of El Salvador.

Today we cannot secure security for one state at the expense of the other. Security can only be universal, but security cannot only be political or military, it must be as well ecological, economical, and social. It must ensure the fulfilment of the aspirations of humanity as a whole.

South Africa reveals similar problems. The inhuman policy of apartheid is at the core of the state of political conflict in Southern Africa. One of the many ways by which apartheid institutionalizes both conflict and environmental degradation is by allocating, through the 'homelands' system, 14 per cent of the nation's land to 72 per cent of the population. Young working-age blacks flee the overcultivated and overgrazed 'homelands' to seek work in the cities, where, on top of the squalor of overcrowded townships, they encounter extreme socio-economic inequality and racial segregation. They fight back. Repression intensifies, and the victims seek refuge over the border - whereupon the South African regime widens the conflict into neighbouring states. The entire region is becoming caught up in the ensuing violence, which could well ignite wider conflict drawing in major powers.

In addition to the interrelated problems of poverty, injustice, and environmental stress, competition for non-renewable raw materials, land, or energy can create tension. It was the quest for raw materials that underlay much of the competition between colonial powers and the subjugation of their holdings. Conflicts in the Middle East inevitably contain the seeds of great power intervention and global conflagration, in part because of the international interest in oil.

As unsustainable forms of development push individual countries up against environmental limits, major differences in environmental endowment among countries, or variations in stocks of usable land and raw materials, could precipitate and exacerbate international tension and conflict. And competition for use of the global commons, such as ocean fisheries and Antarctica, or for use of more localized common resources in fixed supply, such as rivers and coastal waters, could escalate to the level of international conflict and to threaten international peace and security.

Global water use doubled between 1940 and 1980, and it is expected to double again by 2000, with two thirds of the projected water use going to agriculture. Yet 80 countries, with 40 per cent of the world's population, already suffer serious water shortages. There will be growing competition for water for irrigation, industry, and domestic use. River water disputes have already occurred in

North America (the Rio Grande), South America (the Rio de la Plata and Parana), South and Southeast Asia (the Mekong and the Ganges), Africa (the Nile), and the Middle East (the Jordan, Litani, and Orontes, as well as the Euphrates).

How can the world of nature and the community of peoples with their national economies be harmonized? Posing the question this way suggests that the two are separate. But not so. Humanity, the human species, exists and it supported within the world of nature. And I mean that not figuratively but literally.

We are deep-air animals living inside an ecological system. We draw boundaries, of course, on the ecosphere for national and regional purposes. But it is all of one piece.

When, therefore, we optimistically declare that economic development and environmental maintenance can go along hand in hand, this qualifier must immediately be added: only if the maintenance of the ecosphere is made the first priority. Economic development must be secondary, guided by strict ecological standards. These fundamental ideas are far from being universally accepted.

Fisheries, whether coastal or oceanic, are fundamental to the diets of many countries. For some countries, fishing is a key economic sector, and overfishing poses immediate dangers to several national economies. In 1974 Iceland, largely dependent on its fishing industry, found itself embroiled with the United Kingdom in a 'cod war'. Similar tensions exist in the Japanese and Korean seas and on both sides of the South Atlantic. The 1986 declaration of an exclusive fishery zone around the Falkland/ Malvinas Islands has further unsettled relations between Britain and Argentina. Disputes over fishing rights in the South Pacific and the search for tuna by distant-water fleets led to increased competition for diplomatic and fisheries advantages by the major powers in that region in 1986. Fisheries-related disputes may well become more frequent as nations harvest fish stocks beyond the level of sustainable yields.

Environmental threats to security are now beginning to emerge on a global scale. The most worrisome of these stem from the possible consequences of global warming caused by the atmospheric build-up of carbon dioxide and other gases. Any such climatic change would quite probably be unequal in its effects, disrupting agricultural systems in areas that provide a large proportion of the world's cereal harvests and perhaps triggering mass population movements in areas where hunger is already endemic. Sea levels may rise during the first half of the next century enough to radically change the boundaries between coastal nations and to change the shapes and strategic importance of international waterways - effects both likely to increase international tensions. The climatic and sea-level changes are also likely to disrupt the breeding grounds of economically important fish species. Slowing, or adapting to, global warming is becoming an essential task to reduce the risks of conflict.

CONFLICT AS A CAUSE OF UNSUSTAINABLE DEVELOPMENT

Arms competition and armed conflict create major obstacles to sustainable development. They make huge claims on scarce material resources. They pre-empt human resources and wealth that could be used to combat the collapse of environmental support systems, the poverty, and the underdevelopment that in combination contribute so much to contemporary political insecurity. They may stimulate an ethos that is antagonistic towards cooperation among nations whose ecological and economic interdependence requires them to overcome national or ideological antipathies.

The existence of nuclear weapons and the destructive potential inherent in the velocity and intensity of modern conventional warfare have given rise to a new understanding of the requirements for security among nations. In the nuclear age nations can no longer obtain security at each other's expense. They must seek security through cooperation, agreements, and mutual restraint; they must seek common security. Hence interdependence, which is so fundamental in the realm of environment and economics, is a fact also in the sphere of arms competition and military security. Interdependence has become a compelling fact, forcing nations to reconcile their approach to 'security'.

Nuclear War - Threat to Civilization

The likely consequences of nuclear war make other threats, to the environment pale into insignificance. Nuclear weapons represent a qualitatively new step in the development of warfare. One thermo-nuclear bomb can have an explosive power greater than that of all the explosives Used in wars since the invention of gunpowder. In addition to the destructive effects of blast and heat, immensely magnified by these weapons, they introduce a new lethal agent - ionizing radiation - that extends lethal effects over both space and tine.

In recent years, scientists have in addition called our attention to the prospect of 'nuclear winter'. It has been most authoritatively explored by some 300 scientists from the United States, the USSR, and more than 30 other countries - working on a collaborative basis in some cases across ideological divides.

All youth organizations believe that environmental issues stand high on the priority list of global problems. However, their solution depends on the preservation of peace on our planet. The quest of solutions to ecological problems is impossible without the curbing of the arms race, for the arms race absorbs tremendous intellectual and material resources of mankind. The solution of ecological problems also depends on the way of life of young people and their value orientation.

The theory contends that the smoke and dust ejected into the atmosphere by a nuclear war could absorb enough solar radiation to remain aloft for some time, preventing sunlight from reaching the surface of the earth, causing a widespread and prolonged cooling of land areas. There would be severe repercussions for plant life generally and for agriculture in particular, disrupting the production of food to sustain survivors of the war. Great uncertainties remain about the scale and linkages determining environmental effects, but large-scale environmental perturbations are considered probable. A nuclear war cannot be won, and must never be fought. In the aftermath, there would be no difference between so called victor and vanquished. The nuclear-weapon states must spare no effort to conclude a verifiable agreement on banning all nuclear weapon tests.

The findings on nuclear winter are vitally important too for non-aligned nations, predominantly in the South, which are not parties to the East West conflict. They cannot expect to avoid the potentially disastrous environmental consequences of nuclear war in the northern hemisphere. The aftermath of such a war would envelop the world. There is a danger that nuclear weapons will spread to more and more countries and be used in what begins as a limited regional conflict. Beyond the five recognized nuclear-weapon states, at least six others have a widely acknowledged potential nuclear weapons capability; a dozen others are not far behind. The nuclear-weapon states cannot expect the non-nuclear-weapon states to abstain from exercising the nuclear option in the absence of real progress on the road to nuclear disarmament. It is imperative, therefore, that the probable consequences of nuclear war be recognized universally and that all states become involved in efforts to prevent the proliferation - and above all the use of nuclear weapons.

Other Weapons of Mass Destruction

Other forms of war and other weapons of mass destruction have large scale effects or both human societies and the human environment. Biological warfare could release new agents of disease that would prove difficult to control. Recent advances in biotechnology multiply the potentially lethal applications of such weapons. Likewise, the deliberate manipulation of the environment (for example, through artificial earthquakes and floods) would have consequences far beyond the borders of those involved in a conflict, were they ever used. Chemical agents can seriously damage the environment, as demonstrated by the defoliants used in South-east Asia. The dangerous and environmentally unpredictable consequences of biological and chemical weapons have led to international agreements banning their use. But there is need for further efforts to strengthen the regimes to which these agreements contribute. In particular, the Geneva protocol prohibiting the use of chemical weapons should be supplemented by agreements prohibiting the production and stockpiling of such weapons.

Military applications of new technologies now threaten lo make outer space a focus of international competition and conflict.

Most countries in the international community see space as a global commons that should benefit humanity as a whole and be preserved from military competition - a feeling reflected in the 1967 Outer Space Treaty, under which nations agreed not to deploy weapons of mass destruction there. Governments should now agree on measures to prevent an arms race in space and stop it on Earth. Failing such agreement, the arms race could expand, with dire consequences for humanity.

The Costs of the 'Arms Culture'

The absence of war is not peace; nor does it necessarily provide the conditions for sustainable development. Competitive arms races breed insecurity among nations through spirals of reciprocal fears. Nations need to muster resources to combat environmental degradation and mass poverty. By misdirecting scarce resources, arms races contribute further to insecurity.

The coexistence of substantial military spending with unmet human needs has long evoked concern. President Eisenhower, for example, observed at the end his term in office that 'every gun that is made, every warship launched, every rocket fired represents, in the final analysis, a theft from those who hunger and are not fed, who are cold and are not clothed'.

Global military spending in 1985 was well in excess of $900 billion. This was more than the total income of the poorest half of humanity. It represented the equivalent of almost $1,000 for every one of the world's 1 billion poorest. Put another way, military spending surpassed the combined gross national products of China, India, and the African countries south of the Sahara. Moreover, global military spending has risen not only absolutely but proportionately - from an estimated 4.7 per cent of world output in 1960 to over 6 per cent - representing an increase of about 150 per cent in real (constant price) terms. Three-quarters of current expenditure is in the industrial world.

The true cost of the arms race is the loss of what could have been produced instead with scarce capital, labour skills, and raw materials. The plants that manufacture weapons, the transport of those weapons, and the mining of minerals for their production all place enormous demands on energy and mineral resources and are a major contributor to pollution and environmental deterioration.

The distorting effects of the 'arms culture' are most striking in the deployment of scientific personnel. Half a million scientists are employed on weapons research world-wide, and they account to: around half of all research and development expenditure. This exceeds the total combined spending on developing technologies for new energy sources, improving human health, raising agricultural productivity, and controlling pollution. Military research and development - $70-80 billion world-wide in 1984 - is growing at twice the rate of military spending as a whole. At the same time, there is a paucity of resources available for monitoring global climatic change, for surveying the ecosystems of disappearing rain forests and spreading deserts, and for developing agricultural technologies appropriate to rainfed, tropical agriculture.

Nations are seeking a new era of economic growth. The level of spending on arms diminishes the prospects for such an era - especially one that emphasizes the more efficient use of raw materials, energy, and skilled human resources. It also has a bearing, albeit indirect, on the willingness of rich countries to provide development assistance to developing countries. Clearly, there is no simple correspondence between reduced defence spending and increased aid. There are other reasons aside from domestic resource constraints for a reluctance to expand aid, and nations cannot wait for disarmament before devoting more resources to ensuring sustainable development. Nonetheless, increased defence spending puts pressure on other budgetary items, and aid is an easy target, despite being a relatively small outlay for most donor countries.

Although redeployment is clearly possible, resources currently employed in military applications cannot be redeployed quickly or easily elsewhere in other sectors or other countries. There are technical problems in achieving such a transformation, not least the contribution made by military spending to jobs in economies with high unemployment. And beyond the technical problems are questions of political will. Nonetheless, some countries - China,

Argentina, and Peru, for example - have recently shown that it is both technically and politically possible to make substantial shifts from military to civilian spending within a short time.

WORLD ARMAMENTS AND THE GROWTH OF THE 'ARMS CULTURE'

Traditionally, nations have adhered to an 'arms culture'. They find themselves locked into arms competitions fuelled among other things by powerful vested interests in the 'military-industrial complex' as well as in the armed forces themselves. Industrial nations account for most of the military expenditures and the production and transfer of arms in international society. However, the influence of this 'arms culture' is not confined to these nations. It is present also in the developing world, fostered both by the desire of many governments to seek security through acquisition of arms and by a burgeoning world arms trade.

Poverty generates tensions and conflicts, urban and rural violence. The indigenous people are still awaiting solutions for their problems. All this depends on money and nevertheless we are spending money on our nuclear programmes. They say that this has peaceful objectives. This is not true because precious money is being spent on this.

The greatest crime: the death of hope, the death of all of the rights we all have, especially that of the young of believing in a future, the hope for a normal life, a difficult life but something that appears as a challenge to live it the best we can. We have a right to this chance.

Since the early 1960s, military spending in developing countries as a whole has increased fivefold. Their share of total spending increased from under one-tenth to almost a quarter of a far larger total. Some developing countries, such as the Republic of Korea, have achieved a high level of development in spite of military spending. But systematic analysis suggests that increases in military spending have had negative effects on economic performance.

Moreover, defence expenditure is one of the most import-intensive of activities, usually creating a large secondary demand for imported spares, ammunition, servicing, training, and fuel. It has been estimated that 20 per cent of the external debt acquired by non-oil developing countries in the decade to 1982 could be attributed to arms imports. And high levels of arms spending motivated by a variety of reasons have undoubtedly contributed to the severity of the crises of development in Africa, where military spending rose, in real terms, by 7.8 per cent per annum between 1971 and 1982, and arms imports rose by 18.5 per cent. it should be noted in this connection that in the case of the Frontline States they have been compelled to expand their armed forces because of the threat from South Africa.

The development of an 'arms culture' in many developing countries presents particular dangers in the context of environmental and poverty-induced stresses. There are already numerous simmering disputes in the Third World - over 40 unresolved - many arising from boundaries defined in colonial times.

Sophisticated weapons can help convert the potential into actual conflict. According to the UN Group of Governmental Experts on the Relationship Between Disarmament and Development:

There can no longer be the slightest doubt that resource scarcities and ecological stresses constitute real and imminent threats to the future well-being of all people and nations. These challenges are fundamentally non-military and it is imperative that they be addressed accordingly. If this is not recognized,... there is a grave risk that the situation will deteriorate to the point of crisis where, even with low probability of success, the use of force could be seen as a way to produce results quickly enough. This is far from being a remote possibility. In recent years, there has been a marked tendency in international relations to use or to threaten to use military force in response to non-military challenges to security.

The situation in many developing countries presents particular dangers in the context of environmental and poverty-induced stresses. Large-scale movements of refugees, competition for scarce water and fertile lands, deposits of oil and raw materials, ill-defined boundaries, and so on all add to tensions and increase possibilities for conflict. The importation of armaments by developing countries has increased also because of these real or potential conflicts. It is sometimes encouraged by the arms manufacturers because of the important profits that can themselves sustain the manufacture of arms in the exporting countries. The export of arms have been evaluated at more than $35 billion annually. The arms trade is estimated to have absorbed over $300 billion over the last two decades, three-quarters in the form of sales to developing countries.

TOWARDS SECURITY AND SUSTAINABLE DEVELOPMENT

Principles

The first step in creating a more satisfactory basis for managing the interrelationships between security and sustainable development is to broaden our vision. Conflicts may arise not only because of political and military threats to national sovereignty; they may derive also from environmental degradation and the pre-emption of development options.

There are, of course, no military solutions to 'environmental insecurity'. And modern warfare can itself create major internationally shared environmental hazards. Furthermore, the idea of national sovereignty, has been fundamentally modified by the fact of interdependence in the realm of economics, environment, and security. The global commons cannot be managed from any national centre: The nation state is insufficient to deal with threats to shared ecosystems. Threats to environmental security can only be dealt with by joint management and multilateral procedures and mechanisms.

Environment must also be an approach to development. Environment is a social justice issue and environment even is a peace and security issue. The barriers to achieving sustainable development are great, as might be expected in a major historical transformation, but they are far from insurmountable.

We approach the millennium in a world in which global interdependence is the central reality, but where absolute poverty and environmental degradation cloud our vision of a common future, and where a geopolitical climate dominated by nuclear terrorism and increasing militarization saps the idealism of the young and the will to dream in us all.

Cooperative Management

Already, environmental stresses are encouraging cooperation among nations, giving some indication of ways to proceed. Antarctica is subject to a far-reaching agreement that provides a collective approach to management. There are now various institutional systems, often of complex and advanced form, to foster bilateral and regional cooperation for marine fisheries in order to regulate maximum sustainable yields and the distribution of catches. One of the main threats to the oceans the dumping of highly toxic wastes has so far been managed by the London Dumping Convention. As for international water bodies, impressive progress has been made by the bilateral U.S.-Canadian Commission for the Great Lakes. The Mediterranean Convention, only one of the many such treaties concluded within the context of the UNEP Regional Seas Programme, brings together coastal nations in an arrangement to monitor and combat pollution at sea.

Some of the most challenging problems require cooperation among nations enjoying different systems of government, or even subject to antagonistic relations. The 1986 Chernobyl reactor accident in the Soviet Union has resulted in two agreements covering international cooperation in cases of such accidents. In the future, the nation concerned will immediately alert neighbouring states; they, in turn, will offer assistance at cost and free of liability. The 1979 Convention on Transboundary Pollution has provided a framework for monitoring and assessing damage from pollutants causing acid rain in Europe.

Cooperation on environmental issues among developing countries has often been made difficult by poor communications. Nonetheless, many now participate in UNEP's Regional Seas Programme. The nations of the Sahel have formed a regional organization to deal with desertification, and there ie emerging a body of successful case histories with respect to river basin development: Witness the joint management programmes in Africa for the Senegal River Basin.

SPENDING ON MILITARY VERSUS ENVIRONMENTAL SECURITY

The world spent well over $900 billion on military purposes in 1985, more than $2.5 billion a day. The real cost is what the same resources might otherwise be used for:

- An Action Plan for Tropical Forests would cost $1.3 billion a year over the course of five years. This annual sum is the equivalent of half a day of military expenditure worldwide.
- Implementing the UN Action Plan for Desertification would cost $4.5 billion a year during the last two decades of this century - the equivalent of less than two days of military spending.
- One of the greatest environmental hazards in the Third World is lack of clean water for household use, contributing to 80 per cent of disease. The UN Water and Sanitation Decade, although given only a small fraction of support needed, would have cost $30 billion a year during the 1980s. This is the approximate equivalent of 10 days of military spending.
- To supply contraceptive materials to all women already motivated to use family planning would cost an additional $1 billion per year on top of the $2 billion spent today. This additional $1 billion is the equivalent of 10 hours of military spending.

The Importance of Early Warning

Since it is often uncertainty and insecurity that prompts international conflict, it is of the utmost importance that governments become aware of imminent environmental stress before the damage actually threatens core national interests. Governments are usually not well equipped with this kind of foresight.

It would be highly desirable if the appropriate international organizations, including appropriate UN bodies and regional organizations, were to pool their resources and draw on the most sophisticated surveillance technology available - to establish a reliable early wanting system for environmental risks and conflict.

such a system would monitor indicators of risks and potential disputes, such as soil erosion, growth in regional migration, and uses of commons that are approaching the thresholds of sustainability. The organizations would also offer their services for helping the respective countries to establish principles and institutions for joint management.

Disarmament and Security

Action to reduce environmental threats to security requires a redefinition of priorities, nationally and globally. Such a redefinition could evolve through the widespread acceptance of broader forms of security assessment and embrace military, political, environmental, and other sources of conflict.

A broader approach to security assessment would no doubt find many cases in which national, regional, and global security could be enhanced through expenditures quite small in relation to the levels of military spending. Four of the most urgent global environmental requirements - relating to tropical forests, water, desertification, and population - could be funded with the equivalent of less than one month's global military spending. It is difficult to shift budgetary resources, but individual governments have already shown that transformation is possible, given political will. In some of the countries most seriously affected by environmental stress and poverty, the sums required to alleviate these conditions are small in relation to what is now spent on disaster relief, let alone military activities. However, these sums must be spent quickly, before deteriorating conditions require much larger expenditures.

But in terms of the aggregate resources involved in arms spending and the potential throat to the environment from war, the greatest need is to improve relations among those major powers capable of deploying weapons of mass destruction. This is needed to achieve agreement on tighter control over the proliferation and testing of various types of weapons of mass destruction nuclear and non-nuclear including those that have environmental implications.

A substantial number of agreements already show the potential for negotiated, multilateral solutions. President Reagan and General

Secretary Gorbachev made substantial progress towards strategic arms agreement, which must be carried forward to reverse the alarming trends of several decades. Apparently, the two major powers came close to agreeing on intermediate range systems in Europe, to be followed by agreements banning forward deployment of shorter range systems. It would alleviate significantly the pressures exercised by nuclear weapons on the security order in Europe. In addition, they are moving towards, a 50 per cent reduction agreement on strategic systems, followed by total elimination agreements. They also need to agree on effective measures to prevent an arms race in space. Successful negotiations would contribute significantly to stemming the spread of nuclear weapons as the major nuclear-weapon states would deliver on their promise to build down their nuclear arsenals. Such progress is consistent with the basic needs of our times and the right of humanity to have the spectre of nuclear destruction removed from the face of the Earth.

Nations must turn away from the destructive logic of an 'arms culture' and focus instead or their common future. The level of armaments and the destruction they could bring about bear no relation to the political conflict that triggered the arms competition in the first place. Nations must not become prisoners of their own arms race. They must face the common danger inherent in the weapon of the nuclear age. They must face the common challenge of providing for sustainable development and act in concert to remove the growing environmental sources of conflict.

ASIAN SECURITY ENVIRONMENT AND INDIA'S OPTIONS

Asian security environment is in a state of deep turmoil. The single event which has occasioned it is the giant rise of China during the past couple of decades, reaching higher and higher levels of economic and military strength. All neighbors of China including those further afield, are engaged in working out strategies to cope with China should it turn into a rogue state sometime in future.

Even the US is looking for new equations of power as the centre of political and economic balance shifts towards Asia, led by China whose long-term vision of itself remains unfathomable. Setting aside its suspicions of many decades and making an exception to its consistently held non-proliferation policies, the US offered to India a civilian nuclear agreement which will boost its economic and military strength. The rapprochement has been followed by another agreement for joint defense framework that will be in place for ten years envisaging a closer military relationship and arms sale to India. China has not been very happy over these developments as it already sees itself as being the reason for them.

China has been singled out by US as its most likely bete noir of the future because of its galloping economic growth. Economists assess that the Chinese economy will outgrow US economy by the third decade of this century, giving it almost an equal status. But the Indian economy is also expected to grow almost uniformly during the same period, equaling the size of US economy and growing beyond by 2050s. Thus, while China becomes the largest economy in the world in the next 20 years and the most powerful nation in Asia, it will also have to share the high table with India, and Japan which before the spurt in Chinese growth, was the biggest economy in Asia. These three powers Japan, India and China, will have jointly or singly the greatest sway over Asian security in the coming years. History has already decided that they cannot love each other. And since rising to such eminence requires assurances of availability of markets and resources, the relationship among the three is likely to be marked by mutual rivalry, jealousies and recriminations. This accounts for the turmoil which is already visible in Asian security. If careful and visionary steps on future strategy are not taken now by all the nations of Asia, dark times will lie ahead. By opting for India, also a fellow democracy and hence sharing common values, the US wants to preempt those dark times.

US have thus become an active participator in the power play in Asia with a new vantage hold on Asian security. With its new alignments with India, it will try to balance off any attempt by China to dominate over Asia. Furthermore, its own impact on Asia and its security will stay unabated as it plays the role of mentor in the region.

The Japanese have also lately, been displaying a special interest in India, compelled by similar reservations on China. Since 2004, India has become the largest recipient of its overseas aid. In addition they are also mulling over how the constitutional embargoes, placed by the victorious US on a defeated Japan at the end of World War II, restricting their defense forces by size and role, can be amended. Japan is spending not more than 1% of its GDP on its defense whereas the figure for US is 4%. Some clever maneuvering is taking place in this respect and the size and lethality of the Japanese Coast Guard, not identified as a self-defense force, is being furiously expanded. The Japanese, like China and India, is also entering space in a big way. All the three countries have set somewhat identical targets for space and research programs for lunar orbit and manned flights to moon, because the common belief is that space can become the platform for future wars if they cannot be avoided.

Another source of future aggression can be the economic tool of currency reserves. China is no longer a Marxist country even though it is a one party ruled authoritarian communist state. It turned capitalist a long while ago, of course with Chinese characteristics and opened itself to foreign investments, trade and globalization with its instant connectivity. The boom in economy which came in their wake has enabled it to accumulate reserves of which nearly $ 1.4 trillion is invested in US treasury bonds. Japan, the number one economy in Asia until overtaken by China, holds reserves of just less than $ 1 trillion. Such enormous wealth, in the context of cash imbalances in other Asian countries, gives them opportunities for purchasing or heavily investing in state assets of the weaker Asian nations and thereby acquiring undue hold over such countries. It can effectively turn out to be a new form of colonialism. This calls for the establishment of appropriate review committees in such countries to exclude what can prove to be politically mandated sinister investments. Lesser nations have, thus, to remain on guard to preserve their economic integrity and safety.

Infact the nations of South East Asia, neighbours of China and Japan, have already been vigilant for quite sometime. Five of these, Indonesia, Malaysia, Thailand, Philippines and Singapore in 1967 created ASEAN, Association of South East Asian Nations, gradually enlarging it between 1984 and 1995 to include Brunei, Vietnam, Laos, Myanmar and Cambodia. These nations primarily got together to expand intra regional trade and to move towards a single market and customs union. The secondary objective was to create a forum for joint assessments for any predatory assault from more powerful nations of the North and across the Pacific. While the ASEAN has not been able to accomplish much so far by way of integration and common policies, it has given its members a sense of being a close knit group with some common concerns the most important of which remains not getting over shadowed by more powerful and not necessarily benign neighbours like China, Japan and the US.

In 1993 these nations took another step with national security as a special focus to set ARF, Asean Regional Forum, with a considerably expanded membership. ARF includes several distant countries like US, Canada, Australia, Russia and European Union, besides all major Asian countries like India, China, Japan and North Korea. The logic for creating such an omnibus forum was to have all likely adversaries on one platform so that all aggressive design towards the region could be controlled and stalled. ARF has not so far deliberated upon any major security issue but the hope is that in time to come, when regional rivalries are likely to be exacerbated,. ARF could play the role of a mini General Assembly of the UN, India, by being a member of ARF, is now enabled to have its say on any troubling issue, arising in South East Asia.

Their rivalries were again on display when another forum called East Asia Summit was being set up. To the chagrin of China, India was invited to participate in it by Japan, Indonesia and Singapore, with tacit support from the US. By the time the East Asia Summit was inaugurated in 2005, Australia and New Zealand had also become its members. The Chinese ability to dominate over the institution was thus greatly diminished. The EAS is a futuristic organization, to play a role when in future security related issues in the region would become highly complex. Again, through its membership, India will be enabled to present its view forcefully on any or all issues including security.

The region's cautious attitude towards China flows from the historical legacy when the Chinese communist party was blatantly supporting insurgencies and smaller communist parties in the neighbourhood. Chinese war with Vietnam in 1979 and propping up of the murderous government of Pol Pot in Cambodia had added to their misgivings. The Chinese attack on India in 1962 and subsequent withdrawal had already added another dimension to the mystery of Chinese decision-making process. Since then and particularly after the Tiananmen Square uprising of 1989, China adopted a low profile and has been focused on economic development, avoiding distractions which could spoil its concentration. Chinese rapid economic development from the 1990s has revived those anxieties again since China has a number of territorial disputes with its neighbours which have remained unresolved.

China is squatting over 18,000 sq km of Indian land in Aksai Cheen in Ladakh and claims ownership of the entire state of Arunachal Pradesh, an area of 84,000 sq kms. It is showing no signs of resolving these land disputes, leaving one wondering whether it wants the disputed status quo to remain just that way. The aim seems to be keeping India destabilized in these regions. The Arunachal Pradesh issue was recently raked up by China with many shrill and hostile comments emanating from state controlled media in China. China's long and consistent support to Pakistan, including aiding of the latter's nuclear weapon development against India, violating all norms of non-proliferation, is an abiding indicator that China does not wish India well at all.

Certain projects undertaken by China in the neighbourhood strengthens the suspicion that it wants India hemmed in from all sides, so that it remains a regional power only in South Asia and does not reach the status of an Asian or global power.

Among these projects are port development at Gwadar in Pakistan which could also be a resting place for ships of Chinese Blue Water Navy, Karakoram highway connecting Pakistan with Western China, surveillance outposts on Myanmar Islands, a road from Yunan to Bay of Bengal through Myanmar, beefing up of ports of Myanmar and Srilanka etc. The emphasis on port development suggests an intention to use them during forays of Chinese navy into the Indian Ocean. These projects when ready will also help China to expand its trade and investments further to the West. They are, thus a double purpose activity, which should alert India and require it to go by a worst-case scenario for its security and prepare accordingly for the challenges they represent.

At this point it must be stated, the sense of threat is not unidirectional: as their economy strengthens China also is becoming conscious that India can prove to be a menace. Their biggest worry arises from the presence of Dalai Lama and over 100,000 Tibetans in India. Although India has long ago accepted Tibet to be an autonomous region of China, the undiminishing strength of Tibetan nationalism and the magnetism of Buddhist monasteries in Tibet for mobilization of Tibetan sentiments against Han settlers and authorities there, create a deep suspicion in the Chinese mind that India will not hesitate to exploit any worsening of Chinese situation in Tibet. Selection of a new Dalai Lama when the present one dies could create such a scenario if the Chinese seek to enforce their choice on the Tibetan people. The entire Tibetan diaspora including those in India could be expected to explode against the Chinese with repercussions inside Tibet. In such an event China's relationship with India will plummet and the borders would become active. It is probably because of such anticipation that the Chinese are delaying settlement of the border disputes with India.

The security scenario in East Asia remains troubled over the territorial disputes of China with its other neighbours. In East China Sea, China and Japan have laid rival claims over some islands and rights to explore gas and oil in the region. Neither side is giving in lest it is interpreted as weakness. The disputed Senkakus islands, presently in Japanese hands, lie in this patch of waters. Taiwan also claims Senkakus. In South China Sea, five countries, China, Vietnam, Malaysia, Indonesia and Philippines dispute ownership over Spratly and Paracel islands. A code of conduct signed by the five has taken away the sting but resolution of the problem of conflicting claims remains a distant dream. While India has no direct concerns over these disputes, deterioration in the situation could result in the blocking of Malacco straits through which India's bulk of trade with Eastern countries passes. Such disputes and the tension of catching up with the US have made China determined to upgrade its military capacity as fast as it can. The Chinese military budget hides much more than what it reveals and can be conservatively placed between dollar 50 billion to dollar 80 billion. Its military spending is rising in double digits every year. India's military budget is less than half in comparison. Two consequences flow for India from this. One is that India stands out as a much weaker nation militarily before China. The other is that the People's Liberation Army of China will always try to influence Chinese party leadership to remain jingoistic towards India. That is why Chinese official media often displays a tough and uncompromising attitude towards India.

While China thus remains a potent danger to India on its Eastern and northern flanks, many dangers abound in South Asia itself. In it an anarchic security environment prevails, driven by the flow of history and individual state systems which have developed. The nature of relationship among states of the region is influenced by internal ideologies and power equations. Foreign policy remains a hostage to internal environments and the urge for regional cooperation recedes to the background. Efforts at power balancing with India sends regional co-operation to the bottom of the list of priorities.

The South Asian Association for Regional Co-operation has not made any progress because states like Pakistan and Bangladesh have unwarranted fears arising out of asymmetry of power between them and India. Absence of common democratic norms and desire for collective security also creates hurdles. Many of the states in the region have so far failed to develop an orderly state of governance and enlightened polity. Until all states of the region adopt a minimum set of guidelines for governance such as democracy, secularism and welfare for the people, co-operation in the region will remain elusive and problems of security will keep on surfacing.

Since these states emerged as independent entities after the departure of the British colonial power, an environment of conflict, major or minor, prevails in the region. The most serious of this conflictual situation is between India and Pakistan, dating from partition itself. Militant ethnic identity and extremist religious ideology account for some others. Authoritarianism and misgovernance have also spawned a whole lot of them. These conflicts have led to security deficits and political disasters and most of the region has failed to grow to its potential unlike the nations of South East Asia and Far East. What is worse is that they harbour deep suspicions about India's motivations. The security situation on the Indian borders, therefore, remains perpetually problematic. Except for Maldives and Bhutan that have no issues with India, the remaining four, Pakistan, Nepal, Bangladesh and Srilanka feel unease about India and are capable of taking steps, potentially harmful to the security of India.

Most of the states on India's borders including Afghanistan can be designated failed or failing states. The most dangerous region in the area is Pak-Afghanistan, characterized as ground zero by leaders and security experts of the world. An insurgency, powered by confusing strands of nationalism, misguided religious fanaticism, abiding hatred for the West in general and US in particular, historical misgovernance and repression and absence of credible civil society institutions, rages there. Pakistan was the prime mover of this phenomenon and now is turning out to be its prime victim. Its duplicitous policy of clandestinely supporting Taliban in Afghanistan and battling Pakistan Taliban in its North West is splitting its polity and armed forces and causing militant religious extremism, to spread into its hinterland such as Southern Punjab. Pakistan is imbibing more and more of the virus from Al Qaida whose leaders are still holed in safe havens in Pakistan. As Pakistan totters on account of its internal contradictions it represents a flash point for India and truly speaking for the world itself. The irrational and unthinking leadership of Pakistan has often displayed keenness in the past to go nuclear against India. It is not beyond the realm of possibility that they could share their nuclear technology with Al Qaida and other extremist entities. Pakistan, in the past, has proved to be the worst proliferator of nuclear technology and material. Since leadership there does not bind itself to any ethical or moral code, history can repeat itself.

It is a moot question whether India knows how to deal with Pakistan. It has relied in the past on the dialogue process but though romanticized, it has always proved to be essentially substanceless. Experience of many years shows Pakistan is unable to deliver on Kashmir and terrorism. Kashmir is its objective and terror its tool. There is plenty of evidence now that Pakistan also seeks to subvert the Indian Muslims by appealing to their Islamic instincts. Such propaganda does work as several cells have been discovered in the US, Europe and elsewhere where young natural born Muslim citizens respond to their religiously activated instincts and turned disloyal to the countries of their birth and upbringing. The threat from Pakistan is not just a territorial threat: it is also an ideological threat and is, therefore, to be combated at that plane. It should also be noted that Islamization is growing in the North East region of India, thanks to the collaboration of the Pakistani and Bangladeshi intelligence services. This development offers an easy tool for exploitation by evil-minded powers in the region.

There are many scholars and security experts who think that Islamic religious extremism has now got converted into an ideological movement which cannot be controlled by military means. Even in moderate Muslim countries like Malaysia, Indonesia and Maldives, its onward march has become a cause for concern. If it is a valid and true assessment, the US and NATO efforts in the Pak Afghan region can be expected ultimately to end in fiasco. This should be a cause for anxiety to India as it is investing heavily in Afghanistan in the hope that a stable and democratic order will emerge there.

Islamic terrorism, it should be understood clearly, is a joint project of Pakistani establishment and extremist organizations in Pakistan like Lashkar-e-Taiba, Jaish-e-Mohd, Harkat-ul-Jehadi Islam etc. for training, financing and operating jihadis all across the world against US, Jews and India, wherever Muslim interests have come under pressure and to establish Muslim Caliphates worldwide. Lashkar trained Mujahids have fought in Tajikistan, Uzbekistan, Chechen, Dagestan, Bosnia, Afghanistan and Iraq. Only recently a rift has arisen between the Pakistani Establishments and Pakistan terrorist organisations over the former's military actions against Taliban in the North West region due to US pressure. In the eyes of the leaders of the Lashkar, the current leaders of Pakistan have turned unislamic and need to be punished. The latter are, therefore, fearful and will not call off terrorist operations in Kashmir and other parts of India.

As for other troubled countries of South Asia, Nepal has not stabilized after the demolition of the monarchy and embourgeoising of its Maoists. The Maoists seem bent on seizing all controls in Nepal and are systematically moving towards this objective. SriLanka continues to grapple with ethnic and identity conflicts even after the defeat of Tamil Tigers and death of their supremo, Prabhakaran. The Sinhala leadership will have to demonstrate a great deal of pragmatism and statesmanship to find a new and acceptable equilibrium for all the communities living there. Bangladesh presents a pitiable case with a bursting population growth, abject poverty and growing extremism in its polity and is unable to trust India. It is evident that SAARC has failed and needs to be replaced by another body which will promote democratic values, interdependence and conflict resolution. India should take a lead in the matter and invite only such South Asian states to participate who will not let their political hang ups to come in the way of expansion of regional trade, investments, water management, intraregional connectivity and counter terrorism.

The need for counter terrorism has brought the four central Asian states of Kyrgyzstan, Uzbekistan, Tajikistan and Kazakhstan into a regional institution with China and Russia, called the Shanghai Cooperation Organisation, in 2001. Besides dealing with Islamic terrorism this forum can lead to useful arrangements for accessing gas and petroleum products in Caspian Sea area. Institutions like SCO, Asean, and SAARC etc are all created on the model of European Union which dilutes the sovereignty of its members over some major political and social areas and reduces drastically the sharpness of balance of power politics. However the Asian regional institutions are far from accomplishing such results because of their members own sense of insecurity and fears of loss of identity but there seems to be no better way of ensuring their security. India's decision to be a part of such bodies is a visionary decision. India's voice is valued by the smaller nations of the East and that will add leverage to its opinions in South Asia also.

Because Britannia ruled over the waves the British were able to create an empire over which the sun never set. In the near future a deep contestation is likely to arise over who rules over the Indian Ocean. The Chinese want to control the sealanes as more than four fifths of the crude oil requirements of China pass through the Ocean. Bulk of raw materials like iron ore, coal and bauxite, essential for Chinese growth, like wise pass through the same routes. In the next twenty years, Chinese needs for energy and other raw resources are expected to nearly double. China is therefore investing heavily for creating s blue water fleet, with aircraft carriers, nuclear submarines and paraphernalia capable of projecting force in the Indian Ocean apart from the Pacific. India senses a threat from such developments, since four fifths of its own energy requirements like oil from Persian Gulf, liquefied gas from Qatar and Indonesia, come over sea routes. The smaller nations in the region are alarmed by the growth of sea power of India and China and are beefing up their own navies. Hopefully, the rivalries in the Indian Ocean will be contained through prudent diplomacy and non-belligerent engagements.

Only three other trouble spots affecting Asian security, remain to be considered and they are Palestine, North Korea and Iran. No one can predict what shape a solution of the Palestinian question will take since each side remains adamant on its terms, the Palestinian Arabs on sharing of ownership of Jerusalem and vacation of some Jewish settlements from earlier Arab owned land and Israeli refusal to concede on the two points. India has to tread very carefully while dealing with them since it upholds the humanitarian and just demands of the Arabs and at the same time has a very close security relationship with the Israelis through which flows highly sophisticated equipment, essential for its safety and defence. No foreseeable change in this policy is likely to occur.

North Korea has hugely damaged Indian interests in the past by supplying long-range nuclear capable missiles and missile technology to Pakistan against receipt of nuclear weapon technology in return. But no new damage is expected. North Korea is an exceptionally frail economic entity and all its neighbours are worried over its ongoing nuclear weapon programme and its intentions. North Korea like Fidel Castro in Cuba is run only by one man Kim Jong-il, dictator of the country. He is believed to be not in good health. His sudden collapse can open up several possibilities; a civil war, a gradual unification process German style with South Korea, attempt at annexation by China or a proxy war involving US, India is just likely to remain a distant watcher, going along with solutions that UN may offer.

Iran's is a perplexing case for India's security and foreign policy. Although a signatory in 1985 of the Nonproliferation treaty, NPT, the world believes it has violated its commitments and is secretly engaged in a nuclear weapon development exercise. Essentially Iran is a fundamentalist Islamic country with links to Hezbollah in Lebanon and Hamas in Palestine, both accepting terror as a tool of policy. It is feared that the two could be a beneficiary of a successful Iranian nuclear weapon programme. If that happens it will be the thin end of the wedge and nuclear munitions could travel to other terrorist groups in other parts of the world. India, therefore, takes a bold and negative view on this programme. At the same time India depends a great deal on energy imports from Iran and hence must keep Iran pacified. US worries over the Iranian nuclear developments are similar. The Obama administration has probably already commenced track II discussions with Iran to evolve a satisfactory solution. India is also engaged with Iran for a gasline to India through Pakistan. The talks are somewhat stalled on the issue of price of gas but the real stumbling block is whether trust can be placed on Pakistan's assurances about the safety and continuity of the supplies through its territory. Accepting the assurance cannot but be a huge gamble. This whole region, Central Asian Republics, Iran, Iraq the Gulf, US, China and Russia today are heavily involved in the geopolitics of oil, gas and pipelines and none of these countries will easily accept being upstaged by others. India's stakes in the region are also enormous but the horrifying factor of Pakistan cannot be overlooked. A policy, indemnified by major countries, though still risky, may be the best option for India. This survey of Asian security reveals that security problems lie scattered along the length and breadth of Asia. At the same time it is to be noted that such problems do not come in the way of increasing globalization of economic relations, trade, investments, inter- dependence and connectivity. Mutual economic benefits may help in keeping a lid over political disputes, at least over the foreseeable future. Economic prospects perhaps hold the key to integrate security related political complexities of Asia as demonstrated by countries of Europe who are now the members of the European Union.

CHINA AND POWER CHANGING IN FAVOR OF WORLD PEACE

The Russia-India-China trilateral is an idea whose time has come, and will become increasingly more important in setting the global agenda, says Nivedita Das Kundu.

The international balance of power is changing in favour of world peace. Russia, India and China (RIC) have been interacting trilaterally since 1996. The 11th round of the Russia-India-China (RIC) Foreign Minister's meeting was held on April 13, 2012 in Moscow. The impetus of the RIC Foreign Ministers' recent meeting was strengthened as it was held within a fortnight after the March 29 BRICS summit in New Delhi. RIC's main agenda has been to oppose unilateralism and to promote a pluralistic democratic international order. The three countries believes that the diverse threats and risks cannot be addressed by military power alone but need to be appraised through political, social and economic prisms.

Russia-India-China's possible axis formation is an important political idea that emerged in the post-Cold War period. It was advocated by Russian President Yeltsin in 1993 and Prime Minister Yevgeny Primakov in 1996. Indo-Russian, Sino-Russian and Sino-Indian relations have begun to unfold a new trend now. If this trend continues it will stimulate the process of multi-polarity which will be of far reaching significance for international relations.

Countries like Russia, India and China need a multi-polar world in order to promote their national interest across and autonomy of decision-making. To construct a multipolar world, the Russia-India-China triangle would be indispensable. Although there are some unresolved issues between these countries, the movement towards a better understanding between these three states is evident. The relations between the three flourished during the Cold War period. Even after the end of the Cold War, the relationship was maintained as Russia proved to be India's tested and trusted friend.

Similarly, the China-India relationship became smoother in the eighties and after the 1993 accord economic relations acquired an added momentum. The three countries have many converging interests that could add substance to trilateral cooperation. They back the primacy of the United Nations in solving crises and support the principle of non-intervention in internal affairs of sovereign states. In the long term, it is the mutual confidence which will help these three powers to play a larger role in global politics and to respond jointly to the challenges of the new century. There is, however, a need to coordinate the actions as the international environment has become more intricate and complicated. The commonality of key national interests and the long-term friendly relations in the field of culture, economy and science and technology create a real possibility for cooperation between these three great powers.

The three nations share wide-ranging interest on many major international issues, and are committed to build a just and fair, new international political and economic order. There are advantages of trilateral cooperation despite the obvious asymmetries, given the fact that they are amongst the world's largest continental-sized entities and civilization states.

All three countries have had a long history of interaction, exchange, cooperation and close relationships. In the post-World War II period, there have been phases of tremendous warmth and bonhomie among them. There have also been periods of near-total breakdown and actual hostilities, as happened during the 1962 India-China war. However, what has become clear to all three is that any restructuring of relations would be based on a qualitatively different strategic reality. There is, for instance, no doubt that there could be no resurrection of any kind of alliance relationship clearly directed against or targeting any third country or any agreement offering unconditional support to the other.

One of the major areas of cooperation for the three countries is energy security. Russia is an energy-surplus country, whereas China and India are energy-deficient. If these three states can work together, they can invest in joint projects that could facilitate the flow of oil and gas from Russia into China and India. The trilateral cooperation can improve the overall energy security scenario in Asia and the world.

They can also cooperate in combating separatist movements. With each other's cooperation, they can refrain from supporting these movements in each other's country, exchange their experience in solving ethnic problems and can cooperate in opposing terrorism and extremism.

Sustained economic development of Russia, India and China has become the engine of the global economy. There are many similarities in the socio-economic conditions of the three countries and the way they are responding to globalization. The prospects of cooperation in technology, energy, raw materials, etc. are extremely broad. The population of each country should recognise the benefits of Russia-India-China cooperation so that it could gain popular support. Globalisation offers new opportunities and brings new challenges to China, India and Russia. In order to realise the opportunities and to respond to challenges, there is a need for a permanent mechanism for a regular exchange of views and coordination of actions.

RIC trilateral cooperation has great importance in terms of geopolitics as the three countries are home to around 2.4 billion, 40 percent of the world's total population and account for 22.5 per cent of the total area of the world. Undoubtedly, the three countries have great human resources, huge potential of market and rich endowment of natural resources.

All the three countries are faced with the tasks of developing their economy. China has common borders with both Russia and India. All three countries advocate non-alliance and non-confrontation. The relationship among the three countries affects the basic principles of Asian security. It will definitely have a positive impact on Asian security if their ties could be further improved and more countries are persuaded to observe these principles.

The trilateral cooperation has made much headway in the past few years since the first meeting in Moscow in September 2001. The trilateral format was initiated by holding meetings of the ministries of foreign affairs on the margins of the United Nations General Assembly sessions in New York in the year of 2003 and 2004.

A landmark stand-alone meeting of the foreign ministers was held in Russia in June 2005 in Vladivostok. As a result, a clear-cut profile of the troika took shape. The agenda of the ministerial meeting in this format includes an exchange of views on key international and regional problems, including the war on international terror, illicit drug trafficking and other major challenges.

The intensification of trilateral economic interaction acquired an added importance in the ensuing years. At the October 2007 meeting of the three ministers in Harbin, China, the three countries provisionally divided these lines of preparation in a way that the issue of agriculture was coordinated by China, that of health care by India, and emergency prevention and response by Russia.

In February 2007 and later in October 2007 when meetings of the foreign ministers of the three countries were held in New Delhi (India) and in Harbin (China) respectively, it was decided to give a structured and dynamic character to relations in this format to promote practical cooperation. The initiation of the consultation mechanism between the heads of territorial departments of the ministries of foreign affairs of Russia, India and China became a key agency in implementing these objectives. It was decided to hold such events on a regular basis, at least once a year, and since then yearly meetings of the RIC foreign ministers are taking place regularly.

In recent years, the trilateral has been marked by closer coordination on key international issues. During the recent RIC meeting in Moscow, the three countries have taken similar positions on the issues of the Syrian crisis and on Iran's nuclear standoff.

They were supportive of Kofi Annan's peace initiative on Syria. According to RIC, Iran has the sovereign right to peaceful nuclear energy and has strongly argued for resolving this issue through political and diplomatic dialogue and through consultations between Iran and the International Atomic Energy Agency (IAEA).

The RIC joint statement also reiterated their concerns on Afghanistan, where increasing focus on the exit of the International Security Assistance Force (ISAF) was discussed and RIC focused on post-ISAF exit responsibilities of these three countries. They are all immediate neighbours of Afghanistan and victims of terrorism and drug trafficking emanating from Afghanistan.

The joint statements mentioned their commitment to ensuring stability in Afghanistan and reaffirmed their commitment to contribute towards ensuring stability and security within the UN framework or through other regional initiatives, including the Shanghai Cooperation Organisation (SCO), as Russia and China are full member or observer of the SCO and India is an observer. The growing closeness amongst RIC is clearly noticeable in various fora from the United Nations to the G-20 Summits, within the SCO, during Asia-Europe meetings, during climate change meetings, during East Asian summits, and so on.

There are strong complementarities among the three countries, in terms of natural resources, services capability, skilled labour, manufacturing capability and technology. They are all strong on entrepreneurial activity and in innovation and technology activities.

However, the current levels of trade, investment and economic interaction between them are far below their potential. There is, therefore, considerable scope for cooperating on technology and innovation. The RIC has already set up subsidiaries like the RIC trilateral experts meeting on disaster management, the trilateral business forum, and the trilateral academic scholar's dialogue, and held other trilateral projects and conferences in these specialised fields. However, for all three, food and commodity security will emerge as a major concern and that is one area in which closer interaction and some understanding would be essential as the three states go forward to integrate in the global market.

The regular meetings of the three countries' foreign ministers are playing a key role in promoting the trilateral cooperation. The main task of the troika forum is to create a good climate among the three countries and to improve the security paradigm in the region and to strengthen mutual understanding and trust, which is essential for finding the best solutions for certain problems at the bilateral level. The principles laid down in the trilateral dialogues are those of equality, mutual trust and consensus. Trilateral cooperation has gained strong momentum and as long as patience and perseverance are maintained, cooperation among the three countries will go on to scale new heights.

TRIANGULAR RELATION BETWEEN INDIAN, RUSSIA AND CHINA

The bilateral relationships between Russia and China, Russia and India, and China and India, it can be argued that windows of opportunity have certainly opened up for new alignments in global politics. The three major second-tier powers in the international system share a desire for more strategic autonomy vis-à-vis the only remaining superpower, the United States. The political declarations signed during the various bilateral and trilateral interactions of three states reflect the close identity of views the three nations hold on a range of international issues, including terrorism, Iraq, the Middle East, the role of the UN, non-proliferation, and regional security.

However, there are equally strong, if not stronger, constraints that prevent this remarkable convergence of interests from evolving into a trilateral strategic partnership, what has been referred to as a "strategic triangle."

Bilateral Impediments

The most difficult aspect of this strategic partnership is the highly uncertain nature of the Sino-Indian bilateral relationship. China has tried hard to maintain a rough balance of power in South Asia by preventing India from gaining an upper hand over Pakistan. China has consistently assisted Pakistan's nuclear weapons and ballistic missile programmes to counterbalance India's development of new weapons systems. India's preoccupation with

Pakistan reduces India to the level of a regional power, while China can claim the status of an Asian and world power. It is instructive to note that even as India and China share similar concerns regarding Islamic terrorism in Kashmir and Xinjiang respectively, China has been rather unwilling to make a common cause with India against Pakistan.

China's rapid economic growth in the last decade has given it the capability to transform itself into a military power. Its rapidly modernising military is a cause of great concern for India. China's military may or may not be able to take on the United States in the next few years, but it will surely become the most dominant force in Asia. As China becomes more reliant on imported oil for its rapidly growing industrial economy, China will develop and exercise military power projection capabilities to protect the shipping that transports oil from the Persian Gulf to China. The capability to project power would require access to advanced naval bases along the sea lines of communication and forces capable of gaining and sustaining naval and air superiority.

China's assistance to Myanmar in constructing and improving port facilities on two islands in the Bay of Bengal and the Andaman Sea is the first step to securing military base privileges in the Indian Ocean. This can be used as a listening post to gather intelligence on Indian naval operations and as a forward base for future Chinese naval operations in the Indian Ocean. China's increasing naval presence in the Indian Ocean is occurring at the same time the Indian naval expansion has relatively slowed, and this can have great strategic consequences, because India's traditional geographic advantages in the Indian Ocean are increasingly at risk, with deepening Chinese involvement in Myanmar. China has also been actively occupying islands, reefs, and islets throughout the highly disputed South China Sea, occasionally resulting in skirmishes with rival claimants. Though not of any direct strategic consequence for India, this shows that China is serious about making its military presence felt in Asia and would like to be taken seriously. Moreover, Chiha blocked India's membership in the Asia-Pacific Economic Cooperation (APEC) organisation, and India became a member of the

Association of Southeast Asian Nations (ASEAN) Regional Forum (ARF) despite China's opposition. China has been non-committal on India's membership in the SCO and has obliquely warned against India's military presence in Central Asia. It was again China that drafted the highly one-sided and condemnatory UN Security Council Resolution 1172 after India's nuclear tests.

On its part, India seems to have lost the battle over Tibet to China, despite the fact that Tibet constitutes China's only truly fundamental vulnerability vis-à-vis India. India has failed to limit China's military use of Tibet despite its great implications for Indian security, even as Tibet has become a platform for the projection of Chinese military power. India's tacit support to the Dalai Lama's government-in-exile has failed to have much of an impact either on China or on the international community. Today even the Dalai Lama seems ready to talk to the Chinese, because he realises that in a few years Tibet might get overwhelmed with the Han population and Tibetans themselves might become a minority in their own land.

Conversely, reports of Chinese intrusions across the Sino-Indian border keep appearing time and again, especially into the eastern sector of the Line of Actual Control in another of the northeastern Indian state, Arunachal Pradesh. China lays claim to 90,000 square miles of land in Arunachal Pradesh and does not recognise Arunachal Pradesh as part of Indian territory. The opening up of Nathula trade route that connects Tibet and Sikkim is also fraught with dangers, because there are concerns that threats to the internal security of India posed by China could get worse with this opening.

Even though China has solved most of its border disputes with other countries, it is reluctant to move ahead with India on border issues. No results of any substance have been forthcoming from the Sino-Indian border negotiations even as the talks continue endlessly and the momentum of the talks itself seems to have flagged. So far only the maps of the middle sector of the LAC, the least controversial part of the boundary, have been exchanged, and those too yet require confirmation. China has adopted shifting positions on the border issue, which might be a well-thought position to keep India in a perpetual state of uncertainty. In the Indian context, China is ready for an early settlement of the border dispute if India concedes strategic territory.

China's claims along the LAC also seem to be growing and may therefore indicate the reluctance so far to exchange maps on the western and eastern sectors. With China controlling about 35, 000 kilometers of territory in Aksai Chin in the western sector and laying claim to almost all of Arunachal Pradesh (about 90,000 square kilometers) in the eastern sector, no early resolution of the boundary dispute is in sight. On its part, China sees a close Indo-U.S. relationship as an attempt by the United States to encircle it, especially as it comes along with increasing U.S. military presence and influence throughout Central and South Asia after 9/11. China has reacted strongly against the idea of a "democratic quad" consisting of India, Japan, Australia, and the United States and their joint military exercises.

Despite the rhetoric of a new phase in the relationship, the problems between India and China are substantial and complicated, with no easy resolution in sight. Also, the lack of substantial bilateral trade and India's growing trade deficit with China means there is no real economic dimension to boost the relationship. India and China are two major powers in Asia with global aspirations and some significant conflicting interests. The geopolitical reality of Asia ensures that it will be extremely difficult, if not impossible, for *Hindi-Chini* (Indians and Chinese) to be *bhai-bhai* (brothers) in the foreseeable future. The other pillar of the strategic triangle, the Russia-India bilateral relationship, also does not seem very promising on closer examination.

It seems to be a classic case of more style and little substance. In bilateral terms, it is the nature and content of Indo-Russian economic and trade relations that would ultimately constitute the foundation and give substance to any strategic partnership. However, despite sharing an extraordinary defence relationship, the Indo-Russian trade relationship hardly inspires any confidence, because their bilateral trade has shown persistent decline for the last three years. If anything, the momentum of Indo-Russian economic cooperation seems to be slackening on such crucial issues as civilian nuclear energy and other aspects of energy security, because various opportunities in energy security cooperation remain unexploited. The success or otherwise of strategic partnership in future would be decided by the progress in trade and economic relations between the two nations. And, as of now, it seems to be on a rather weak wicket. And even the bilateral defence relationship has come under pressure as India adjusts to the changing nature of modern warfare and shifts its defence priorities to the purchase of smart weaponry, which Russia is ill equipped to provide.

Already, India's increasing defence ties with Israel and the gradual opening of the U.S. arms market for India has made Russia relatively less exciting for India. The U.S. offer to India of F-16s, the Patriot antimissile system, C-130 stretched medium-lift transport aircraft, and P-3C Orion maritime surveillance planes may only be a reflection of what is still to come. The Indian military has been critical of an over-reliance on Russia for defence acquisition, which was reflected in the Indian Naval Chief 's view that they should rethink India's ties with Russia in light of the Russian demand of $1.2 billion more for the aircraft carrier, Admiral Gorshkov, purchased by India in 2004. India is also sensitive to the fact that Russia also enjoys an excellent defence relationship with China. It is the largest supplier of defence equipment to China, with the result that the modernisation of Chinese military owes a lot to Russian supplies. Not only is this of direct strategic consequence for Indian security but it also creates a cascading effect whereby Russian military technology and know-how gets transferred to Pakistan via China.

Therefore, the prospects of Indo-Russian defence and political cooperation will be assessed by India in the light of Russia's defence supplies and cooperation arrangements with China. Reports of Russia transferring special military technologies to China developed with Indian resources and exclusively for Indian armed forces are causing consternation in India. On the other hand, there are concerns in Russia about the growing Indian strategic alignment with the United States even as Russia has been adopting an increasingly confrontational posture vis-à-vis the United States and the West.

The China-Russia bilateral relationship is also not as free from friction as it appears on the surface. Despite dramatic expansion of Sino-Russian relations in recent years, Russia and China are bound to run sooner rather than later into the limits that geography imposes on two large and ambitious neighbours. Russia has reasons to worry about China's rising profile in East and Northeast Asia about Chinese immigrants overrunning the Russian Far East and about China's economy dwarfing its own. It has been argued that it would take enormous effort on the part of Russia and China to avoid geopolitical confrontation.

Given the divergence between their geopolitical and strategic national interests, it is anybody's guess how far Russia and China would be able to maintain the current positive trend in their relationship. The greatest danger to this relationship comes, perhaps, from a weakened Russia unable to control instability along the lengthy Sino-Russian border and Central Asia. Despite the renunciation of territorial claims under the Sino-Russian treaty, it is very possible that if China continues to grow at the present rate, it might opt for a revision of the Sino-Russian border. And, even though China is the largest buyer of Russian conventional weaponry, many in Russia see this as counterproductive because China might emerge as the greatest potential security threat to Russia, worse than the United States could ever become.

China, meanwhile, is working towards diversifying its military imports from sources other than Russia, the European Union being a major one. Suspicion of China's motives is strong in Russia, especially in the military. This is reflected in Moscow's refusal to sell China an in-depth production license for its SU-27 and SU-30 jets, thereby keeping China dependent on supplies from Russia. People-to-people contacts between the two societies also remain lukewarm at best, and bilateral economic relations, despite the best efforts of both governments, have been slow to pick up.

Despite its historically adversarial relationship with Japan, Russia is improving its military and economic relations with that country, mainly to prevent China from seeking regional hegemony. In the Russian Far East, where local nervousness has been growing over the large number of Chinese tourists, attitudes towards Japan are the most favourable in Russia. Japan is also attracted by the large oil and gas deposits in eastern Russia and has lobbied Russia successfully to build an oil pipeline to the Sea of Japan, skirting China.

The breakdown of the 2001 interstate agreement to construct an oil pipeline from Russia to China has also adversely affected Sino-Russian relations. The pipeline should have been completed by 2005 and should have supplied China with 20 million metric tons of Russian oil a year by 2010 and 30 million metric tons after 2010. China's unexpectedly tough position on Russia's entry into the World Trade Organisation (WTO) can be considered as a revenge for this oil pipeline imbroglio.

Finally, while trade between Russia and China has begun to grow and China will remain among Russia's five major trading partners, China's trade with Russia remains unimpressive. Russian businesses, which have started to step up their activities around the globe, will also be competing with their Chinese rivals in the coming years, thereby increasing the strain in Sino- Russian relations.

The Centrality of the United States

The problems in bilateral relationships between China and India, Russia and India, and Russia and China get further complicated with the special relationships that the United States has been able to cultivate with each of the three nations. This is especially true after September 11, 2001, because the U.S. relationship with each of the three, especially with Russia and India, has taken a turn for the better. Though Russia, China, and India are obviously pursuing their own interests in their engagement with the United States, this imposes severe constraints on their attempts at coming together and forging a strategic triangle, because all three attach the highest importance to their ties with the United States.

As Russia has realised the importance of reviving its ailing economy, it has cast its lot overwhelmingly with the West and, in particular, with the United States. There is a realisation in Russia that Russia's security can be ensured only by membership in a powerful and ever-growing Western union. All other considerations have been subordinated to this attempt to get closer to the United States. So, even as Russia has quietly acquiesced to the U.S. decision to renounce the ABM treaty and the expansion of NATO right up to Russia's borders, it has used multilateral channels like the UN Security Council to put up token resistance to the U.S. global preponderance. It is instructive to note that even on Iraq, Russia chose to let France take the heat in the UN debates while it played safe by not overtly antagonising the United States.

September 11, 2001, gave Russia a significant opportunity to prove its utility to the United States on the issue of global terrorism. Putin has used this global "war on terrorism" not only to bolster his own position vis-à-vis domestic issues like Chechnya, but he has also sought to position himself as the head of an antiterrorism alliance straddling Europe and Asia. Russia made a major contribution to the war in Afghanistan by sharing intelligence, stepping up efforts to bolster the Northern alliance, and even accepting U.S. military presence in the region. It is another matter, though, that Russia can do little about the expansion of the U.S. political and military presence in the Gulf, and South and Central Asia under the garb of the war on terrorism. Russia's decision to go along with the NATO enlargement also has to do with a realisation that it was inevitable, whether Russia liked it or not. It, therefore, decided to use NATO enlargement to its best advantage by bargaining some concessions for itself, especially a new "partnership" with NATO though without a right to veto over NATO's decision. This pragmatism may also result from the fact that Russia's security today is not so much threatened by the United States as it is by transnational terrorism, ethnic and religious extremism, illegal migration, proliferation of illegal arms, and drug trafficking.

Russia today faces an enormous challenge of resolving the contradictions between its desire to emerge once again as a pre-eminent power on the international stage and the realistic compulsions of reconciling itself to the expanding political, strategic, and technological influence of the United States. And as of now it seems to have concluded that cooperating with the United States can perhaps give Russia both a voice on major global developments and U.S. assistance in shoring up its economy. Russia also realises that a strong and sustainable bilateral relationship with the United States is significant for a whole range of its vital interests from the war on terrorism to non-proliferation and economic growth.

It is also instructive to note that despite Russia's opposition to the U.S.-led war in Iraq, it has gravitated closer to the U.S. positions on major international issues. It has abandoned talk of expanding its nuclear assistance to Iran and pushed that country to subject its nuclear programme to strict international inspections. Russia has teamed up with China to bring new pressure on North Korea to negotiate on its nuclear weapons programme. It has also not been at the forefront of the opposition against U.S. postwar Iraq policies at the UN. This had led some to speculate that the emerging U.S.-Russian global partnership could attain even greater significance than the relationships that the United States currently enjoys with its traditional European allies. These positive trends in the U.S.-Russian relationship are, however, in danger of coming under severe stress because of Putin's steady accretion of power over Russian politics, society, and economy, thereby increasing concerns in the West about the course Russia has taken under Putin's presidency. Putin's reign will be followed by his nominated successor, his Deputy Dmitri Medvedev, while Putin will be the Prime Minister—that is, the real power controlling the destiny of Russia. Going against Ukraine's popular opinion, Putin openly supported the presidential candidate who favoured closer ties to Russia and even campaigned on his behalf. Putin lost his prestige on the international stage when Yanukovich had to make way for Yushchenko as Ukraine's president after allegations of electoral fraud forced Ukraine's supreme court to intervene. Putin has used Russia's economic levers, especially its oil and gas, to bind its neighbours into an ever-tighter dependency. In Moldova and Georgia, Putin has been accused of openly abetting separatist groups by refusing to keep his commitments to withdraw Russian troops.

Putin has moved Russia towards soft authoritarianism by increasing restrictions on free media, by decreeing that provincial governors would no longer be elected but appointed, and by distributing Russian assets to cronies. Even as the U.S. president, George Bush, has been championing his favourite theme of spreading democracy around the world, Putin has been accused of rolling back democracy in Russia. And Bush has come under increasing pressure to confront Putin on a whole range of issues. Russia is reasserting itself as a major player on the global stage with a booming economy, a defence modernisation programme, and a willingness to confront the West. But the United States realises that it is important to keep Russia on its side in dealing with a range of international problems, including the war on terrorism, persuading North Korea and Iran to abandon their nuclear ambitions, and the ongoing effort to secure nuclear materials across the former Soviet Union. And Russia is also acutely aware that despite several years of economic growth, driven largely by the high price of oil, Russia remains a power in decline and that a good relationship with the United States is important to maintain its global profile as a major player of consequence. Therefore, despite some ups and downs, it can be safely assumed that both the United States and Russia would like to keep their relationship on an even keel.

China, on its part, has also moved considerably closer to the United States, especially with its strong support of the antiterror coalition in the immediate aftermath of 9/11. It is interesting, however, in this context to note that China's emphasis has been on SCO with respect to its own stance on antiterror cooperation as opposed to any global coalition led by the United States. In some ways, international developments post–9/11 have helped by shifting the focus of the U.S. national security policy from containing China as its future rival to the elimination of the transnational terrorist networks. It has been an emerging opinion that China has been the biggest beneficiary of post–9/11 global climate as it moved it off the U.S.'s enemies list. This does not mean, however, that China would not be concerned with Russia's deal making with the United States on issues ranging from missile defence to Iraq, leaving China as the only major opponent of the U.S. policies. China has been trying to build a close relationship with Russia by emphasizing their common opposition to various

U.S. policies, like the U.S. pursuit of the BMD and its disregard for multilateral agreements.

China, fearing its marginalisation in the emerging international security environment, has also been trying to project an image of a responsible global player. Its active role in bringing North Korea to the negotiating table has been well appreciated in the United States. Gradually, but with some deft diplomatic footwork, China has been able to use the post–9/11 environment to come to the right side of the United States. China has not only supported the U.S. invasion of Afghanistan to dislodge the Taliban and install the Hamid Karzai government, but it has also been collaborating with the United States in the sphere of counterterrorism. Despite making some routine noises about the U.S. moves in Iraq, China has not been unduly disruptive of the U.S. policies as France and Germany have been. It has also been helping in the reconstruction of Afghanistan and playing a constructive role in using its leverage over Pakistan to nudge it towards greater cooperation with the United States. Though frictions remain, particularly the burgeoning U.S. trade deficit with China, by and large Sino-American relations are on an upswing.

India, being the weakest of the three nations, has to operate its foreign policy within different parameters. Its relations with the United States, Russia, and China are far thinner than the ties among the other three. However, the exclusive superpower status of the United States imparts a special quality to India's ties with the United States.

During the cold war, India's relations with the United States and former Soviet Union (now Russia) were viewed in a zero-sum context. The extent to which the international environment has changed can be gauged from the fact that now Russia itself has emerged as a close ally of the United States.

India has made a serious attempt to upgrade its bilateral relationship with the United States in recent years. It has engaged the United States on a host of issues from non-proliferation and arms control, trade, and cultural exchanges to military-technical cooperation. There is no denying the fact that India would like to consolidate this upward movement in bilateral relations. There are strong domestic constituencies in both India and the United States that believe that close and cooperative relations between the two nations will endure over the long run because of the convergence of their democratic values and vital national interests.

This is despite a feeling in some quarters in India that the United States has not supported it strongly enough vis-à-vis Pakistan's abetment of terrorism on the Indian territory. A substantial part of Indo-U.S. relations remain hyphenated to Pakistan, despite protestations to the contrary, especially after Pakistan's newfound geographical relevance in the U.S.-led coalition's operations against Afghanistan. Despite this, however, Indian foreign policy today is strongly geared towards influencing the U.S. administration in its favour with some even suggesting an alignment with the United States to contain China's growing influence in Asia. The Indian political establishment might not be enthusiastic about openly joining hands with the United States to contain China, there is less aversion to closer Indo-U.S. ties than ever before.

It can also be argued that in the long run, India and the United States are bound to come even closer as Pakistan's utility in the war on terrorism declines and that containing fundamentalism in Pakistan itself becomes a U.S. foreign policy priority. The United States also hopes that India would join its Proliferation Security Initiative and missile defence programme, further cementing their bilateral ties. The Pentagon has been designating India as a "friendly" foreign country for the last two years along with nations like Austria, Brazil, Bulgaria, Finland, South Africa, and Kuwait. This is significant, because India's refusal to turn down a U.S. request for troops to Iraq apparently did not have any effect on this designation. The United States has also lifted the decades-old export restrictions on equipment for India's commercial space programme and nuclear power plants.

To cap it all, the July 2005 U.S.-India civilian nuclear cooperation agreement has taken U.S.-India bilateral ties to a new level, as it overturns three decades of old technology-denial regime and gives India access to U.S. nuclear fuel and reactors and paves the way for Indian integration into the global nuclear order. The nuclear pact between the United States and India has engendered claims by the Indian opposition parties that India is in danger of losing its strategic autonomy in the realm of foreign policy. While this is a gross exaggeration of the state of U.S.-India bilateral ties, India clearly realises the importance of cultivating the United States in its foreign policy calculus, and U.S.-India ties will only grow stronger in the coming years if the present strategic trends in global politics are any guide.

PREDOMINANT POWER IN THE INTERNATIONAL SYSTEM

While the United States remains the predominant power in the international system, the dispute over Iraq has demonstrated that most of the major global powers do not share American perspectives on major problems in the international system and the appropriate means for resolving them. Many countries see a need to balance the U.S. might in the global system, but there is little that they are capable of doing given the enormous differences in capabilities. This desire to balance the United States and an opposition to so complete a U.S. dominance of the international system is shared by Russia, China, and India, though perhaps to different degrees.

According to standard international relations theory, states in the international system will act to prevent any one state from developing a preponderance of power. A state will join whichever state seems weaker to maintain a balance of power in the international system. States can try to balance power unilaterally by developing armaments or by forming alliances with other countries whose power resources help to balance the major player in the international system. A balance of power system is seen by the realist school of thought in international relations as both inevitable and beneficial, because it prevents any one state from becoming the top dog in the system, thereby enhancing global security. Realists of all hues agree that balancing is the principal strategy that states employ to prevent any other state from upsetting the balance of power.

Given the current distribution of power in the international system wherein the United States enjoys an overwhelming preponderance of power since the demise of its cold war rival, the former Soviet Union, the question arises as to why do we not see other major powers in the international system trying to counterbalance the U.S. dominance. Some realists like Kenneth Waltz have argued that "balancing tendencies are already taking place" and that it was only a matter of time before other major powers found a serious balancing coalition. In fact, for Waltz unipolarity is the least durable of international configurations and inevitably will provoke actions and responses by the dominant and weaker states that will ultimately return the system to a more traditional balance of power order.

According to other realist scholars such as Stephen Walt, the United States exhibits a long-standing commitment to work within "a set of multilateral institutions that limit its ability to either threaten or abandon its major allies." Furthermore, the United States remains isolated geographically from other great powers and continues to deploy strategic weapons that are oriented towards defence rather than offence. Washington, therefore, as per Walt, poses little if any threat to others and thus provokes no measures to counteract its pre-eminence in world affairs.

While most realists focus on the traditional form of balancing—internal defence buildups or external alliance formations, some realist scholars have advanced the concept of "soft balancing," whereby states will try to contain the U.S. might by entangling it in a web of international institutional rules and procedures or ad hoc diplomatic maneuvers. The United States might also find itself excluded from regional economic cooperation, and its ability to project military power may be undermined by restricting or denying military basing rights. On the other side of this theoretical debate are the liberals who point out that U.S. predominance enjoys a high degree of legitimacy primarily because of Washington's consistent championing of liberal ideals and its history of supplying a wide range of public goods to the international community.

But some liberals, such as Charles Kupchan, assert that Europe is likely to pose a growing challenge to U.S. hegemony in the foreseeable future. He argues that, with an increase in Europe's wealth, military capacity, and collective character, Europe will desire a greater role in international affairs and will be prone to challenging America's primacy.

There is, as of now, no theoretical consensus among scholars as to whether balancing is taking place at all vis-à-vis U.S. preponderance and, if it is occurring, what form is it taking. This debate has gained additional momentum after the demonstration of U.S. military supremacy in Afghanistan and Iraq in recent years and the seemingly unilateral foreign policy pursued by the George W. Bush administration. This chapter looks at a small subset of interstate relations among Russia, China, and India and examines the possibility of a Russia-China-India strategic triangle materialising in the near future. The proposal for a Moscow-Beijing-Delhi strategic triangle had originally come from the former Russian prime minister, Yevgeny Primakov, during his visit to India in 1998, arguing that such an arrangement would be a force for greater regional and international stability. It did not, however, elicit as enthusiastic a response from China and India as Russia had, perhaps, hoped for. Though the three countries have focused on improving the nature of their bilateral relationships in the last few years, they have maintained a safe distance from the Primakov proposal.

But this idea of a strategic triangle took a tangible form when the foreign ministers of Russia, China, and India met on the margins of the United Nations General Assembly in New York in September 2002. Although nothing concrete emerged out of this meeting, this was the first major attempt by the three nations to deliberate on world affairs, and these annual meetings have continued since then. Increased bilateral engagements among the political leaderships of three states in the last few years are also an attempt to impart a new dynamic to this process.

The concept of a strategic triangle has been used by the students of international politics to make sense of relationships among three major powers. It is generally referred to with regard to a triangular relationship among three states that can have a major impact on regional and/or global balance of power. A strategic triangle can, however, take various forms—two of the three states in the triangle can decide to balance the third, all three states can decide to work together to balance a more powerful adversary, or each of the three can work against the other in an attempt to become the predominant power. Which triangular configuration would evolve ultimately depends on the strategic environment and the interests of the three states in question. The case for a Russia-China-India strategic triangle has been built by various constituencies to offer a counterweight to the U.S. global and regional hegemony.

Russia has an extremely important role in this process. Russia's loss of power and influence on the world scene has been a major cause of concern for virtually all the Russian leaders. There has been a growing and pervasive feeling among Russia's elites and population that they have surrendered Russia's once-powerful position on the world stage for a position of little international influence and even less respect. It is in this respect that Russia has been trying to establish itself as the hub of two bilateral security partnerships that can be used to counteract American power and influence in areas of mutual concerns.

While Russia has witnessed a downward slide in its status as a superpower in the last decade, China is a rising power that sees the United States as the greatest obstacle in achieving its pre-eminent position in the global political hierarchy. As a consequence, it realises the importance of cooperating with Russia to check American expansionism in the world, even if only in the short term. In fact, Kenneth Waltz has gone to the extent arguing that "wrong" U.S. policies towards Russia and China are moving these two states close to each other and might even lead to the formation of a new balance of power against the United States.

India, conversely, has different considerations, because it is still a far way off from becoming a significant global power. However, India has always tried to voice the concerns of the so-called third world, strongly arguing for respecting the sovereignty of all countries and opposing the use of force in international politics. The concerns that the United States is probably becoming too powerful and unilateral, and that a unipolar U.S.-dominated world would not be in the best interests of weaker states like India, has made the idea of a strategic triangle attractive for certain sections of the Indian strategic elite. Moreover, all the three countries also realise that there is enormous potential in the economic, political, military, and cultural realms if the bilateral relationships among them can get adequately strengthened. And all of then have made some sincere attempts in this regard in the last couple of years. But huge obstacles remain in moving towards a trilateral strategic partnership, making the very idea of a strategic triangle in the context of Russia-China- India interstate relations rather unrealistic.

GEOPOLITICAL IMPORTANCE OF CENTRAL ASIA

As the geopolitical importance of Central Asia has increased in recent years, all the major powers have been keen to expand their influence in the region, and India is no exception. It shares many of the interests of other major powers such as the United States, Russia, and China vis-à-vis Central Asia, including access to Central Asian energy resources, controlling the spread of radical Islam, ensuring political stability, and strengthening of regional economies. But unlike China and Russia, its interests converge with that of the United States in Central Asia and some have even suggested that it is in U.S. interests to have a greater Indian presence in Central Asia to counter growing Chinese or Russian involvement.

Central Asia is crucial for India not only because of its oil and gas reserves that India wishes to tap for its energy security but also because other major powers such as the United States, Russia, and China have already started competing for influence in the region. India's concern about rising Chinese influence in Central Asia was also reflected in India's desire to become a member of the Shanghai Cooperation Organisation (SCO). While ostensibly the SCO is aimed at tackling the security concerns in Central Asia, including extremism and separatism, it also serves as an important instrument in keeping control of the region and limiting U.S. influence there. India has been granted an observer status, but China made sure that Pakistan was also invited, thereby diminishing India's influence. China has a major geopolitical advantage in Central Asian oil politics. Oil resources in the region are of vital importance to China's future oil security and will become an important basis for China's future military strategy. In the event of an unexpected military crisis, China would have to rely heavily on oil resources in mid-Asia to sustain military operations. The extension of the pan-Asian global energy bridge from Central Asia to Iran would link China to the Middle East.

This lifeline from the Caspian Sea to China, incorporating the Middle East, would most benefit China's long-term strategic energy security policy. It would leave China in a much less vulnerable position with respect to both oil reserve depletion and transportation risks. By drastically shifting the most important and busiest global energy artery from the Strait of Malacca to a line across mainland China, the creation of new geopolitical tendencies inside Asia would be inevitable. China would undoubtedly benefit from such a pivotal geostrategic position, particularly as its coastal regions would serve as the refining link between Middle Eastern and Central Asian crude oil—and the Asian-Pacific market.

Chinese aspirations as an "energy bridge" in Central Asia are long term and will require massive international investment in pipeline infrastructure and coastal refineries. The Chinese National Petroleum Company (CNPC) has an oil-swap agreement with Iran. Oil purchased by China from the Uzen oil field in Kazakhstan is pumped to a refinery near Tehran, with China receiving an equivalent amount of Iranian crude exported from Iran's Gulf coast. China's other deal with Kazakhstan includes a commitment to build a 3,000-kilometer pipeline from the oil fields to the Xinjiang province of China, and a 250-kilometer pipeline to the border of Iran (via Turkmenistan). Indian and Chinese state-owned oil companies were engaged in a bidding war to acquire a Canadian company with oil fields in Kazakhstan.

China's National Petroleum Corporation won the bid against India's ONGC after offering a higher sum for Petro Kazakhstan. The Caspian Sea region in Central Asia is another region that is going to see major powers, including China and India, jostling for influence, given its new-found importance as a still-growing source of oil and gas. The area is distant from world markets, generating uncertainty whether Caspian oil will increasingly be sent east or will continue to flow west through Russia or Turkey. In all probability, China is likely to emerge as a new energy hub for Caspian oil and more pipelines will be built to western China, even as India is yet to make any significant headway in exploiting the region's resources.

Exploration and development of the Sakhalin-I oil and gas fields in Russia

India's ONGC has a 20 per cent stake in exploration and development of the Sakhalin-I oil and gas fields in Russia and has been keen to import natural gas from Sakhalin. But China outmaneuvered India by offering a $6 billion loan offer to the Russian Oil company, Rosneft, which then asked India to outbid China if it wanted to be considered for the exports. India's OVL also lost out to China in the acquisition of BP's oil assets in Russia. In one of the first big-ticket oil asset acquisitions by China in Russia, TNK-BP, which controls the OAO Udmurtneft fields in Russia, decided to opt for China's Sinopec in the place of OVL. Though India has expressed its desire to buy nearly a quarter of its annual oil imports in the next decade from Russia, and Russia plans to increase the share of its energy exports to Asia from the current 5 per cent to around 25 per cent, India will have to compete with other Asian nations, most significantly China, which are as eager to court Russia.

While the Chinese have a natural advantage of having a common border with Russia, their diplomacy also seems to be more proactive. Energy issues are driving China and Russia into the arms of each other politically, leading to the mobilisation of the Shanghai Cooperation Council to focus on energy issues, with the possibility of it evolving into a military alliance to rival NATO.

Sino-Russian ties have improved considerably following a plethora of agreements and declarations on energy security cooperation. Russia could become an important supplier of oil to China in the coming years. The two states have performed a feasibility study on a $1.6 billion, 2, 200-kilometer oil pipeline project to bring Serbian oil to northeast China which the Chinese government views as one way for alleviating its dependence on the Middle East oil supplies.

Russia is a world-class gas producer, which fits well into the Chinese strategy to diversify its energy requirements and thus alleviate its dependence on oil. For such a venture to be economically viable, however, significant international confidence and cooperation is required at a multinational level; investment and demand by Japan and Korea is required to realise such a scheme. Russia is also investing in nuclear power reactors in China.

India and China's relationship with energy-rich "rogue states"

A key area of friction and a barrier to engagement between the democratic West and autocratic Beijing is China's relationship with energy-rich "rogue states." Chinese companies, backed by political intent and government finances, are willing to invest in countries with high political risk. With competition for scarce energy resources intense, China has pursued deals with international pariah states that are off limits to Western companies because of sanctions, security concerns, or ethical policy and the threat of international condemnation.

China's relation with state sponsors of terrorism provides a great deal of money, allowing these countries to continue to harbour terrorists and to maintain a policy of oppression and exploitation of their people. This highlights the ideological affinity between China and other authoritarian regimes that are also anxious for market transition while maintaining singleparty rule—Myanmar, Vietnam, Cambodia, Laos, Iran, Sudan, and North Korea. China remains unconcerned as to the source of vital energy, whether Iranian, Kazakh, Sudanese, or Angolan.

China considers anyone who helps with its oil security problem to be a friend of Beijing. China's unconditional assistance and opaque commercial transactions, which do little to encourage these rogue States to improve their governance systems, is viewed in Beijing as necessary in order to guarantee its own continued economic growth. India, conversely, seems to be aligning itself with the West and is investing significantly in trying to evolve a strategic partnership with the United States. The desire of the George W. Bush administration to achieve full civil nuclear energy cooperation with India as part of its broader goals of promoting nuclear power and achieving nuclear security has marked a new phase in the rather unstable bilateral relationship between the world's oldest and the world's largest democracies. The nuclear agreement creates a major exception to the U.S. prohibition against nuclear assistance to any country that doesn't accept international monitoring of all its nuclear facilities.

India, with sixteen nuclear plants, plans to build seven more and has been promised U.S. help to triple its collection by 2020. China remains the only major power that has taken an ambivalent stand of the nuclear deal. While it has indicated that it is willing to promote bilateral cooperation with India in civil nuclear energy, it has also hinted that it might step up its nuclear cooperation with Pakistan. Given the strained relationship between Iran and the United States, India's traditionally close ties with Iran have emerged as a major factor that is influencing how certain sections of U.S. policymakers are evaluating the Indo- U.S. partnership.

Though India has tried to carefully balance its relations with Iran and the United States, because of intense U.S. pressure, especially after the signing of the nuclear deal, India has moved closer to the United States on the issue of the Iranian nuclear programme. As discussed earlier, these complications are bound to increase, because India will be forced to make some difficult diplomatic choices. The United States, preoccupied with the global war on terrorism, is becoming increasingly concerned with Chinese diplomatic activity, particularly in Asia and the Middle East, where its own presence in these regions could be marginalised. China's record of arms sales and support to energy-rich Middle Eastern countries and state sponsors of terrorism in the Gulf region continues to agitate Washington. Asia's oil imports from the Middle East are set to increase rapidly, primarily because of rising demand in China and India and Japan's continuing requirement to import all of its oil requirements.

Ensuring reliable and stable flows from the Gulf region will be Asia's biggest challenge. This may result in the political and economic dependence of many Middle East states shifting from the West towards Asia. As it is America's dependence on Middle

East is much less than that of other major global economies as only 17 per cent of its oil imports flow from the region. In fact, it is China that will be importing almost 70 per cent of its oil from the Middle East by 2015. Unless new sources of oil production are exploited, Middle East reserves as a percentage of global stocks will be proportionally greater by 2025, as other key production areas see their resources dwindle. Middle East producers accounted for 31 per cent of the world's oil supply in 2000, and this figure could grow to 70 per cent by 2025. The Middle East will therefore continue to be the most significant region for oil-energy production.

China will continue to maintain a strong interest in oil production in both Iraq and Iran. These two energy partners are an insurance measure against reduced production from Central Asian oil fields. Iran has explicitly stated its desire for China to replace Japan as the country's largest energy trading partner. China is also considering to revive a $1.2 billion deal that it signed with Iraq during Saddam Hussein's regime in 1997 to develop the Iraqi oil field of al-Ahdab. Energy also remains the backbone of the Sino-Saudi relationship.

Until 1993 China was a net oil exporter, but it has since become the secondgreatest oil consumer after the United States. More than half of Chinese oil imports originate in the Persian Gulf, with 15 per cent in Saudi Arabia. Total Saudi-Chinese trade grew 59 per cent in 2005 to $14 billion and may reach $40 billion in the next four to five years. By 2010 the Middle East might account for 95 per cent of China's imported oil. Saudi Arabia has also emerged as a major investor in Chinese refineries. In 1999 Saudi Arabia's Aramco Overseas Company provided a $750 million investment—25 per cent of the total project—in a petrochemical complex in Fujian capable of processing eight million tons of Saudi crude oil per annum. Saudi Arabia, in cooperation with several members of OPEC, intends to build a new refinery in Guangzhou involving a total investment of $8 billion. China is assiduously attempting to enlarge its sphere of influence throughout the Persian Gulf, and its relationship with Saudi Arabia is a key component of this strategy.

The move in 2005 by the Chinese state-owned CNOOC to take control of the California-based oil exploration and production company Unocal Corporation in a $19 billion bid sent shock waves through the U.S. Congress. Although the Chinese maintain that their interest in Unocal was purely commercial in accessing substantial oil and gas reserves in Southeast Asia, the United States feared a broader Chinese strategy to secure global energy resources. China remains concerned over U.S. aspirations to dominate the Persian Gulf in order to secure its own energy requirements while simultaneously containing China's expansion in the region. Some in Beijing, therefore, consider the United States as a major threat to China's future energy security and remain reluctant to rely on the United States for the security of China's seaborne oil imports, thereby resulting in a focus on developing a blue-water navy to protect its sea lanes of communication. The Iraq war and its aftermath also seem to have reinforced China's fears that it is locked in a zero-sum contest for energy with the United States and added urgency to its mission to lessen dependence on Middle East oil supplies. However, if the American predominance of the Middle East weakens and China's global profile rises in region, India, along with several other regional states, will consider that a threat to its energy security with the distinct possibility of military conflict over the region's valuable resources.

AMERICA'S GLOBAL IMAGE REMAINS MORE POSITIVE THAN CHINA'S

Publics around the world believe the global balance of power is shifting. China's economic power is on the rise, and many think it will eventually supplant the United States as the world's dominant superpower.

However, China's increasing power has not led to more positive ratings for the People's Republic. Overall, the U.S. enjoys a stronger global image than China. Across the nations surveyed, a median of 63% express a favorable opinion of the U.S., compared with 50% for China.

Globally, people are more likely to consider the U.S. a partner to their country than to see China in this way, although relatively few think of either nation as an enemy. America is also seen as somewhat more willing than China to consider other countries' interests. Still, both of these world powers are widely viewed as acting unilaterally in international affairs.

And the military power of both nations worries many. China's growing military strength is viewed with trepidation in neighboring Japan, South Korea, Australia and the Philippines. Meanwhile, the Obama administration's use of drone strikes faces broad opposition – half or more in 31 of 39 countries disapprove of U.S. drone attacks against extremist groups.

Respecting individual liberty remains the strong suit of America's image. Even in many nations where opposition to American foreign policy is widespread and overall ratings for the U.S. are low, majorities or pluralities believe individual rights are respected in the U.S. Across the nations surveyed, a median of 70% say the American government respects the personal freedoms of its people. In contrast, a median of only 36% say this about China.

Of course, attitudes toward the U.S. and China vary considerably across regions and countries. In Europe, the U.S. gets mostly positive ratings. During the presidency of George W. Bush, anti-Americanism was common throughout much of Europe, but President Barack Obama has been consistently popular among Europeans, and since he took office in 2009, Obama's popularity has given America's image a significant boost in the region.

Currently, more than six-in-ten in Italy, Poland, France and Spain have a favorable opinion of the U.S. European perceptions of China are much less positive – among the eight European Union nations polled, Greece is the only one in which a majority expresses a favorable view of China. Moreover, ratings for China have declined significantly over the last two years in a number of EU countries, including Britain, France, Poland and Spain.

As has been the case in recent years, America's image is the most negative in parts of the Muslim world, especially Pakistan (11% favorable), Jordan (14%), Egypt (16%), and the Palestinian territories (16%). Only 21% of Turks see the U.S. positively, although this is actually a slight improvement from last year's 15%. But the Muslim world is hardly monolithic, and America receives largely positive ratings in predominantly Muslim nations such as Senegal in West Africa and Indonesia and Malaysia in Southeast Asia.

Elsewhere in the Asia/Pacific region, the U.S. receives particularly favorable reviews in the Philippines, South Korea and Japan, and a majority or plurality in all three countries say it is more important to have strong ties with the U.S. than with China.

By a wide margin, the Japanese give China its worst ratings – only 5% express a positive view. Territorial disputes have increased tensions between these two historic rivals over the past few years, and 82% of Japanese describe these disputes as a big or very big problem.

Territorial frictions with China are also considered major problems in South Korea and the Philippines, although unlike Japan, South Koreans and Filipinos are divided in their overall assessments of China. Even though roughly seven-in-ten Australians (71%) are concerned about the growing strength of the People's Liberation Army, a majority (58%) nonetheless has a favorable opinion of China, their country's largest trading partner.

In three predominantly Muslim Asian nations surveyed – Indonesia, Malaysia and Pakistan – large majorities express a positive overall view of China. Additionally, many Pakistanis and Malaysians welcome China's growing military power.

Chinese investment in Latin America and sub-Saharan Africa has increased significantly over the past decade, and views toward China are largely positive in both regions. Attitudes toward the U.S. also tend to be favorable, and overall the U.S. receives slightly higher ratings than China in these two regions.

Additionally, America enjoys a soft power advantage over China among Latin Americans and Africans. American scientific and technological achievements, ways of doing business and popular culture are embraced by many. The appeal of U.S. soft power is generally stronger today in Latin America and Africa than it was during the final years of the Bush administration.

These are among the major findings of a new survey by the Pew Research Center conducted in 39 countries among 37,653 respondents from March 2 to May 1, 2013.1 The survey also finds rising tensions between the American and Chinese publics. Just 37% of Americans express a positive view of China, down from 51% two years ago. Similarly, ratings for the U.S. have plummeted in China – in a 2010 poll conducted a few months after a visit to China by President Obama, 58% had a favorable impression of the U.S., compared with 40% today. Young people in both countries express more positive attitudes about the other, a finding that is part of a broader pattern – in many countries, both the U.S. and China receive more favorable marks from people under age 30.

CHANGING PERCEPTIONS OF POWER

Since the 2008 financial crisis, perceptions about the economic balance of power in the world have been shifting. Looking at the 20 nations surveyed in both 2008 and 2013, the median percentage naming the U.S. as the world's leading economic power has declined from 47% to 41%, while the median percentage placing China in the top spot has risen from 20% to 34%.

This trend has been especially apparent among some of America's closest allies in Western Europe. Today, for example, 53% in Britain say China is the leading economy; just 33% name the U.S. Roughly six-in-ten Germans (59%) say China occupies the top position, while only 19% think the U.S. is the global economic leader (14% say it is the EU).

Many believe China's economic might is growing, but the U.S. is still generally seen as the world's leading economy in Latin America, Africa and in much of China's own backyard. More than six-in-ten in Japan (67%), the Philippines (67%), and South Korea (61%) name the U.S. as the leading economic power.

Bibliography

Allison, Graham, *Nuclear Terrorism: The Ultimate Preventable Catastrophe*, New York: Times Books, 2004.

Anil, K.C.: *Military and Democracy in South Asia : Challenges, Politics and Power*, Sumit Enterprises, Delhi, 2009.

Barber B.R.: *Strong Democracy. Participatory Politics for a New Age*. Berkeley, University of California Press, 1984.

Bhat, T.P. : *India and China : Trade Complementarities and Competitiveness*, Bookwell, Delhi, 2008.

Brooks, Constance : *Disaster Preparedness*, Washington, DC, Association for Research Libraries, 1993.

Buzan, Barry & Eric Herring: *The Arms Dynamic in World Politics*, London: Lynne Rienner Publishers, 1998.

Chitkara, M.G. : *China-Pak Relations Challenges Before New Millennium*, APH, Delhi, 2001.

Damrosch, L.F.: *Law and Force in the New International Order*, Boulder, Westview Press, 1991.

Deepak, B R : *India and China : 1904-2004 : A Century of Peace and Conflict*, Manak, Delhi, 2005.

Drewes, Jeanne : *Computers: Planning for Disaster*, Law Library Journal, Winter, 1989.

Friedman, G.: *The Future of War of Cyber Crimes*, N.Y., Random House, 1996.

Ghose, S.K.: *Politics of Violence: Dawn of a Dangerous Era*, Springfield, Nataraj, 1992.

Goel, Suresh : *Military, Security and Intelligence Agencies*, MD Publications, Delhi, 2009.

Hoffman, Bruce, *Inside Terrorism*, New York: Columbia University Press, 1998.

Huntington, S.P.: *The China Modernisation Military and the State*, N.Y., Vintage Books, 1964.

Keane J.: *Democracy and Civil Liberty*, London, Verso, 1988.

Kunju, N. : *Indo-Pak : Nuclear Cold War*, Reliance, Delhi, 2002.

Laquer, Walter, *The New Terrorism: Fanaticism and the Arms of Mass Destruction*, Oxford: Oxford University Press, 1999.

Norton, Augustus R., and Martin H. *Greenberg, Studies in Nuclear Terrorism*, Boston: G.K. Hall & Co., 1979.

Posen, B.R.: *The Sources of Military Doctrine*, Ithaca, 1984, Cornell Univ. Press.

Qureshi, A. Iqbal : *Islam and the Theory of Interest*, Kitab Bhavan, New Delhi, 1994.

Rhodes, Richard, *The Making of the Atomic Bomb*, New York: Simon and Schuster, 1988.

Schroeer, Dietrich, *Science, Technology, and the Nuclear Arms Race*, Ontario: John Wiley & Sons, 1984.

Sidney Fox: *Klaus Dose, Molecular Evolution and The Origin of Life*, New York: Marcel Dekker, 1977.

Stephen Reyna : *The Political Economy of African Famine*, Philadelphia, Gordon and Breach Science Publishers, 1991

Whitaker, D. J.: *The Terrorism Reader*, New York: Routledge, 2001.

White, J. R.: *Terrorism: An introduction: 2002 update*, Belmont, CA: Wadsworth, 2002.

Worster, Donald : *Dust Bowl: The Southern Plains in the 1930s*, New York, Oxford University Press, 1979.

Index

A

Armed Clash, 209, 211, 219.

C

Climate Change, 57, 58, 59, 60, 61, 62, 63, 64, 66, 67, 68, 69, 70, 72, 73, 75, 76, 78, 79, 80, 81, 82, 86, 87, 88, 223, 225, 227, 229, 231, 232, 233, 235, 236, 237, 238, 239, 240, 241, 274.
Climate Framework, 83.
Conflict Model, 11, 12, 13, 14, 15, 22.
Conventional Arms Control, 202, 205.
Cooperation in South Asia, 42, 44.
Cooperative Security, 222, 223, 224, 226, 227.

D

Developments, 4, 5, 30, 33, 43, 44, 46, 75, 122, 132, 136, 138, 154, 156, 157, 163, 164, 165, 173, 174, 176, 181, 190, 201, 221, 237, 259, 268, 269, 283, 284.

E

Emerging Agenda, 81.
Energy Security, 32, 34, 40, 42, 218, 225, 272, 273, 279, 292, 293, 294, 298.
Environmental Security, 65, 85, 86, 88, 224, 227, 254.
Environmental Stress, 242, 243, 245, 256, 257.

F

Food Security, 65, 78, 223, 225, 227, 228, 229, 231, 233, 235, 236, 237, 239, 240, 241.
Foreign Policy, 26, 27, 30, 31, 32, 34, 101, 110, 159, 285, 290, 300.
Future Security Environment, 90, 91, 94, 98, 101, 102, 103, 104, 113, 117, 121, 122, 133, 137, 140.

G

Geopolitical Calculations, 29, 104.
Geopolitical Importance, 291.
Geopolitical Strategy, 105.
Global Governance, 76, 88.
Globalization, 81, 127, 142, 184, 185, 189, 191, 193, 194, 195, 260, 270, 272.

H

Horizontal Proliferation, 154, 156, 157, 167, 176.
Human Security, 63, 65, 66, 67, 68, 69, 70, 76, 86, 224, 225.

I

Internal Factors, 197.
International Factors, 200.
International system, 215, 275, 287, 288.

M

Militarized Interstate Disputes, 14, 17.
Military Development, 46.
Mitigating Options, 218.

N

Nuclear Cooperation, 156, 172, 175, 176, 177, 179, 180, 181, 182, 183, 286, 295.
Nuclear Doctrines, 156, 157, 163.
Nuclear Policies, 163.
Nuclear States in Conflict, 7.

P

Peace, 9, 10, 13, 14, 27, 32, 36, 38, 41, 42, 43, 44, 46, 64, 66, 76, 86, 88, 99, 101, 113, 115, 122, 123, 128, 136, 138, 139, 142, 143, 144, 145, 146, 150, 151, 152, 158, 160, 195, 197, 198, 200, 207, 208, 209, 211, 212, 214, 222, 242, 245, 248, 250, 254, 270, 274.
Policy, 2, 5, 8, 26, 27, 30, 31, 32, 33, 36, 39, 42, 43, 45, 54, 65, 69, 71, 74, 78, 97, 98, 99, 102, 104, 107, 115, 121, 123, 127, 134, 138, 162, 163, 164, 172, 180, 184, 185, 187, 191, 205, 215, 220, 224, 226, 227, 228, 231, 232, 248, 259, 276, 280, 284, 288, 291, 300.
Preventive Options, 215, 218.
Proliferation Trends, 156.

R

Regional Factors, 198.
Rising Tensions, 57, 299.

S

Security Architecture, 43, 201, 202, 206, 208.
Security Challenges, 57, 61, 225.
Security Dilemma, 12, 154, 155, 156, 161, 165.
Security Disputes, 157, 160, 163.
South Asia Conflict, 1, 4.
South China Sea, 29, 31, 98, 209, 211, 212, 213, 214, 215, 216, 217, 218, 220, 221, 263, 276.
Strategic Restraint Regime, 202, 209.
Sustainable Development, 62, 69, 76, 77, 80, 81, 84, 85, 86, 87, 88, 218, 242, 247, 250, 251, 254, 258.

T

Threat Perceptions, 44, 46, 154, 156, 157, 160, 161, 162, 184, 185, 191, 196.
Towards Security, 254.
Trade-Conflict Model, 11, 12, 13, 14, 15, 22.

W

World Peace, 142, 152, 270.

❑❑❑